D0131385

UFOs

THE DEFINITIVE CASEBOOK

UFOs

THE DEFINITIVE CASEBOOK

JOHN SPENCER

HAMLYN

EDITOR ANNA MUMFORD

ART EDITOR BOB GORDON

PICTURE RESEARCH RACHEL DUFFIELD

PRODUCTION CONTROLLER CHRISTINA ROBILLIARD

First published 1991
Hamlyn is an imprint of Octopus Illustrated Publishing
Michelin House, 81 Fulham Road,
London SW3 6RB
part of Reed International Books

Reprinted 1992

© Copyright Text John Spencer 1991
© Copyright Illustrations and Design Reed International Books Limited 1991

All rights reserved. No part of this publication may be reproduced, stored in a
retrieval system, or transmitted in any form or by any means, electronic,
mechanical, photocopying, recording or otherwise, without the prior written
permission of the Publisher and copyright owner.

ISBN 0 600 57223 4

Typeset by Dorchester Typesetting Group Limited
Produced by Mandarin Offset - printed in Hong Kong

The Publishers would like to thank the following organizations
and individuals for their kind permission to reproduce the
photographs in this book.

Aerofilms 75, 76
Martin Bower 19B, 22, 93B, 116-7
Steuart Campbell 111
Peter Day 100T
Mary Evans Picture Library 17, 24, 25, 28B, 29T, 34,
46T&B, 49, 53, 59, 62, 64, 69R, 79, 80L, 81, 82B, 83,
85TL, TR&B, 88, 90, 93T, 102, 107, 123, 173, 187B,/Project
Hessdalen 118, 119T&B
Fortean Picture Library 14, 15, 21B, 26B, 35, 38, 43, 54, 69L,
71L&R, 78, 87, 115, 120, 185,/Fotorama 26T,/Tsutomu
Nakayama 63,/B Skinner 121, C Svahn 80R
Stanton T Freidman 18
John Frost Newspapers 51
The Ronald Grant Archive 11
Robert Harding Picture Library 50-1
Cynthia Hind 147, 153, 156,/ © Ministry of Information,
Zimbabwe 150
The Hutchison Library 157,/T Bedow 145
The Kobal Collection 33, 57, 101
MUFON 39L&R, 58

NASA 12,/SPL 137, 187T
Novosti Press Agency 128
Popperfoto 27, 28T, 66, 82T, 114, 129, 140
Science Photo Library 2-3, 29B, 40-1,/J Baum 131,/J Finch 40,
133,/D Parker 135,/M Paternostro 136
South American Pictures/Tony Morrison 189
Spectrum 105T&B, 108-9, 141, 175
John Spencer 60, 95, 103
Syndication International/Associated Press 163
TRH Pictures 130R,/Grumman 130L
© VUFORS 167,/P Norman 172, 174
Zefa 178

Although every effort has been made to trace the copyright
holder, we apologize in advance for any unintentional omissions
and would be pleased to insert the appropriate
acknowledgements in any subsequent edition of this
publication.

Illustrations on pages 30-1, 36-7, 44-5, 96-7, 112-13, 138-9,
154-5, 164-5, 170-1 and 182-3 by Tony Roberts. Illustration on
page 21 by Keith Scaife. Models and photographs on pages
19B, 22, 93B, 116-17 by Martin Bower. These compositions
are artists' impressions based on witnesses' reports.

CONTENTS

FOREWORD

As the International Director of the Mutual UFO Network (MUFON), the world's largest and most geographically widespread independent UFO research organization, I am aware, perhaps more than most, that the UFO phenomenon is a truly global one. Unidentified Flying Objects are experienced by people all over the world and *UFOs: The Definitive Casebook* shows this continent by continent.

The *Casebook* also highlights areas of large countries – remote or less technological countries – where UFOs are rarely, sometimes never, reported. It becomes apparent that UFO reporting is confined to those areas that have UFO investigators to whom these events can be reported. Those of us involved in the study of this phenomenon are convinced that if there were more people to whom sightings could be reported, then more cases deserving of serious study would reach UFO researchers.

During my twenty years at MUFON I have determined at least two important things: first, that the UFO subject is serious and deserves to be treated with greater respect by scientists, world governments and the public than it presently is; second, that this subject is bringing people together across the world, and in a way that brings out their best talents. Thousands of people are donating hundreds of hours per year without financial compensation to helping those who do not seem to understand their own experiences or who may be unwilling victims of traumatic experiences.

The annual MUFON International UFO Symposium attracts hundreds of people from all over the world who come together in a spirit of joint endeavour that breaks down international boundaries. Both the Mutual UFO Network (MUFON) and the British UFO Research Association (BUFORA) are organizations to which the author and many of the contributors belong. They have a stated objective to educate the public in a responsible and authoritative manner, to encourage other groups and organizations around the world to share their work, and to proceed towards a solution to this intriguing and mysterious subject. This book is part of that process.

WALTER H. ANDRUS JR.
INTERNATIONAL DIRECTOR
MUTUAL UFO NETWORK

INTRODUCTION

Unidentified Flying Objects are a subject which is much misunderstood: partly because of poor media attention, partly because of inadequate support from the scientific community and partly because of the absurd claims of cult followers who attach themselves to the subject. The end result is that authoritative data rarely gets to the general public and the UFO phenomenon as a whole attracts ridicule. *UFOs: The Definitive Casebook* aims to redress that imbalance.

We do not know what UFOs are: some cases make it very clear that they are a physical reality; other cases seem to be caught up in a sociological event; some cases have mythological and others psychological components. Some UFO reports are humorous and appear to be relatively unimportant while a great many have serious, often frightening implications for individual people and for the world as a whole. Too many people have been touched by UFOs, directly and indirectly, for the UFO phenomenon to be wished away. These people and the rest of the world deserve a reasoned attempt to provide them with the answers that they seek – whatever those answers may be. *UFOs: The Definitive Casebook* proves one thing very clearly: that at some level, or in some way, the UFO phenomenon is real.

To compile a world database of over forty years of research from all around the world was a daunting task. I could not have easily done so without the support of friends and colleagues across the world who supplied data, gave their opinions, guided me to sources of data, or simply kept me going when the coffee ran out. From an endless list I would particularly like to mention: Hilary Evans, Cynthia Hind, Paul Norman, Eduardo Russo, Walter H Andrus Jnr, Budd Hopkins, Thomas (Eddie) Bullard, Bertil Kuhlemann, Jenny Randles, Steve Gamble, Bob Digby, Philip Mantle, Andy Roberts. None of these people are responsible for any opinions expressed in the book other than those they make in their own section introductions.

My thanks also to the artists and illustrators, Tony Roberts, Martin Bower and Keith Scaife for their astonishing visualizations that portray the mystery and awe of key events.

I would like to give special thanks to three other people who each gave very special support in their own way: my wife, Anne, who became researcher and cartographer despite the demands of our home and her own business; Anna Mumford, of Paul Hamlyn Publishing, who gave tremendous back-up and installed a hot-line direct to my desk; Kathryn Howard, a UFO abductee who, when I needed a fresh perspective on the subject, provided it (in trumps!).

There are people missing from this list who, for various reasons, cannot be acknowledged individually: the hundreds of good UFO investigators whose cases make up the databases – space simply prohibits a full cross-referenced list; psychologists and some scientists who prefer to remain anonymous at least for the moment; witnesses whose cases are not included out of respect for their wish that their stories remain out of the public domain – the perspective they provide is vital.

In researching the data, I have used many case files including my own, and taken the opinions of many more experienced than myself. For specific references I have referred to many publications (see Bibliography page 192). None of the books, journals or authors mentioned are responsible for the opinions expressed, some of which are no doubt contrary to their own. Such is this subject.

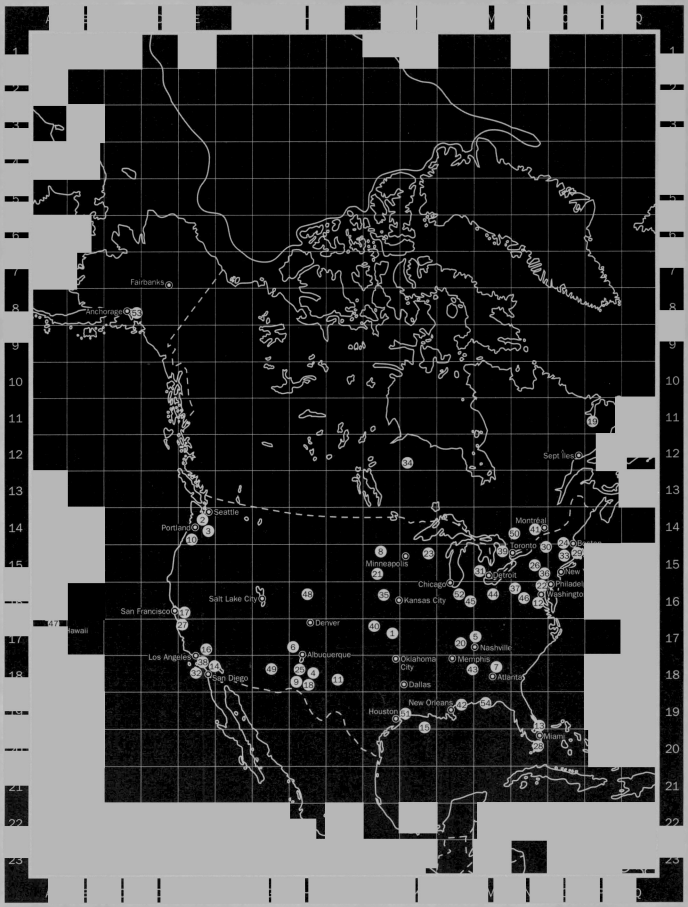

Fairbanks

Anchorage 53

19

Sept Îles

34

Montréal
Seattle
41
Portland
50
10
Toronto 30 24 Boston
39 33 29
8 23 26 New Y
Minneapolis 31 Detroit 36
21 22 Philadel
Chicago 52 37 Washington
Salt Lake City 48 35 Kansas City 45 44 46 12
San Francisco 17
27 Denver 40 1
Hawaii 47
16 20 5
Los Angeles 6 Nashville
38 14 Albuquerque Oklahoma Memphis
32 49 25 4 City 43 7 Atlanta
San Diego 9 18 11 Dallas
New Orleans 42 54
Houston 51 13
15 Miami
28

NORTH AMERICA

SOMEWHERE 'OUT THERE', THERE MUST SURELY BE TECHNO-DEMOCRATS, JUST LIKE OURSELVES, IN SEARCH OF NEW FRONTIERS AND HORIZONS, WILLING TO GO 'WHERE NO MAN HAS GONE BEFORE'.

KEY TO MAP OF NORTH AMERICA

① Aerial Cattle Rustlers, Le Roy, Kansas
② Maury Island, Washington State
③ Kenneth Arnold Sighting, Mount Rainier, Washington State
④ Roswell Incident, Roswell, New Mexico
⑤ Captain Thomas Mantell, Godman Field, Kentucky
⑥ Aztec, New Mexico
⑦ Chiles/Whitted, Montgomery, Georgia
⑧ Fargo, North Dakota
⑨ White Sands, White Sands Proving Grounds, New Mexico
⑩ The Trent Photographs, McMinnville, Oregon
⑪ The Lubbock Lights, Lubbock, Texas
⑫ Washington Flap, Washington D.C.
⑬ Desvergers Encounter, West Palm Beach, Florida
⑭ George Adamski, Desert Centre, California
⑮ Gulf of Mexico
⑯ Tujunga Canyon, California
⑰ Livermore, Oakland, California
⑱ Daniel Fry, White Sands Proving Grounds, New Mexico
⑲ Goose Bay, Labrador (Canada)
⑳ Kelly-Hopkinsville, Kentucky
㉑ 'Jennie', Nebraska
㉒ Lochraven Dam, Baltimore, Pennsylvania
㉓ Joe Simonton, Eagle River, Wisconsin
㉔ Betty and Barney Hill, Concorde, New Hampshire
㉕ Socorro, New Mexico
㉖ Gary Wilcox, Tioga, New York State
㉗ Cisco Grove, California
㉘ Flynn Incident, Everglades, Florida
㉙ Exeter Flap, Exeter, New Hampshire
㉚ Great North Eastern Blackout, North Eastern United States/Canada
㉛ Swamp Gas Debacle, Ann Arbor, Michigan
㉜ Catalina Island Film, California
㉝ Betty Andreasson, Ashburnham, Massachusetts
㉞ Stephan Michalaq, Falcon Lake, Ontario/Manitoba border (Canada)
㉟ Patrolman Schirmer, Ashland, Nebraska
㊱ Shane Kurz, New York State
㊲ Callery Chemical Plant, Butler, Pennsylvania
㊳ Dapple Grey Lane, Los Angeles, California
㊴ St Catherine's, Ontario (Canada)
㊵ The Delphos Ring, Kansas
㊶ Michel Imbeault, Montréal, Canada
㊷ Pascagoula Encounter, Mississippi
㊸ Jeff Greenhaw, Falkville, Alabama
㊹ Captain Coyne, Mansfield, Ohio
㊺ Flatter/Donathan, Blackford County, Indiana
㊻ Polaski Encounter, Greensberg, Pennsylvania
㊼ Tsutomu Nakayama, Hawaii
㊽ Carl Higdon Abduction, Medicine Bow National Forest, Wyoming
㊾ Travis Walton Abduction, Snowflake, Arizona
㊿ Falconbridge, Ontario (Canada)
(51) Cash/Landrum Encounter, Dayton, Texas
(52) 'Kathie Davis' Abductions, 'Copley Woods', Indiana
(53) Japan Air Lines, Anchorage Airport, Alaska
(54) Gulf Breeze Case, Gulf Breeze, Florida

LAST BASTION OF ETH

Each year the President of the United States of America addresses the nation with a State of the Union message. This speech is purely political; that is to say, heavy on platitudes, and short on substance. A few troublesome issues are admitted to, but these are traditionally glossed over as nothing 'the spirit of the American people can't conquer if we only put our minds to it, and our shoulders to the wheel.'

I can see that I might easily be accused of a similar sort of equivocation here. As editor of the monthly journal of MUFON, the Mutual UFO Network, I suppose I can be seen as a party loyalist, one who adheres publicly to the perceived party line, and tends to put a gloss on the overall status of the situation, whether or not merited by reality.

All I can say in my defence is that is certainly not how I think of myself. (Nor, judging from my mail, do all members of MUFON.) I hope I am capable of giving a more or less objective assessment of the present state of American ufology, warts, roses and all. I also understand that what follows is only one person's opinion. Another ufologist might see the current situation in a different colour or light altogether and certainly they are welcome to their opinion.

So, what is the nature of the beast, then, as I perceive it? Frankly, fairly encouraging, though not without its moments of low humour and open rancour. Before we enter into specifics, however, it might prove fruitful to look first at our background.

That America should be the haven (if not the last bastion) of the so-called Extra-terrestrial Hypothesis (ETH), should not come as a surprise, either, given our nature and circumstances. Although Americans are arguably no more a technological culture or society than, say, the Germans or the Japanese, we have always prided ourselves that we were. For example, it was American ingenuity and industry, was it not, that felled Hitler's Fortress Europe? (Never mind for now that Soviet armies had a small helping hand in turning back the Fascist tide.) Moreover, it was American know-how that manufactured the world's first atomic bomb. (And a military mind-set we tend to overlook that decided to drop it.)

Certainly, the remarkable economic and industrial recovery of a war-ravaged world owes a great deal of debt to its American constituency, however tarnished or lagging our present performance. The point is that, for better or worse, it is, perhaps, the American character that has cast the longest shadow over the collective post World War Two global village. Muscovites crowd into McDonald's rather than New Yorkers into McGorky's.

Some commentators believe that we Americans are our own worst critics. In fact, our mania for introspection is much more political and ethical than it is, say, psychological or metaphysical. Given our industrial and technological background (itself a product as much of circumstance as character) it was only logical that we would see ourselves in the UFO phenomenon.

Somewhere 'out there', there must surely be techno-democrats just like ourselves, in search of new frontiers and horizons, willing to go 'where no man has gone before'. Such was the only *logical* assumption that could be made about these mysterious little green men in their magnificent flying machines. It was just not in our make-up to think otherwise. As America's taste for fast food suffused the world market place, so did perhaps premature adoption of the ETH suffuse ufology, again, for better or worse.

On the other hand, as with any empire, rebellion was bound to set in, and this is exactly what we see happening today. That these mini-revolutions have

adopted their own individualistic and local 'style' was inevitable. Of course the failure of the ETH to prove itself contributed to the situation, too. Still, the revolts have fallen back on their own culture and circumstance in a sort of intellectual nationalism, or chauvinism. Thus we have several separate 'schools' of which faerie folklore, tribal culture, psychological and mystical are all examples.

However, none of these schools has come any closer to ultimately resolving the central issue – the unknown nature of the UFO phenomenon. Nor do I mean to suggest that these generalized separate approaches are in any way monolithic, or that there are not schisms. But the point is that American ufology, first and foremost, is a product or manifesta-

The mother ship in *Close Encounters of the Third Kind* which compounded technological America's extra-terrestrial view of the subject.

tion of its own peculiar time and place. Like its contemporaries, it is riddled with holes and factions.

There is an exaggerated tendency to 'choose sides', based on belief and feeling about a specific case, or personal loyalty to the principles involved, rather than a dispassionate examination of the evidence itself. This was most recently exemplified by the spectacular and apparently on-going Gulf Breeze Case in Florida (see page 67), which saw – if not old friends – at least old acquaintances, suddenly at one another's throats over its validity.

Interestingly, the argument could be made that each country and people get not only the ufologists they 'deserve', but seemingly specialized outbreaks of the phenomenon itself, as well. In the US, of late, that involves apparently physical and photographed objects seen by large numbers of witnesses, as in Gulf Breeze, accompanied by a strong undercurrent of abductions and a whiff of mutilated animals. In England, the strange Wessex crop circles (see page 121) beneath the great Chalk Horse have yet to be put in their proper context, and the same can be said of the French humanoids of an earlier day, and now, the Soviet 'invasion' and Brazilian accounts of flying refrigerators and death-dealing ray beams. Whether these specialized outbreaks can best be thought of as a case of the seeker blind to anything but the sought, or alternatively as a sort of perverse prank on the part of the phenomenon itself remains to be answered.

Our native proclivity for picking teams has surfaced in the one area of ufology where one would naturally assume it might least rear its ugly head: in the realm of government and military intelligence documentation. The present controversy centres around an alleged presidential briefing paper which describes the existence of Majestic 12, or MJ-12, an ultra-secret special studies group reportedly founded in the wake of the Roswell Incident (see page 18). Those awaiting definite confirmation of MJ-12 may find themselves condemned to a permanent UFO purgatory. Meanwhile, the waters have been rendered even more murky by the recent revelation (or confession, depending on your point of view), made by a major MJ-12 player, of having actively participated in a military intelligence disinformation and surveillance campaign directed against certain individuals and UFO organizations.

In the wake of Whitley Strieber's bestselling *Communion* and *Transformation*, in both of which he describes his own abduction, it seemed for a time as if the abduction scenario might swamp the stage entirely. Such apprehensions have proven largely unfounded, although several competing camps have been set up as a consequence of personality and philosophical differences. Strieber and associates have established the Communion Foundation, with its own quarterly newsletter, and urged members not to fraternize with other 'orthodox' UFO organizations. Budd Hopkins and associates have responded with the Intruder Foundation. Yet a third group, TREAT (for Treatment and Research on Experienced Anomalous Trauma) is underway, and a fourth abduction-related group is rumoured to be on the horizon.

The space shuttle, a symbol of North America's technological achievement which features so strongly in the consciousness of its people that the Extra-terrestrial Theory predominates.

At the moment, TREAT seems to have the best chance of bridging the immense gap between ufology and establishment science, if by the latter we include professional psychotherapists and other mental health practitioners. A working arrangement with a major east coast university appears imminent, which could lead in turn to academic respectability, increased funding, access to a super-computer and other tangible benefits. MUFON itself is presently engaged in an ambitious programme to standardize reporting procedures and computerize its database. The Fund for UFO Research continues to solicit support in the field. Subscriptions in the membership groups are up, approaching numbers not seen since the mid-fifties.

The number of annual UFO conferences and symposia is on the rise as well, though the quality of the presentations varies widely. After a lengthy absence, there are now two national news-stand magazines devoted to the subject, though again the contents of each issue fluctuate dramatically in terms of reliability. So called tabloid TV programmes regularly feature UFO stories, and of course the taller tales remain a favourite staple of the supermarket press. Jacques Vallée has returned to the publishing fold with *Dimensions* and *Confrontations,* studies which link folklore with UFOs. We have also seen, in 1990, the hardback appearance of Ed Conroy's well received *Report on Communion* and *The Gulf Breeze Sightings* by Ed and Frances Walters. An eagerly anticipated study by reporter Howard Blum, *Out There,* was also published towards the end of 1990. Other books that impinge on or envelope the UFO subject, favourably or critically, are too numerous to mention, but balance would hardly be served if we did not refer to the revised paperback appearance of *UFO Abductions: A Dangerous Game,* by skeptic Philip Klass. Several English titles have also received limited distribution here, although Timothy Good's *Above Top Secret* was picked up by a major American publisher. The amateur press has been extremely preoccupied as well, and both MUFON and CUFOS, the Center for UFO Studies, continue to produce monthly and bi-monthly journals respectively. Journals back in business include *The Journal of UFO Studies* along with *Caveat Emptor,* a local equivalent on a somewhat more folksy scale than England's *Magonia.* No doubt I have left much out in this brief summary, and my apologies to anyone particularly offended.

Just as in the political arena, ufology has its own extreme elements. The more vocal of these have begun to raise rumours abroad of a secret diplomatic treaty between our government and the diminutive (one is tempted to say, demonic) 'grays'. What is encouraging about the present picture is the unlikelihood of any extreme minority, however vocal or active, assuming the mainstream mantle. There is a certain inertia or gravity in human affairs which may well work to our advantage, although in the meantime, the rumour mongers are not exactly performing a public service in our best interest.

In-fighting and factionalism abound, but this strikes me as a by-product of human nature and behaviour as opposed to anything fundamentally inherent to ufology, American or otherwise. Although sheer cantankerousness can be distracting and wasteful of both precious time and energy, it also demon-strates that US ufology is anything but moribund, and that the spirit of American individualism is alive and well, if not particularly inclined towards harmony and co-operation.

Unfortunately, there is at least one other alarming proclivity that should be addressed, and that is the temptation, in this most litigious of societies, to settle some issues in a court of law rather than through open dialogue and public opinion. These civil actions to date have mostly been lodged against other nationals, whose laws allow for financial retribution in the case of libel. Some of us here wait with bated breath and crossed fingers for similar suits to be filed in this country. While the prospect of legal action may indicate to some people a 'coming of age' for ufology, it is safe to say it is not the one most American ufologists have in mind as they continue to court public opinion and scientific respectability.

Now, where do we stand vis-à-vis our contemporaries? Despite the difficulties of the science involved (the distance between stars, the unlikelihood of so *many* extraterrestrials suddenly showing up on our doorstep, etc.), the ETH must remain a viable *theory.* Theories, after all is said and done, are all we have. But if one theory can be convincingly shown to be better than another, then Americans will be among the first to welcome it and applaud. So far this has not been the case. Arguing that abductions, for example, are predominantly psychological in origin, and *therefore,* so is the science of ufology at present is a far cry from an *overall* viable theory. In fact, so scarce is our scratch on the surface, that hard and fast facts are difficult to come by that would support *any* overall theory, including those of mass psychokinesis, psychotronic control systems, and a number of other hypotheses, half- or full-baked, that have been offered up over the last half century. I also include here the ultraskeptical, Shakespearean notion that all this has been 'much ado about nothing'.

It may behove us all to keep an open mind, be patient, and remember that the U in UFO stands for unidentified. That may not be an especially popular or American point of view, but neither was the two-minute hamburger until we won the war.

DENNIS STACY is both a full-time writer and the editor of *MUFON Journal*, the house magazine of the Mutual UFO Network. His editorship is characterized by impartial and well-informed commentary so vital in a country where extreme views and high passions often run free.

PRE 1900

NAME AERIAL CATTLE RUSTLING

DATE 20 APRIL 1897

PLACE LE ROY, KANSAS
MAP REF: J17

EVENT AERIAL CATTLE RUSTLERS

On 20 April 1897, farmer Alexander Hamilton filed an affidavit stating that earlier that week he had watched a huge object glide down from the darkness and come to rest in a field some 200 yds (183 m) from his home. Together with his son and one of the farmhands he had approached to within 150 ft (46 m) of the object, which he described as approximately the length of an American football field and made of something coloured deep red. It was like an enormous cigar in shape and beneath it appeared to be a cabin made of glass; within it the farmer and his companions could see six occupants which they described as 'the strangest beings ever saw'.

An enormous wheel, located beneath the craft, began to spin and the airship rose to an altitude of some 300 ft (92 m). The farmers noticed that a rope, reaching down from the craft, was attached to a heifer which was caught against the barbs of a fence nearby. As the object rose it pulled the calf up with it and disappeared into the darkness trailing the unlucky animal behind it. The following day what remained of the calf was recovered from a nearby farm: legs, head and skin.

Should Hamilton's credibility be called into question, it must be pointed out that he had been a member of the House of Representatives and that people who had known him for over thirty years testified in an affidavit that they had never heard a word of his questioned and 'do readily believe his statement to be true and correct'. Furthermore the affidavit was signed by the sheriff, the deputy sheriff, a justice of the peace, a postmaster, the registrar of deeds, a banker, an attorney, and others.

Hamilton said of the encounter 'Every time I drop to sleep I see the cursed thing, all its bright lights and hideous people. I don't know whether they are angels or devils . . . I don't want any more to do with them.'

1940s

NAME MAURY ISLAND

DATE 23 JUNE 1947

PLACE MAURY ISLAND, WASHINGTON STATE
MAP REF: E14

EVENT CLOSE ENCOUNTER OF THE SECOND KIND

The 24 June 1947 is regarded as the birth date of the modern era of UFOs when Kenneth Arnold had his 'flying saucer' sighting at Mount Rainier in Washington State, USA. However, on the day prior to this sighting an event was unfolding – the precise meaning and implications of which have been a mystery to ufologists ever since.

Harbour patrolmen Harold A. Dahl and Fred L. Crisman owned a boat and on the day in question Dahl and other companions were sailing it in Puget Sound, near Maury Island (Tacoma harbour) when they saw six UFOs above them. One of the UFOs, described as saucer- or doughnut-shaped, jettisoned material, some of which fell on to the boat injuring one of the companions and killing his dog.

By the time this story had become known Kenneth Arnold was already associated nationally with the flying saucer phenomenon. He was drawn into the Maury Island investigation principally due to the intervention of Ray Palmer, the editor of *Fantasy* magazine.

Dahl claimed to have been visited by a 'man in black', a character of repression soon to appear repeatedly in American UFO stories and a feature that would last at least a decade or more. He apparently strongly suggested to Dahl that it would be in his interests not to discuss his sighting.

The 'men in black' were a feature of the early days of UFOs. They reputedly sought to repress witnesses, but their identity is unknown: FBI, AEC or ET?

Kenneth Arnold was concerned that professional people should investigate the case and suggested calling the 4th Air Force Base at Hamilton Field and requested the involvement of two intelligence officers; Captain William Davidson and Lieutenant Frank Brown.

When Brown and Davidson arrived they were shown an assortment of the debris from the UFO, it was laying on the floor of the room in which they met. Davidson and Brown seemed to have played down their concern and even refused to accept samples of the material when offered, apparently giving the impression that they thought the witnesses were the victims of a hoax. However, at the last minute Crisman gave them a carton containing the material and they stowed it in their car, subsequently apparently placing it on their B-25 aircraft which stood by to fly back to Hamilton Field, in California.

It has been speculated that the material was in fact radioactive slag being dumped illegally by the Atomic Energy Commission (AEC) and that the 'man in black' was in reality an agent of the AEC determined to suppress the story before it got out of hand. Whatever the truth, the mystery deepened considerably when the B-25 containing the intelligence officers and the material apparently caught fire and crashed. Its two crew members survived but the two officers died with the plane.

A newspaper report shortly after the incident suggested that the crash involved sabotage because the 'plane may hold flying disk secret'. The report also suggested that there was some evidence the plane was carrying 'classified material'.

Unfortunately, with two prime players lost in the aircraft accident the case, for the moment, defies any more substantial conclusion.

NAME	KENNETH ARNOLD SIGHTING
DATE	24 JUNE 1947
PLACE	MOUNT RAINIER, WASHINGTON STATE MAP REF: E14
EVENT	DISTANT DAYLIGHT SIGHTING – BUT THE BIRTH OF 'FLYING SAUCERS'

In the clear skies of Washington State, lone pilot Kenneth Arnold was peacefully admiring the breathtaking scenery of the Cascade Mountains. He was flying a Callair plane especially modified for mountain search and rescue and although not formally engaged on such a mission, Arnold was searching for a crashed C-46 marine transport plane. He was spurred on by both a humanitarian desire to relieve the anguish of relatives of the lost crew and also the financial incentive of a $5,000 reward for discovery of the wreck.

Having completed his day's work installing fire fighting equipment for the Central Air Service at Chehalis, a small town in Washington State, Arnold took off at around 2 o'clock heading for Yakima. With Mount Rainier ahead and a DC-4 above and behind to his left, Arnold was suddenly startled by a flash of light.

To the left and north of Mount Rainier he saw what appeared to be a formation of nine objects in flight.

Kenneth Arnold initiated the media coverage phenomenon with his coining of the phrase 'flying saucers' in 1947.

15

While thinking they must be jet planes he was also noticing that they were moving in a curious way; flipping up and down like the bows on the tail of a kite or, to use a phrase that was later to make history, moving 'like a saucer would if you skipped it across the water'.

Given their distance – estimated at 25 miles (40 km) away – Arnold was unable to make out their shapes clearly but believed that when they passed in front of the snow-covered Mount Rainier he could then see their outlines distinctly. It is questionable to what degree Arnold could accurately have identified the outlines of the objects if they were at the distance he suggested, it may indicate they were far closer to him than he thought. If that was the case they must have been moving more slowly, possibly at the speed of terrestrial aircraft. The shapes were disturbing, however; he thought they were jet planes but could find no tails. This description coupled with his later drawings of the objects show that he believed he was looking at boomerang shaped craft.

Arnold did as much as possible to analyze the observation including opening his window to get a clear view. The objects were flying directly across his field of vision between Mount Rainier and Mount Adams. Using these peaks as reference points Arnold estimated the objects were moving between 1,300-1,700 miles (2,092-2,736 km) per hour, far faster than any plane of the day could have achieved. Of all of his estimates which have been called into question the most difficult to determine with accuracy was the distance from the aircraft to the objects and the length of their formation, which he estimated at 5 miles (8 km). He estimated the individual size of the objects at approximately two-thirds that of the DC-4 aircraft which was sharing the

sky with him – equivalent to about 67 ft (19 m).

Within a short time the objects were gone and Arnold continued his search for the plane though he later admitted his mind was no longer on the job. After a cursory search of the Tieton reservoir he eventually flew into Yakima at 4 pm.

On arriving and desperate to tell someone about the sighting, Arnold went to see the general manager of Central Aircraft, Al Baxter, who in turn called in other pilots to hear the story. Someone suggested that possibly the craft were guided missiles from Moses Lake Base, Washington. Arnold felt satisfied that this must be the case.

However, by the time Arnold arrived back in Pendleton, Oregon his story had out-raced him. There was a large group there to listen to him recount his sighting and again Arnold concluded they were probably guided missiles. He did not believe they could be manned because the flipping motions and the speeds would – he believed – be impossible for the human frame to withstand. Arnold also reported his sighting to the local FBI officials on the basis that they could be some sort of Russian weapon.

Widespread news coverage ridiculously distorted the encounter. As Arnold put it 'After three days of this hubbub I came to the conclusion that I was the only sane one in the bunch.' One of those distortions was to make sociological history; picking up on Arnold's phrase that the objects were moving 'like a saucer would if you skipped it across the water', the expression 'flying saucer' was born and it was the birth of a catch phrase that has attracted media attention ever since. Although Arnold described basically boomerang shapes and his use of the word saucer was to describe the erratic up and down motion of the

objects, the term was very quickly being used to describe saucer shapes. It must be admitted that Arnold seems to have jumped on his own bandwagon. By the time his story was told in the first edition of *Fate* magazine in the spring of 1948, the cover illustration depicting the encounter was a gross distortion of the original story. The objects are seen in close proximity to Arnold's plane and they are clearly saucer shapes with just a slight modification at the rear to pay lip-service to Arnold's 'boomerang' description.

During the next two months something very extraordinary was happening (or press attention was creating the impression of something happening); some 850 sightings were reported across the United States during that time and earlier sightings were uncovered.

For Arnold, his sighting was to change his life completely and he became an active flying saucer researcher and a devotee up until his death on 16 January 1984. He had many further sightings during his life and they seemed to have convinced him of an extraordinary interpretation of the UFO phenomenon: that the objects are masses of living organisms that live in our atmosphere.

The objects were never identified. Today the sighting would be low priority because there was no corroborative witness, the sighting was of short duration, indefinite distance and dubious clarity.

Nevertheless, the media attention which was generated from those few minutes over Washington State gave birth to the UFO phenomenon.

Artistic licence was heavily employed in this magazine jacket illustration which depicts Arnold's sighting. The UFOs apparently moved 'like a saucer would if you skipped it across the water'.

FATE

SPRING
1948
25c

VOLUME 1   NUMBER 1

THE TRUTH ABOUT THE FLYING SAUCERS
By KENNETH ARNOLD

MARK TWAIN AND HALLEY'S COMET
By HAROLD M. SHERMAN

INVISIBLE BEINGS WALK THE EARTH
By R. J. CRESCENZI

TWENTY MILLION MANIACS
By G. H. IRWIN

The FLYING DISKS

NAME THE ROSWELL INCIDENT

DATE 2 JULY 1947

PLACE ROSWELL, NEW MEXICO
MAP REF: H18

EVENT CRASH RETRIEVAL

The most intriguing of all crash retrieval stories, and the only one definitely supported by physical evidence, is the Roswell incident of July 1947, which occurred just a few days after the Kenneth Arnold sighting (see page 15).

In the early evening of 2 July a disc shaped UFO was seen flying over Roswell, New Mexico and heading towards the north-west.

The following morning, 75 miles (127 km) in that general direction, ranch manager William Brázel and his son and daughter discovered scattered wreckage on their farm and alerted the local sheriff's office of Chaves County. Sheriff Wilcox of Chaves County contacted Roswell Army Air Base and Major Jesse A. Marcel.

To say that the government took the report seriously would be an understatement; Brazel was incarcerated for a period of several days and encouraged not to discuss the event on grounds of national security. Meanwhile Major Marcel and his team collected the debris

from the ranch. It must be stressed that contrary to some rumours there was no disc recovery at this point – Marcel confirms that small pieces of debris were put into the boot of a car – and there were no alien bodies recovered. The debris was returned to the Roswell Army Air Base and, on the orders of Colonel Blanchard, was flown on to Wright Patterson Air Force Base in Ohio. Although apparently detailed to accompany the debris, Marcel was diverted by his superiors at Fort Worth and did not go to Wright Patterson.

What was recovered has been the source of considerable speculation: that the material was a

ABOVE General Roger Ramey and Colonel Thomas Jefferson DuBose display the remains of a weather balloon, allegedly the material recovered by Major Jesse Marcel. Marcel said, 'It was definitely not a weather or tracking device . . .'

ABOVE RIGHT *The Roswell Daily Record* of 8 July 1947 announcing the capture of the flying saucer. RIGHT A model artist's reconstruction showing the retrieved saucer and what may have later taken place at Wright Patterson Airbase.

thin, foil like metal that could not be dented even by forceful blows, that it was a light, balsa-wood substance which would not burn even under a direct flame, and that there were strange hieroglyphs on the debris.

The Roswell incident has been further complicated by apparently conflicting information, some of which may have been issued by the government. If so, it was probably to divert attention from what was really going on. In particular, a press release was issued by Roswell Army Air Base on 8 July which stated 'Roswell Army Air Field was fortunate enough to gain possession of a disc through the co-operation of

one of the local ranchers and of the Sheriff's office at Chaves County.' Another report by radio station KSWS in Roswell which was being put on to the ABC wire service was apparently interrupted by an incoming teletype message ordering the station with these words 'Do not transmit. Repeat. Do not transmit this message. Stop

communication immediately.'

A reconciliation of the contradictions in this case has been offered by the claims of witness G. L. Barnett who stated to friends that he had seen another crash site near Socorro, New Mexico where a damaged but complete saucer was discovered along with dead alien bodies. The speculation is that the

machine exploded over Brazel's farm dropping debris but continued in the air to Socorro before finally being downed. It is suggested that the government may have issued the statement about the retrieved saucer at Brazel's farm in order to divert attention from the recovery going on nearby. This seems to be a diversion fraught with risks though, if true, it does seem to have worked.

There is no question that debris was recovered from Brazel's ranch. In order to explain the situation to an eager public Brigadier General Ramey, commander of the 8th Air Force district at Fort Worth together with his adjutant displayed the recovered debris for the press. The wreckage shown was clearly that of a Rawin weather balloon which it was claimed was the cause of the event.

Almost certainly this was a device to cover up the truth and the real wreckage was by this time on its way to Wright Patterson Air Force Base.

A proper analysis of the Roswell incident must take account of the circumstances surrounding the immediate area and time of the incident. New Mexico in 1948 was the site of the White Sands Proving Grounds, where German scientists brought over during the war were giving birth to the American space programme, and Los Alamos was the site of the recently developed atomic bomb. The possibility that the government was trying to secretly recover a damaged device of its own must on this account alone be high on the list of explanations for Roswell.

If the Roswell incident proved nothing else, it indicated that the government was prepared to cover up *something*, and prepared to use the newly born flying saucer phenomenon to do it with.

NAME	CAPTAIN THOMAS MANTELL
DATE	7 JANUARY 1948
PLACE	GODMAN FIELD, KENTUCKY MAP REF: M17
EVENT	UFOLOGY'S FIRST MARTYR

In the early afternoon of 7 January 1948 the control tower crew at Godman Field, Kentucky reported a sighting of a bright disc-shaped object to their base operations officer. Approximately one hour and twenty minutes after the sighting, when the object was still visible, four National Guard P-51 Mustang training craft led by Captain Thomas Mantell were diverted from their flight to investigate the sighting.

The aircraft climbed toward the object. At 15,000 ft (4,572 m) the other planes turned back as they did not have the equipment required to supply oxygen which would enable them to fly higher. They attempted to contact Mantell by radio. Mantell made one transmission at 15,000 ft (4,572 m) saying he had the object in sight and was still climbing to investigate. The plane crashed, scattering wreckage for over a mile. Mantell was dead; this young man was ufology's first martyr.

Analysis of the wreckage indicates that Mantell did not attempt to bale out of the plane and suggests that the plane broke up from diving at excessive speed, presumably out of control. It is suggested that Mantell blacked out from oxygen deprivation as he flew above the plane's capability to supply oxygen. The question is, what was it that drove Mantell higher and higher? One theory is that it was a Skyhook weather balloon; one binocular observation described the UFO as parachute-like with bright sun reflecting from the top. Another theory is that Mantell was chasing the bright image of a planet which would account for his

inability to 'close-in' on the target. Mantell's experience should have taught him to react better and it is speculated that he may have overreacted to the UFO sighting as a result of six months of media hype following the Arnold sighting of the previous year.

Mysterious rumours abound concerning this case; that Mantell described the object as 'metallic . . . tremendous in size', that his body was not in the plane when the wreckage was recovered, and that his funeral was 'closed casket' because of extraordinary wounds on

his body. None of these claims can be regarded as definitively substantiated and it is certainly the usual procedure for plane crash victims to be buried 'closed casket' due to their injuries.

Whether Mantell was a victim of his own excitement, or whether he was struck down by an alien force resisting his pursuit of their saucer can now never be proven. However, the light Mantell chased was, by any sensible definition, a UFO and therefore we can rightly regard Mantell's death as the first attributed to a UFO encounter.

ABOVE An artist's impression of Mantell's P-51 Mustang training plane climbing towards the UFO high over Godman Field in Kentucky. Other planes in the flight turned back at a lower altitude but Mantell pressed on. Minutes later he was dead. Speculation with regard to what he was chasing continues to this day. Was it a weather balloon, a star, the planet Venus, or a craft from another world?

RIGHT Captain Thomas Mantell.

NAME AZTEC

DATE 25 MARCH 1948

PLACE AZTEC, NEW MEXICO
MAP REF: H17

EVENT CRASH RETRIEVAL

According to the newspaper columnist Frank Scully in his book *Behind the Flying Saucers* a most extraordinary discovery was made by the United States Air Force in 1948. According to the story he was told by his informants a flying saucer had crashed near Aztec, New Mexico and was recovered by the United States military. Inside the craft were sixteen dead humanoid alien cadavers. The disc had been detected by radar units and indeed it is thought that radar signals may have disrupted the craft's controls, bringing it down accidentally.

The disc was 100 ft (30 m) wide and had a central cabin around 6 ft (183 cm) high. It was made of a light metal so strong that neither heat nor diamond drills could affect the surface; there were no rivets or signs of welding. Fortunately, damage to one of the saucer's portholes enabled the investigators to break in and open its hatchway.

After successfully dismantling the object, its components and the cadavers were then transported to what is now Wright Patterson Air Force Base. Further investigation of the object apparently revealed still working control panels displaying hieroglyphic symbols and a book of hieroglyphs on plastic like paper. The cadavers were described as approximately 3 ft 6 in (107 cm) high with large heads, large slanting eyes and diminished nose, mouth and ears. The bodies were apparently very thin with long arms and webbed

A modelmaker's reconstruction of the Aztec crash retrieval. A more exciting incident than Roswell (see page 18) but less authoritatively substantiated. Many believe this one to be a hoax.

fingers. Dissection revealed that there was no blood but instead a liquid smelling similar to ozone. Curiously, and apparently contradictorily, the bodies had no digestive tract but perfect teeth. Whether or not Scully was the victim of a hoax, Aztec remains just one of many similar crash retrievals reported in the United States over the years.

NAME CHILES/WHITTED

DATE 24 JULY 1948

PLACE MONTGOMERY, GEORGIA
MAP REF: M18

EVENT CLOSE ENCOUNTER OF THE FIRST KIND

Just after the formation of the US Air Force's Project Sign, one of its many attempts to investigate UFOs, it received the report of two Eastern Airline pilots, Captain C. Chiles and First Officer John Whitted.

In the early hours of the morning they were flying an Eastern Airlines DC-3 near Montgomery when both pilots witnessed a UFO heading towards them at 'terrific speed'. So close was the encounter that the DC-3 had to veer sharply to the left and the UFO passed by only 700 ft (213 m) from the plane. The UFO's deceleration was so violent that it rocked the DC-3.

The pilots were close enough to it to take some note of the object itself; it appeared to radiate an intense blue light and the pilots saw a double row of windows along the side. As it disappeared behind the plane they saw a red-orange exhaust. They estimated its speed at between 500-700 miles (805-1,127 km) per hour.

There was corroboration of the sighting from witnesses at Robbins Field, Georgia who described an object tallying very closely with the description given by the pilots.

NAME FARGO

DATE 1 OCTOBER 1948

PLACE FARGO, NORTH DAKOTA
MAP REF: J15

EVENT AERIAL DOG FIGHT

Captain Edward A. Ruppelt's official Blue Book explanation of the Fargo encounter was 'In this incident the UFO was a balloon.' Considering the facts of the case below it is difficult to decide whether this conclusion represents great imagination on the part of the US Air Force or an astonishing lack of it.

It was approximately 9 o'clock in the evening of 1 October 1948 when Second Lieutenant George Gorman of the North Dakota Air National Guard was piloting an F-51 towards Fargo, North Dakota. As he was being given instructions to land he was informed that there was a Piper Cub nearby, which he confirmed visually. At the same time he saw another craft moving very rapidly under his right wing. He contacted the tower for further identification but they confirmed no aircraft near him, other than the Piper Cub.

Closing in, Gorman saw that the object displayed a light some 8 in (20 cm) in diameter. It was globular and hazing at the edge. Gorman watched the object move into a sudden turn passing over the control tower; Gorman dived towards the object but could not catch up with it. As it started gaining altitude it banked left and Gorman attempted to follow. At this point they were 7,000 ft (2,130 m) high, the object made a sharp turn again and was heading straight for Gorman's aircraft. The effect was so startling that Gorman was forced to make a dramatic dive and the light passed over the canopy some 500 ft (152 m) above him. As the UFO circled above, Gorman gave chase again. One account suggests that the manoeuvring was so intense that Gorman blacked out temporarily.

Air traffic control was now visually confirming Gorman's sighting, traffic controller Errol Jensen announced 'You were right. There is something.' He was examining the object through high-powered binoculars and he passed these to witness Manuel Johnson, who confirmed the sighting.

As the object closed in again it suddenly shot upwards, Gorman chased it to 14,000 ft (4,260 m) and his plane then went into a power stall, its engine dead. The object disappeared towards the north-west-north direction. The combat had lasted nearly thirty minutes.

Gorman reported 'I am convinced there was thought behind these manoeuvres. I had the distinct impression that its manoeuvres were controlled by thought or reason. I am also certain that it was governed by the laws of inertia, because its acceleration was rapid, not immediate and although it was able to turn fairly tightly, at considerable speed, it still followed a natural curve.'

A most remarkable balloon!

NAME WHITE SANDS

DATE 24 APRIL 1949

PLACE WHITE SANDS PROVING GROUNDS, NEW MEXICO
MAP REF: H18

EVENT DISTANT DAYLIGHT SIGHTING

On a clear Sunday morning near the White Sands Proving Grounds, Naval Commander R. McLaughlan and a tracking crew of four launched a large weather balloon. This followed an earlier launch of a small similar balloon at 10.30 a.m.

They were tracking their target at approximately 10,000 ft (3,048 m) when one of the team, Charles Moore, spotted a white egg-shaped object; he pointed it out and the UFO was confirmed visually by all the personnel. For about one minute they tracked the object until they saw it shoot up and vanish.

If their interpretation of the data was correct, it follows that when they had first started tracking the object it had been 56 miles (90 km) high and travelling at 7 miles (11 km) per second, the escape velocity needed to break out of the Earth's gravitational pull. During one part of the observation the craft had made an 80 degree turn at that velocity, quite beyond the capabilities of even today's technology.

Interestingly, the object was similar in shape and colour to the object which landed at Socorro, New Mexico on 24 April 1964 (see page 46), fifteen years to the day following this sighting.

NAME THE TRENT PHOTOGRAPHS

DATE 11 MAY 1950

PLACE McMINNVILLE, OREGON
MAP REF: E14

EVENT CLOSE ENCOUNTER OF THE FIRST
KIND

In the early evening of 11 May 1950, on a small farm near McMinnville, Mrs Trent was outside feeding her rabbits when she saw the close approach of a large disc-shaped object. She called to her husband, Paul Trent, who brought with him their camera, and Mrs Trent was able to take two black and white photographs as the object passed across the sky in the direction of the north west.

A local newspaper picked up the story and published the photographs, which were later featured in *LIFE* magazine, causing something of a national sensation. At the time they were some of the best flying saucer photographs available. William Hartmann, investigating for the Condon committee, acknowledged that these photographs were the only ones that the committee had not dismissed (the Condon committee was notorious for its unscientific, dismissive attitude towards the UFO phenomenon). He stated that the photographs were consistent with the witness's testimony 'that an extraordinary flying object, silvery, metallic, disc shaped, tens of meters

One of two photographs taken by Mrs Paul Trent on 11 May 1950 over the Trent farm at McMinnville, Oregon.

in diameter, and evidently artificial, flew within sight of two witnesses.'

In the four decades since the photographs were taken there have been many more sophisticated analysis techniques employed to study the photographs such as 'edge enhancement' (which would show any cut-outs photographed through glass, or expose any supporting wires or struts for example) and colour-contouring. None have yet suggested that the photographs were faked, and the indications suggest that some large object flew over the Trent's farm that day.

NAME THE LUBBOCK LIGHTS

DATE 28 AUGUST 1951

PLACE LUBBOCK, TEXAS
MAP REF: I18

EVENT ANOMALOUS LIGHT PHOTOGRAPHS

Witnessed on many occasions and photographed several times are the famous Lubbock lights which appear from time to time over Lubbock in Texas. Many explanations have been offered for the arrow shaped formation; inevitably, fleets of flying saucers have featured prominently. However, other suggestions have included lights reflecting on the underbellies of ducks, and a natural light phenomenon not yet understood by science, but perhaps a cousin of the Aurora Borealis (see page 42), or St Elmo's fire.

The lights have become something of a tourist attraction. As one American put it, Lubbock used only to have the Lights and Buddy Holly (who was born there) – now they've only got the Lights.

A photograph taken by an unnamed teenage student over Lubbock, Texas.

195Cs

NAME DURING THE WASHINGTON FLAP

DATE 19 JULY 1952

PLACE WASHINGTON D.C.
MAP REF: N16

EVENT RADAR VISUAL ENCOUNTER

It was nearly midnight when staff of the Air Route Traffic Control (ARTC) at Washington National Airport noticed a formation of seven objects on the radar screen, at a position slightly south-east of Andrews Air Force Base. The objects seemed to be moving at approximately 100-130 miles (160-209 km) per hour and were therefore assumed to be a flight of ordinary small aircraft.

Suddenly two of the objects accelerated forward and off the screen at an amazing rate, later calculation indicated in excess of 7,000 miles (11,265 km) per hour, and at this point the radar monitor knew that he was not witnessing normal aircraft movements.

He called for his senior officer and together with two other experts they watched the remaining objects. A suggestion was made that the scope may not be functioning correctly but the technician examined it and agreed that it was in perfect working order.

ARTC called the control tower and a senior officer there confirmed that they were also watching the same unknowns on their radar screens and that they had had information from Andrews Air Force Base that that military installation was monitoring the objects.

Throughout the time of the observations the objects were not only manoeuvring at incredible speed above Washington D.C. but they had the temerity to fly into the 'no go' area above the White House. Perhaps they were considering that much requested 'landing on the White House lawn'.

They were not alone in the sky. Captain S. 'Casey' Pierman of Capital Airlines was flying Flight 807 from Washington to Detroit and sighted the seven objects between Washington and Martinsburg. He reported the objects as 'like falling shooting stars without tails'.

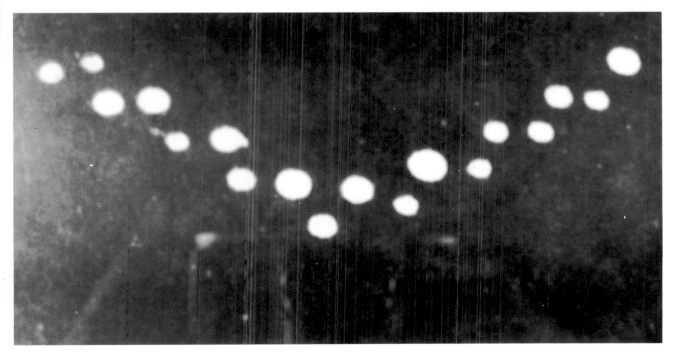

George J Stock photographed this, which was one of seven UFOs he saw over Passaic, New Jersey on 29 July 1952. The sighting came during an intense wave of reports in the vicinity of Washington DC (the Washington Flap) and is typical of many descriptions of the time.

Pierman observed the objects for some twelve minutes before they disappeared at remarkable speed and confirmed much of the detail of the radar reports. He said of the incident 'In all my years of flying I've seen a lot of falling or shooting stars . . . but these were much faster than anything like that I've ever seen. They couldn't have been aircraft . . . they were moving too fast for that.'

Pierman's confirmation of the radar sightings is all the more impressive for his impartiality. He stated 'Please remember I didn't speak of them as flying saucers . . . only very fast moving lights.'

In the pre-dawn light further confirmation was approaching. A new blip had appeared on the ARTC radar screen above Andrews Air Force Base and tower personnel there, when notified, visually observed a large globular orange sphere hovering directly above them. ARTC called for Air Force interceptors which arrived too late; the objects had gone.

Senior Air Traffic Controller Harry G. Barnes at the ARTC made the observation that it seemed as though the UFOs were monitoring radio communication between ground and aircraft and were able to take appropriate action based on what they could hear.

NAME	DESVERGERS ENCOUNTER
DATE	19 AUGUST 1952
PLACE	WEST PALM BEACH, FLORIDA MAP REF: N19
EVENT	CLOSE ENCOUNTER OF THE SECOND KIND

Evidence of possible hostility on the part of UFOs comes from the claims of scout-master D. Desvergers and his experience on 19 August 1952.

Most significant is the reaction of the Air Force. Instead of ordering a routine check by a local intelligence officer from Miami, they instructed Captain Ruppelt, the head of its UFO investigation Project Blue Book, to investigate personally.

At around 9 o'clock in the evening the scout-master and three scouts were travelling by car from a meeting towards their homes when they saw lights in the nearby woods. Desvergers, carrying a machete knife and a torch, left the three boys in the car and went to investigate. One of the scouts apparently saw a red ball of fire above where Desvergers had last been seen; when Desvergers failed to return, one of the scouts ran to the nearest house and telephoned the sheriff.

It was as the sheriff arrived that Desvergers made his reappearance. He was badly frightened, totally exhausted and describing a very close encounter indeed. He stated that when he had reached a clearing he had pointed his torch upward and had seen a huge, metallic, disc-shaped machine hovering above him, which had immediately fired some sort of hot spray at him. He had lain injured for a few minutes during which time the saucer disappeared.

There certainly seems to be some corroboration for the story: Desvergers' arm was scorched, his hat was burned, and the Sheriff discovered scorching in the trees.

Captain Edward J Ruppelt, head of Project Blue Book, the US Air Force's investigation into the UFO phenomenon.

PHOTOGRAPHIC EVIDENCE

For most people, photographic evidence is perhaps the most convincing of all material used to substantiate a sighting. In fact, photographs can easily mislead and confuse rather than clarify a case. Very few credible cases are supported by photographs, and many photographs that do exist are vague and give very little information about the origin of a UFO phenomenon. No photograph, however thought-provoking, has yet been able to prove satisfactorily that UFOs are extra-terrestrial spaceships.

Nevertheless, photographs are of use in support of witness testimony. If the image in the photographs is consistent with the story line given by the witness, then the case gains strength from the added weight of evidence. If the photographs tell a different story, then almost certainly the case is a hoax. Many photographs indicate the presence of UFOs but subsequent analysis proves otherwise. Often, people will 'snap' pictures on holiday only to find, when examining the developed prints, that disc-shaped objects appear in the sky. Sometimes these are established to be lens flares (which can have remarkable symmetry and apparent solidity) or tricks of the light. Modern analysis can expose these photographs as such. In one such case BUFORA received a photograph showing a disc in the sky which had not been noticed at the time the photograph was taken. The witness was convinced of the extra-terrestrial origin of the 'craft' shown but close study of the negative revealed it to be a lens flare.

Occasionally, photographs last a long time before being exposed in this way. The photograph below was taken on 16 July 1952 at Salem, Massachusetts during a wave of sightings. It was case number 1501 in the US Air Force's Project Blue Book. The photograph seems to show lights in the air over the Coast Guard Facility. In fact, the photograph was taken through a glass window, and modern analysis suggests that the images are reflected lights from somewhere inside the building, which quite possibly went unnoticed by the photographer at the time who would have been concentrating on the 'dimming' and 'brightening' of the lights as he lined up to take the photograph. Of course when strange lights appear in the sky over a Coast Guard facility one can understand to some extent how a photographer might leap to false conclusions.

NAME GEORGE ADAMSKI

DATE 20 NOVEMBER 1952

PLACE GEORGE ADAMSKI, DESERT CENTRE,
CALIFORNIA
MAP REF: E18

EVENT THE FIRST CONTACT BETWEEN MAN
AND EXTRATERRESTRIAL

In 1953 62-year-old George
Adamski published a book *Flying
Saucers Have Landed* which claimed
that he had met with
extraterrestrials in the desert in
California. Although there had been
flying saucer sightings for many
years (and indeed Adamski revealed
that he himself had been sighting
saucers since 1946), this was the
first claim of contact between man
and alien. It apparently occurred just
after noon on Thursday, 20
November 1952 approximately 10

miles (16 km) from Desert Centre,
towards Arizona.

To a limited extent the encounter
was witnessed by two families, the
Williamsons and the Baileys who had
asked to be with him when he next
believed he would see a flying
saucer. They reported that from a
distance of approximately a mile
away they saw some details of the
meeting.

Adamski was watching and
photographing a flying saucer some
35 ft (11 m) wide when he noticed a
man beckoning towards him. The
man was approximately 5 ft 6 in
(167 cm), of average weight and
appeared youthful. He had perfect
white teeth, calm green eyes, long
flowing blond hair and tanned skin.
He was wearing a one-piece brown
ski-type suit and oxblood coloured
shoes resembling sandals.

The two used sign language and telepathy to communicate and the alien indicated he was Venusian. In the days when Adamski published his book it was held that Venus was the sister planet of the Earth and likely to produce an identical race of people. Subsequent analysis of the planet indicates that that could not be further from the truth and no humanoid could comfortably live on the planet. The alien apparently believed in God, felt that he and his people followed a more devoted path than us and was concerned about atomic radiation from Earth.

The contact was the first of many; during this first meeting Adamski handed his alien companion a film from his camera and at the second meeting the film was apparently returned, covered in indecipherable hieroglyphs. In subsequent adventures Adamski was taken on journeys to other planets where he met Martians, Saturnians and Jovians.

In 1965 Adamski and Madeleine Rodeffer apparently took 8 mm movie film of the flying saucer visitations in Maryland, USA though the authenticity of that film has been called into question.

Many of Adamski's photographs were taken in the grounds of the Mount Palomar Observatory where Adamski worked and had a small telescope. Over the past forty years controversy has dogged Adamski's claims and the photographs he produced but, more importantly, scientific knowledge has made redundant many of the statements he made. Adamski himself was clearly aware of the controversy. In *Flying Saucers Have Landed* he states 'Surface thinkers might like to conclude that I had had a very original dream. Or that I may be out to make money for myself in the field of science fiction. I can assure such persons that nothing is farther from the truth.'

OPPOSITE ABOVE Flying saucer photographed by contactee George Adamski at 9.10 am on 13 December 1952 at Palomar Gardens in California. Adamski took the picture through a 6 in (15 cm) telescope. OPPOSITE BELOW Photographed by George Adamski on 5 March 1951, the picture apparently shows a cigar shaped 'mother craft' releasing small 'scout ships'. RIGHT The cover of Adamski's book, written with British author Desmond Leslie, which told the extraordinary tale of Adamski's meetings with extra-terrestrials. His were the first claims of this sort and led to a plethora of others in subsequent years. BELOW Mount Palomar observatory, the dome of the 200 in (500 cm) Hale Telescope. Adamski made much of his association with this institution although his main connection with the establishment was his job at a local hamburger cafe.

Flying Saucers Have Landed

Desmond Leslie & George Adamski

On Thursday 20 November 1952 George Adamski claimed man's first meeting with an extra-terrestrial. Using sign language and telepathy the alien indicated that he came from Venus.

NAME GULF OF MEXICO

DATE 6 DECEMBER 1952

PLACE GULF OF MEXICO
MAP REF: K19

EVENT RADAR/VISUAL ENCOUNTER

In the early hours of the morning of 6 December, Captain John Harter and radar officer, Lieutenant Sid Coleman were returning to base following a night practice flight of their B-29 bomber.

They were approximately 200 miles (322 km) from Galveston, 100 miles (160 km) south of the Louisiana coast at 18,000 ft (5,486 m) in bright moonlight when Coleman noticed an unidentified blip on one edge of the radar screen. It was not until the second sweep of the screen that its significance became apparent.

When the blip reappeared the unknown object had moved 13 miles (21 km). By the third sweep Coleman and his staff sergeant had computed the speed of the object: over 5,000 miles (8,047 km) per hour, considerably faster than any aircraft of the day!

Coleman reported the trace to the captain, and indicated the speed of the object; Captain Harter insisted that the set should be recalibrated as it was 'impossible'. While Coleman was recalibrating the set Master Sergeant Bailey noticed another object on the screen. At that point the navigator, Lieutenant Cassidy, reported that he had them on his screen as well.

Within a short space of time there were four UFOs on the screen and the captain radioed from the flight deck 'I've got four unknowns at 12 o'clock. What do you show?' ('12 o'clock' is the code for 'dead ahead'). Coleman reported that the objects were showing up on all three of the plane's radar screens and it was therefore not a malfunction.

Harter needed no confirmation of that; he was watching the objects approaching incredibly fast outside the windscreen. Bailey watched out of the starboard side of the plane as one of the objects, illuminated blue-white, streaked rapidly past the plane, vanishing to the rear. Almost immediately other UFOs were appearing on the radar screen and all heading towards the aircraft!

Fortunately for the aircrew the UFOs were on a course which just missed the aircraft and after six minutes from the time of the first sighting it appeared that the danger was over. It was not!

A third group of UFOs flashed onto the radar screen, radar tracking indicated speeds much the same as before. Again blue-white illuminated objects streaked past the plane. For Captain Harter the dangers were all too real as he was watching the objects cutting across the plane's flight path and – suddenly swerving – they were now heading straight for the B-29!

Suddenly, and almost unbelievably, the objects slowed to the speed of the aircraft and paced it for some ten seconds. As the crew watched, the objects pulled away and then the most amazing part of the sighting occurred.

An enormous UFO apparently joined the formation and, still moving at some 5,000 miles (8,047 km) per hour, it appeared that the smaller craft docked or merged with the larger object. Accelerating to 9,000 miles (14,484 km) per hour the UFO flashed across the scope and disappeared. The encounter was finally over.

Captain Harter contacted his base and when he landed United States Air Force intelligence officers met him and the crew. For some time they were questioned separately and as a group but their story remained quite firm.

Major Donald E. Keyhoe, a prominent ufologist with a military background, interpreted the sighting as: 'The discs had been launched from a huge mothership for some type of reconnaissance mission . . . for a rendez-vous, whoever guided the discs had chosen this point over the Gulf of Mexico. After the B-29 was sighted one group of discs had been diverted for a brief observation or tracking. Then, flying at 5,000 miles (8,047 km) per hour they had been taken aboard the mothership.'

Whether this interpretation is correct or not is open to debate and the visual sightings were unable to confirm a distinct shape to the objects because they were moving so fast. However, the fact is that several members of a highly trained crew all witnessed the same encounter. Added to this it was tracked not only visually but on radar, strongly suggesting the proof of some reality, whatever its exact nature or source.

NAME TUJUNGA CANYON

DATE 1953

PLACE TUJUNGA CANYON, CALIFORNIA
MAP REF: E17

EVENT ABDUCTION

The Tujunga Canyon abduction was, by today's standards, a rather undetailed and unremarkable event. However, it contains certain aspects which make it worthy of note.

The case predates Antonio Villas Boas (see page 181) and Betty and Barney Hill (see page 42) by some years and consequently becomes one of the first reported abductions. A word of caution: the report first arose considerably after the given date, not in fact until 1975 when abduction lore was rife in America. Note, too, that the case contains, at

H G WELLS'S *WAR OF THE WORLDS* COMES TO AMERICA

In 1897, when H G Wells's *War of the Worlds* was published, man had not yet even learned to harness the power of flight. In his original story the Martians reached Earth in bullet-like projectiles fired as if from a gun and proceeded to terrorize the Home Counties in England from within walking machines. In 1953, George Pal's film moved the location to California and updated the walking machines to flying saucers It was a clear reaction to the flying saucer phenomenon. Pal said, 'With all the talk about flying saucers, *War of the Worlds* had become especially timely. And that was one of the reasons we updated the story.' Just as films mirror UFO reports, conversely, detailed analysis shows that some aspects of UFOs follow film and other mythologies; the interaction is a complex one which requires serious research. Genuine reports of aliens often act like their filmed predecessors, yet the films were made before alien reports were offered. Simple copy-cat claims do not explain the complexity of the interaction, which suggests that a genuine experience is being overlaid on a basic belief system which can manifest itself in fact or fiction.

least as reported, the most explicit example of missing time in any abduction case.

According to the report the two witnesses, known as Sara Shaw and Jan Whitely, both in their early twenties, were living in a remote part of the Tujunga Canyon in California. Sara was woken by a moving light out of her bedroom window which apparently terrified her. She feared it might be the headlights of a motorcycle gang seeking to attack the isolated women. The smooth movement of the lights quickly ruled out this possibility as the road towards their cabin was rough and would have caused 'bouncing' motion. Jan was now awake and went to get her dressing-gown, Sara noticed it was 2 a.m. on the clock.

As apparently only a fraction of a second passed she looked at the clock again feeling giddy and confused and noticed that the minute hand had moved on twenty minutes. When Jan checked the clock she confirmed this observation but pointed out that the hour hand had also moved on two hours. Apparently both witnesses had

suffered a two hour, twenty minutes time lapse and this caused them to panic so considerably that they left their home and went to Jan's parents.

Regression hypnosis revealed a classic abduction story, several of which we shall see later in this database. The case has also come under considerable scrutiny from those who believe abductions constitute a psychological phenomenon as it appears that the two girls' sexual relationships may have generated anxieties of which the abduction may have been a manifestation.

NAME LIVERMORE

DATE 27 JANUARY 1953

PLACE LIVERMORE, OAKLAND, CALIFORNIA
MAP REF: E16

EVENT CLOSE ENCOUNTER OF THE FIRST
KIND

While not dramatic by today's standards, the sighting by John Bean on 27 January 1953 had a considerable effect at the time, partly because of the location of the sighting and partly because of the qualifications of the witness.

Bean had been flying for some seventeen years and was knowledgeable about aircraft manoeuvrability. On the afternoon in question he was driving away from the Atomic Energy Commission Research facilities and had pulled into the side of the road to get some papers from his briefcase. He was about to get out of the driver's door to go round to the backseats to obtain his briefcase when he stopped

for a moment to watch a DC-6 descending towards Oakland Municipal Airport. His attention was attracted to a white object crossing the Atomic Energy Commission facilities and he first thought of this as some sort of plant material in the wind. He quickly realized that the object was more solid and indeed swiftly moving. He described it as perfectly round with a metallic sheen something like aluminium.

Bean concentrated on the object and its manoeuvring watching its very abrupt direction changes and the incredible speed of its ascent. Only days before he had watched two F-86 fighters manoeuvring to the limit of their capabilities and he realized that these fighters were amateurs compared to the capabilities of the object he was watching.

A jet aircraft was also approaching for a landing. Bean was therefore particularly fortunate in having three distinct types of aircraft

in sight at the same time, allowing him to make certain comparisons. By any definition the UFO had more power and manoeuvrability than the DC-6 or the jet fighter.

NAME DANIEL FRY

DATE 1954

PLACE WHITE SANDS PROVING GROUNDS,
NEW MEXICO
MAP REF: H18

EVENT CLOSE ENCOUNTER OF THE THIRD
KIND

According to Daniel Fry's testimony his first meeting with extraterrestrials took place on 4 July 1950 thus predating many UFO claims and certainly the contactee claims of George Adamski which had been published in 1953. However, as Fry's book was published in 1954 and since there seem to be some grounds for believing it was inspired in some way by George Adamski's

claims, I have set it into the database at the date of publication rather than at the date of claim. Daniel Fry's was just one of many contactee claims to follow those of Adamski but it is, perhaps along with Adamski's, one of the best known.

According to his claims Dr Daniel Fry witnessed a landing of a UFO on 4 July 1950. He walked up to it and touched it, feeling that it was nothing known to man on this Earth. The hull apparently felt soap like and smooth and a voice came out of the machine warning him, in a strangely American slang, 'Better not touch the hull pal, it's still hot.' Clearly Fry's aliens came from somewhere other than Adamski's who, three years later, were still using telepathy and sign language to communicate.

Fry's contactee, A-Lan (but later shortened to Alan for convenience sake) explained much of the physics involved in the construction and movement of his craft to Fry who

ABOVE Daniel Fry, the contactee who claimed several meetings with space people during the early 1950s. Although his claims pre-date Adamski's, they were not revealed until after Adamski had published his book. LEFT One of the alien spaceships photographed by Daniel Fry.

understood some of it since he was a trained space technician. Indeed, the event had taken place near the White Sands Proving Grounds where Fry was working.

The visitors were trying to 'help you people on earth alter the present flow of events and avert a holocaust which is otherwise inevitable.' Fry was told he had to write a book to communicate the messages to the people of Earth which he dutifully did.

NAME GOOSE BAY, LABRADOR

DATE 29 JUNE 1954

PLACE GOOSE BAY, LABRADOR
MAP REF: P11

EVENT CLOSE ENCOUNTER OF THE FIRST KIND

Reports of sightings of UFOs by pilots are frequent and deflate the claim that only unqualified or deranged people sight such objects. Perhaps the best reported example is that of Captain James Howard over Goose Bay, Labrador in 1954.

Captain Howard was flying a BOAC Stratocruiser from New York to London in the early hours of the evening of 29 June. Some half an hour out, Boston air traffic control informed Howard he must hold position though gave him no reason. It took a request from Howard to Boston control, pointing out his concerns for his fuel levels, to obtain permission to go forward and in doing so he was made to detour far north via Cape Cod. In view of what was to happen later in the flight it is speculated that air traffic control had picked up anomalous returns on its radar and was redirecting traffic as a result of this.

It was some three hours later over the St Lawrence estuary flying at 19,000 ft (5,791 m), way above the cloud level, that Captain Howard

first witnessed seven UFOs in formation. Howard indicated they were moving at a speed to pace the aircraft, i.e. some 230 knots, were some 3 miles (5 km) away from them and were below the cloud level. Once they had passed over the coast, the clouds cleared and Captain Howard saw the UFOs more clearly.

They paced the aircraft for some twenty minutes during which time Captain Howard, his crew and several passengers witnessed and sketched the objects. There were apparently six small globes and one large object but the formation was constantly changing. The objects kept a straight line with sometimes three ahead of the large globe and three at the rear or sometimes four ahead and two at the rear, etc. Howard believed they were solid. Co-pilot Lee Boyd reported the incident to Goose Bay, Labrador and they were asked to describe the sighting, which they did.

Captain Howard could hardly complain that he was not taken seriously. A patrolling F-94 fighter was vectored towards the aircraft and frequencies were lined up to allow Captain Howard to talk directly to the pilots of the fighter. Whatever the explanation for the UFOs they were not radar visible as the fighter indicated they had only the Stratocruiser on radar. Even more mysteriously the objects disappeared as the F-94 approached.

At a fuel stop over at Goose Bay United States Air Force intelligence officers interrogated the crew and told them that there had been other sightings like it in the area. Despite possible corroboration from a ground witness who saw a number of objects flying in the right direction at the right time, lack of radar corroboration unfortunately deprived the case of its most valuable possibilities.

Kelly-Hopkinsville, 21 August 1955. Eight adults and three children experienced a horrifying siege by beings so grotesque as to be almost beyond belief.

NAME KELLY-HOPKINSVILLE

DATE 21 AUGUST 1955

PLACE KELLY-HOPKINSVILLE, KENTUCKY
MAP REF: L17

EVENT CLOSE ENCOUNTER OF THE THIRD
KIND

As evening fell on 21 August 1955 the Sutton family, Elmer, Vera, John, Alene and her brother were hosts to the Langford family, Glenie and her three children Lonnie, Charlton and Mary together with a friend of Elmer's, Billy Ray Taylor and his wife June. Around 7 o'clock Billy Ray Taylor left the house to get water from the farm well and to take a drink. While outside he saw a UFO 'real bright, with an exhaust all the colours of the rainbow'. It apparently landed close to the farm in a dried-up river bed. When he returned inside the house and told the others of his sighting he was not believed, and it was generally thought he had seen a shooting star. Nobody investigated the landing site. An hour later the eight adults and three children were to begin an extended, horrifying siege by beings so extraordinarily grotesque as to be almost beyond belief.

It began with the crazed barking of their dog in the yard and Elmer, known as 'Lucky' Sutton, went with Billy Ray Taylor to the kitchen door of the farmhouse to see what was disturbing the animal. What he saw must have seemed like the product of a nightmare: a glowing, dwarf like creature with enormous eyes and with arms stretched high above its head was slowly and determinedly approaching the house!

These isolated country folk were not accustomed to diplomatic pleasantries and tend to 'shoot first and ask questions afterwards'. Lucky took a shotgun, and Taylor a .22 rifle, and both fired at the entity when it had reached around 20 ft

(6 m) from the farmhouse. The creature scurried away into the night. Indoors, the others heard a scraping sound from the kitchen roof and the men ran back into the yard and saw a similar creature on top of the farmhouse. When fired upon, although the creature fell, it apparently floated gently down towards the backyard before making off on all four limbs.

The entities were of a type unique in UFO lore. Although incorporating some of the features of 'classical' entities, i.e. short slim figures, large round bald heads, etc. there were striking differences. Each had huge yellow shining eyes placed on the sides of their face and an enormous mouth like a crack stretching across the face. The ears were huge elephant like appendages, enormous in comparison to the body.

The creatures appeared to be reluctant to come too close to the bright lights of the farmhouse but the families were concerned because of the ineffectiveness of their weapons and barricaded themselves inside. For some three hours they watched the entities around the farmhouse until they were forced to make a desperate decision to escape. At around 11 o'clock in the evening they dashed from the farmhouse into two cars and 'high-tailed' it the 10 miles (16 km) to the police station at Hopkinsville, arriving in a state of agitation and fear.

They impressed the police to the extent that the Chief, Russell Greenwell, his Deputy George Batts, Sergeant Pritchett and three other officers, along with a local journalist, returned with the family to the farm ready to take up the battle. Just 2 miles (3 km) out of Hopkinsville and on the way back to the Kelly farmhouse they saw two streaks of light overhead and heard a

loud, persistent banging sound.

No trace of either the entities or the UFO could be found although some bullet holes were located. The Chief of Police stated that 'something frightened these people, something beyond their comprehension.' The police called off the investigation until daylight.

But at 2.30 in the morning the nightmare returned!

Glenie, in bed, looked at her window and saw the huge shining eyes of one of the entities staring into the bedroom. She softly called to the other members of the family and 'Lucky' Sutton shot at the intruder which scampered off into the darkness. It was not until past 5 o'clock that morning, 22 August, and approximately an hour before

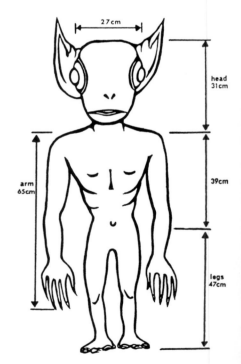

An artist's impression of one of the entities that besieged the Kelly-Hopkinsville farmhouse on 21 August 1955. They never harmed the witnesses, and their approach, with claws raised in the air, may have been a gesture of peace – not an easy intention to express when you look like this!

first light, that the entities were last seen and the nightmare was over.

The aftermath of the night was very difficult for the witnesses. They were accused of religious hysteria and they were harassed following the publicity that surrounded their report. Throughout all of this, however, they stuck to their story and refused to protect themselves from the excesses of the media even by toning down their claims, maintaining that they were being truthful.

No explanation for the encounter has been offered that stands up to reasonable examination. A travelling circus had passed through Hopkinsville that day and it was speculated that they could have lost performing monkeys but the suggestion falls down on so many grounds that it is almost laughable. For one thing there was no report of any lost monkeys, for another monkeys do not fit the physical descriptions of the entities, let alone glow in the dark. Most importantly at least one wounded or dead monkey ought to have been found after a night time barrage of shooting, yet no bodies were ever recovered.

It has to be admitted that there was no proof of malevolent intent on the part of the entities and it has been speculated that these creatures approaching the farmhouse with their hands in the air may have been trying to show they were unarmed and harmless. Given their physical appearance there seems to be no practical way in which a creature like that could ever fail to instil fear.

Whatever the truth of the Kelly-Hopkinsville encounter, it remains today, over thirty-five years later, one of the most extraordinary and terrifying multiple-witness encounters on record.

JIM AND CORAL LORENZEN

One of the first civilian UFO research organizations in the world was the Aerial Phenomena Research Organization (APRO), formed by Jim and Coral Lorenzen. The organization and its founders came under much official monitoring and it is now disbanded. Despite a known study by the Air Office of Special Investigation (AOSI), neither Jim nor Coral Lorenzen were prevented from continuing their work for the US Air Force, suggesting at least no official condemnation of their activities.

NAME 'JENNIE'

DATE 7 OCTOBER 1955

PLACE NEBRASKA
MAP REF: J15

EVENT ABDUCTION

Late in the evening a teenage girl, Jennie, was dressed for bed in her bedroom. Under hypnosis, she told the story of an entity floating outside her bedroom window whom she refers to as 'the explorer' and she states that she felt drawn towards him, perhaps under his telepathic influence. She seems to be trying to protect herself, by pretending that the event is a dream and she says she does not want to listen to him.

The entity floated through the air towards a UFO, described as like two dessert bowls placed together, and willed her to follow. In doing so she moved *through* the bedroom wall and claimed she could even see the dirt and cobwebs inside the wall as she passed through it.

The UFO itself appeared to haze in and out of visibility, apparently allowing vision through its walls to the interior and even through that to the surrounding terrain. Inside the UFO it was very cold. She described the entity as between 3-4 ft (91-122 cm) tall with an egg shaped head, grey complexion, reduced facial features and long, slit like eyes. He was wearing some close-fitting head dress. During the subsequent medical examination blood samples were taken.

On re-awakening the next morning Jennie remembered the event as a dream; whether this is a protective device of her own mind or not is unclear. There is some corroboration of her story as possible physical traces on a nearby

UFO COMES IN ALL SHAPES AND SIZES

The expression UFO has been corrupted over the years and is often held to mean extra-terrestrial spaceship. Nothing could be further from an accurate definition and it is well to remember that the expression means nothing more nor less than Unidentified Flying Object. Of all the reports received by organizations throughout the world, approximately 90-95% are identified. Typically, most of these turn out to be reports of natural phenomena of various sorts. Planets – and particularly the bright planets Venus and Jupiter – are often identified as the cause of UFO reports. Some stars have been culprits, and there are many natural but exotic-looking phenomena that are reported as UFOs. RIGHT Noctilucent clouds are visible at night, at dawn or at dusk and comprise masses of ice high in the atmosphere illuminated by the sun from over the horizon, causing a hazy, glowing shape in the sky. BELOW *Aurora borealis*, the Northern Lights, photographed before dawn near Fairbanks, Alaska. Auroras are luminous displays that occur in the night sky at high latitudes.

elm tree outside her window show as burn markings. However, her father believes that it was hit by lightning.

Interestingly, this case only came to light in 1984 when abduction lore was rife in the American media and details were becoming well known to the previously 'uninitiated'.

NAME	LOCHRAVEN DAM
DATE	26 OCTOBER 1958
PLACE	LOCHRAVEN DAM, BALTIMORE, PA MAP REF: N16
EVENT	CLOSE ENCOUNTER OF THE FIRST KIND

At 10.30 in the evening Alvin Cohen and Philip Small saw an egg-shaped UFO above Lochraven Dam in Maryland. The object was, they estimated, hovering approximately 100-150 ft (30-46 m) above a small metal bridge near the dam, some 250 yds (229 m) from them. They drove closer to investigate.

At some 80 ft (24 m) from the object the car's electrical systems went dead; its dashlights and headlights went out and its motor stopped. In trying to restart the car there was no sound of even the starter motor trying to engage. Both witnesses panicked, jumped out of the car and moved behind it.

After some 20-30 seconds a bright white light accompanied by a deafening noise burst from the object and it started to rise vertically and within just a few seconds it had vanished into the sky above. As the light flashed both men reported feeling heat and both displayed symptoms similar to sunburn. There were other witnesses who confirmed the sound prior to take off.

It was reported to the United States Air Force, but the case remains unsolved and is officially listed as 'unidentified'.

1960s

NAME JOE SIMONTON

DATE 18 APRIL 1961

PLACE EAGLE RIVER, WISCONSIN
MAP REF: K15

EVENT CLOSE ENCOUNTER OF THE THIRD
KIND

A case that has prompted considerable background research into the true meaning of close encounters occurred in April 1961 at Eagle River in Wisconsin when witness, Joe Simonton saw a 'brighter than chrome' saucer shaped object hovering near his farmhouse. His attention had been attracted by a rushing noise which had drawn him out of the house; this happening around 11 o'clock in the morning.

The UFO was apparently approximately 12 ft (3.65 m) high and 30 ft (9.14 m) wide and while he watched it a hatch opened and three occupants looked out at Simonton. Simonton described the occupants as approximately 5 ft (152 cm) tall with dark hair, and human like clothing. Indeed Simonton described the aliens as 'resembling Italians'. Perhaps the most extraordinary event was yet to come.

One of the men waved a jug towards Simonton apparently indicating that he needed water. Simonton took the jug inside the house, filled it and returned it to them by which time he also noticed they appeared to be having some sort of barbecue on board their saucer and were frying food on a grill. In addition to the 'cook-out' Simonton noticed several instrument panels and a dark black interior.

Simonton requested like-for-like and indicated he would appreciate one of the pancakes they were cooking; they gave him three of

them each about 3 in (8 cm) wide. After this contact, lasting only a few minutes, the object apparently rose into the air, took off rapidly towards the south, its downwash actually bending nearby pine trees.

The United States Department of Health, Education and Welfare Food and Drug Laboratory was given pieces of the cake to examine, Simonton had already stated it tasted like cardboard. The official analysis indicated that it was made of perfectly normal Earth type materials but that it contained no salt.

It is the absence of salt which has interested researchers ever since; comparison is drawn to the exchange of foods between humans and faerie folk in Celtic traditions. The turn of the century Celtic researcher Walter Evans-Wentz wrote of the Irish 'little people': 'They never taste anything salt, but eat fresh meat and drink pure water.' Pure water was the request made of Simonton.

Since the physical traces research reveals nothing of extra-terrestrial origin the case probably offers no further analysis. Sheriff Schroeder, of the area, stated that having known Simonton for fourteen years he 'obviously believed the truth of what he was saying.'

NAME BETTY AND BARNEY HILL

DATE 19 SEPTEMBER 1961

PLACE CONCORDE, NEW HAMPSHIRE
MAP REF: O14

EVENT ABDUCTION

Returning from a holiday in Canada to their home in the state of New Hampshire, Betty and Barney Hill were to become the first highly publicized account of a UFO abduction.

Having crossed the Canadian border at approximately 9 o'clock

and having made a short stop in a restaurant at Colebrook the couple set off down highway US 3. Just beyond the village of Lancaster they noticed a bright light in the sky ahead of them which appeared to be getting bigger and brighter as they watched. During the drive they continued to observe the light which was apparently moving behind trees and mountain tops. It was not until they stopped the car that they were able to determine for sure that it was moving, and that the movement had not been the apparent motion given by the twists and turns in the road. By looking at it through binoculars Barney was of the opinion that it was an aircraft or a helicopter.

As they approached the Cannon mountain they became somewhat concerned by their sighting and Betty considered pulling into an open motel to find company and shelter. Had they done so they may have avoided the next extraordinary and frightening events.

While Barney drove, Betty looked through binoculars and saw what appeared to be an enormous craft with a double row of windows. This caused Barney to stop the car and make a more detailed investigation. He left the car, crossed through a dark field and apparently walked up to within 50 ft (15 m) of the object now hovering at treetop height, although he admitted later he was 'fully gripped with fear'. With concern, Betty was looking into the darkness for her lost husband.

Isolated in the dark field Barney, again through binoculars, looked at the object now so close to him and stated that he could see at least a dozen people looking back at him. He particularly remembered the eyes of the crew members which almost hypnotically gripped his attention and then, screaming that

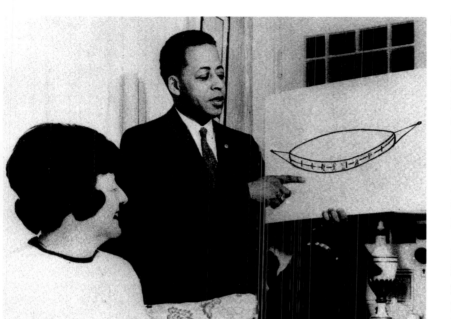

he feared they were about to be captured, he ran back across the field to the car, jumped in and drove off. Betty at this point could not see either the light or the craft but could hear a continuous beeping noise, and they seemed to have drowsed as a sedated feeling overcame them.

Seventeen miles (27 km) from Concorde, according to a sign they saw, Betty and Barney Hill seemed to have recovered from their semi-sedation at the same time as they heard – or think they heard – a separate set of beeping sounds similar to the first. Eventually they reached home.

In the morning following the event Betty discovered spots of metallic 'polishing' on the boot (trunk) of the car. This was just one of many physical traces which suggest, but do not alone confirm, the nature of a real event. She talked at great length to her sister about the sighting, her sister having had a UFO event some years before. Betty was apparently very

Betty and Barney Hill with their dog, Delsey. These are the three witnesses to the first highly publicized abduction. Barney is holding a sketch of the object that captured them.

agitated by the case and drew the attention of another couple living in the house with them by her excited state. Betty's interest in UFO study was then, and has remained to this day, very high. Just two days after the sighting she went to the library to collect a great deal of information about UFOs including reading Major Donald Keyhoe's *Flying Saucer Conspiracy* and just one week after the sighting she wrote to Major Keyhoe about her experience which had only just begun.

Ten days after the sighting Betty had a series of vivid nightmares over a period of a week of a most disorientating kind. She dreamed that the UFO had stopped the car, that alien beings from the UFO had extracted them from the car and taken them aboard their spaceship,

subjecting them to an unpleasant medical examination. In addition to this Betty was given a tour of the spaceship by the aliens who showed her a map apparently depicting their home world. Nightmares are bad enough, but in talking with people at her work she became convinced that these were no ordinary nightmares; they were memories of a real event. A frightening event, and one which suggested a less than benign purpose on the part of the aliens.

In February 1964 the couple began a series of regression hypnosis sessions with Boston psychiatrist Dr Benjamin Simon, the purpose of which was to relieve tensions in the couple which they believed stemmed from the night of their encounter. The sessions appeared to confirm the worst; both Betty and Barney recalled the abduction of Betty's dream as a reality. According to a later analysis of the star map recalled by Betty Hill as shown to her by the alien leader, the aliens' home world orbits either of the stars Zeta Reticuli I or II and the occupants apparently have a purpose here on Earth.

It must be said that Dr Simon's view of the encounter was that he believed the abduction reality 'to be too improbable, and much material was similar to dream material'. Subsequent analysis by other psychologists has suggested that the regression hypnosis would be unable to sort fantasy from fact, particularly where the couple had been convinced that the nightmares were a reality, so it is possible that the event did not occur.

For those who take comfort from this possibility there is one further fact that must be taken into account. Military radar at Pease Air Force Base apparently tracked an anomalous UFO in the skies of New Hampshire at the time and place of the Hill report!

Betty and Barney Hill, 19 September 1961 . . . Afterwards he particularly remembered the eyes of the crew members which hypnotically gripped his attention.

NAME SOCORRO

DATE 24 APRIL 1964

PLACE SOCORRO, NEW MEXICO
MAP REF: H18

EVENT CLOSE ENCOUNTER OF THE THIRD
KIND

At around a quarter to six in the evening, Police Officer Lonnie Zamora was chasing a speeding car when he heard a noise and saw a light in the sky approximately 1 mile (1.6 km) away. He believed it might possibly be a dynamite store that had exploded and he called off the chase to investigate. As he approached, it appeared that the blue-orange flame was descending over the rise of a hill ahead of him.

Having cleared the hill Zamora noticed a shiny object parked off the road about 200 yds (183 m) away. Nearby were two people in white overalls who seemed startled at the appearance of the police car. Thinking that it might be a crashed vehicle Zamora approached with help in mind. He reported over the radio that he was investigating a

possible accident and that he would be out of the car; he stopped the vehicle and got out.

All that he witnessed was the object taking off, its pilots presumably having been startled into an escape. Apparently the object rose on a column of blue-orange flame. Of the object itself Zamora believed it was oval in shape, whitish and had some red 'lettering' on the side.

Zamora ran from the car and ducked over the hill, watching the object rise out of the gully and into the air. The object then appeared to level off and fly horizontally over the dynamite store and away across country. Inspection of the landing site showed four clear impressions in the sand and burn marks in the vegetation. Marks nearby were referred to as the 'footprints' of the entities.

There were reports of corroborative sightings of the blue flame and of someone seeing the police car driving towards the encounter. There were other reports including one made by a

ABOVE Police Officer Lonnie Zamora who reported seeing a landed egg-shaped craft near Socorro, New Mexico in April 1964. Beside it were two humanoid forms. As Zamora approached, the beings and the craft fled. BELOW Inspection revealed ground traces where the craft had stood. On the damaged rocks were metal fragments which were sent for analysis but mysteriously went missing.

principle investigator of the case, Ray Stanford, who saw a similar object in flight shortly afterwards.

No identification has ever been made of the object Zamora witnessed but fairly extraordinary claims have been made to debunk the sighting. One suggestion was that having taken place on land owned by the local Mayor the whole story and physical traces may have been created to increase tourism.

Dr J. Allen Hynek who investigated the case said, 'Of all the close encounters of the third kind, this is the one that most clearly suggests a "nuts-and-bolts" physical craft.'

NAME GARY WILCOX

DATE 24 APRIL 1964

PLACE TIOGA, NEW YORK STATE
MAP REF: N15

EVENT CLOSE ENCOUNTER OF THE THIRD KIND

This particular case is potentially important because of its approximation in time to the Socorro incident (see page 46). According to the witness, Gary Wilcox, it occurred at 10 o'clock in the morning placing it just a few hours before Socorro but I have listed it in this database afterwards as its significance is only appreciated when the details of the Socorro incident are understood.

If true the account gives substantial support to the Socorro claim but it is the opinion of the Socorro principal investigator, Ray Stanford, a well-known and well-respected researcher, that 'my ufologer's intuition tells me this account may be a total hoax, fabricated by Wilcox after he had heard of the Socorro incident.'

Wilcox's report stated that at approximately 10 o'clock in the morning of 24 April 1964 he was spreading manure on his field. He moved into another field ready for ploughing and he saw a light-coloured object there as he approached. At first he gave his sighting a mundane explanation, believing it to be a defunct refrigerator that had been laying in the field for some time. As he got nearer he changed his mind, and believed it might be the wing tank dropped from an aeroplane. Only as he approached much closer did he recognize the fact that it was some 20 ft (7 m) long, egg shaped and glistening aluminium. Near the craft were two short humanoids wearing tight fitting clothing and helmets.

From a box on his chest, one of the humanoids calmed Wilcox's apprehensions and stated 'We have talked with people before.' He then went on, implausibly, to state 'We are from what you people refer to as the planet Mars.' During two hours of conversation with the Martians Wilcox discussed farming and learned from them that they were on Earth to learn about organic materials. They apparently offered explanations of how their craft worked which Wilcox did not understand and said that their visits to Earth were regular. Apparently one of the humanoids asked for a bag of manure and Wilcox went to his barn to collect one. When he returned the craft was gone but he left the bag of manure in the field anyway and the following morning it was gone also.

If this is an early visit by the same occupants of the same craft that visited Socorro some hours later then in the intervening hours they obviously became less talkative and less comfortable around people; leaving as abruptly as they did when officer Zamora interrupted them. They can hardly have been in a desperate hurry to return just to collect their bag of manure!

NAME CISCO GROVE

DATE 5 SEPTEMBER 1964

PLACE CISCO GROVE, CALIFORNIA
MAP REF: E17

EVENT CLOSE ENCOUNTER OF THE THIRD KIND

For those who believe that it is only abductions that cause great fear and extreme reaction in witnesses, the case of Mr S. in Cisco Grove, California merits a study.

Having spent the day hunting with two companions and becoming separated from them he took shelter in a tree, strapping himself to a branch to prevent himself falling out of the tree if he slept.

Mr S. observed three objects with rotating lights from his location and he believed these may have been helicopters searching for him. Reacting to this he left the tree and lit signal fires to attract their attention. Unfortunately, he succeeded.

The unknown silvery objects closed in and apparently despatched two humanoids who approached the fires. They were dressed in silver suits and had extraordinary, prominent eyes. The two humanoids apparently tried to remove Mr S. from the tree and a third robot like entity appeared also. Mr S. fired arrows at the robot, then tore off strips of his clothing, set them alight and threw them at the entities to frighten them away. He apparently succeeded and they took off in their UFO, the downblast of which unfortunately caused him to black out. He regained consciousness at daybreak and discovered the UFO and entities were gone.

Several local people attested to Mr S.'s good character, including a local astronomy teacher who notified Air Force officials. The Air Force explained the case as 'psychological'.

NAME FLYNN INCIDENT

DATE 14 MARCH 1965

PLACE EVERGLADES, FLORIDA
MAP REF: N20

EVENT CLOSE ENCOUNTER OF THE SECOND KIND

Rancher James W. Flynn of Fort Myers, Florida was camping in the Everglades on the night of 14 March 1965 after a day spent training hunting dogs. After midnight he saw a bright light descend approximately 1 mile (1.6 km) away from his location and, believing it to be a plane landing in difficulties, he drove towards it in his swamp buggy, getting as close as he could. Around 1,320 ft (402 m) from the landing site he alighted and went the rest of the way on foot.

As he approached the object he saw that it was a large conical machine hovering near the ground, some 75 ft (23 m) wide and 30 ft (9 m) high. Portholes were visible because of the yellow lights shining through them. Flynn could see no occupants. Deciding to offer friendship, Flynn stepped near the object and raised his hand in a gesture of greeting. He was greeted by a beam of light which struck him on the forehead and knocked him unconscious.

When he came to he was partially blinded and bruised. Although the object had disappeared there was a charred circular ground trace near where the object had been hovering and trees nearby were also burned. Flynn spent five days at Fort Myers Hospital who confirmed that his vision and muscular reflexes were impaired.

Unfortunately Flynn's encounter came at a time of maximum difficulty for the Air Force, indeed during a major flap in the locality, and they were doing their very best to play down the sighting. Attempts were made to discredit Flynn which backfired when many leading citizens, police officers and doctors vouched for him. The Air Force's suggestion that Flynn may have hoaxed the encounter ignored the remarkable ground and tree traces and his own physical impairments which his doctor believed 'could not have been faked'.

In the end the Air Force settled for the somewhat useless statement that, when questioned, they had nothing on their files concerning the Flynn incident.

NAME EXETER FLAP

DATE 3 SEPTEMBER 1965

PLACE EXETER, NEW HAMPSHIRE
MAP REF: O15

EVENT MULTIPLE NIGHT LIGHT SIGHTINGS

In the spring of 1965 the area of Exeter, New Hampshire was subject to a local wave of UFO sightings, many of which were investigated by journalist John G. Fuller and related in his bestselling book *Incident at Exeter*. Not untypical of the wave, though perhaps most documented, was the sighting of 18-year-old Norman J. Muscarello on 3 September 1965. His sighting was confirmed by police patrolmen Eugene Bertrand and David Hunt.

Muscarello was hitch-hiking to the south of Exeter at 2 o'clock in the morning when he saw a group of five red lights in a line, over a house some 100 ft (30 m) from his position. He watched as the lights moved behind trees and houses, out over a large field and commented that they were so bright that he could not see structure behind them, possibly indicating only that it was hidden by their brilliance. The lights were apparently pulsating and only one light was bright at any given time.

Muscarello observed these lights for approximately a quarter of an hour and at one point they appeared to come so close to him he leapt into a ditch to avoid being hit by them. Eventually Muscarello hitched a lift to Exeter police station and reported what he had seen.

Confirmation came from patrolman Eugene Bertrand who had been in the area in his car at 1 o'clock in the morning. The police officer had spoken to a woman who claims she was too upset to drive because she had been followed in her car by a bright light though Bertrand did not witness this aspect of the report. He did, however, accompany Muscarello to the field and witnessed the bright red lights Muscarello had reported. Bertrand noticed that although the lights were silent they were upsetting farm animals in the area and he called patrolman Hunt to the scene who also observed the lights.

Pease Air Force Base investigated the report some months later and could not find a cause of the sighting. They commented that the observers appeared to be reliable and stable people and believed that their own B-47 aircraft which had been in the area at the time could not have caused the sighting.

During the flap that followed, there was an extraordinary call to the police station in Exeter; a man in a call box claimed that a flying saucer was heading directly towards him, the call was interrupted, the connection broken and he could not be traced.

For several weeks after the sighting Muscarello and his mother staked out the hills to see if they could see the UFOs again and on one evening they did so.

Project Blue Book, however, seems to suggest in its report that the B-47 aircraft or aircraft from an

MISSING INFORMATION

The sheer weight of UFO-related material available for study is astonishing. The late Dr J Allen Hynek, for over twenty years a leading figure in the subject, referred to it as an embarrassment of riches. In fact, so many claims are received that hosts of reports are either uninvestigated or afforded only a cursory examination; their details are logged and are of value mainly in the event of other reports being received which can then be corroborated. Perhaps surprisingly, even photographs fall into this category; if a photograph is indistinct and has no reference points from which detailed analysis can be made, then often there is very little that can be learned from it. However spectacular or clear the image is, its relevance will always depend on the witness's other testimony.

BELOW This photograph was taken by Deputy Sheriff Arthur Strauch near St George, Minnesota while he was out hunting with four companions. While potentially a very interesting image, interpretation of it is limited through lack of authoritative information on the subject.

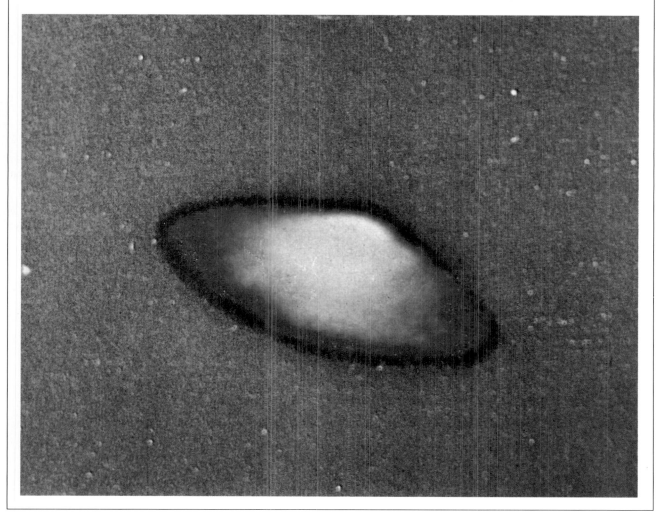

operation known as 'big blast' may have been responsible for the sightings though such conclusions have created great criticism due to their other inaccuracies.

There has been some suggestion that the sightings were of indistinct definition and even by the standards of 1965 rather mundane and only attracted the attention they did because of the high publicity they received rather than the particular qualities of the reports themselves. When questioned about the sighting fifteen years after the event the witnesses stood by their statements. Officer Hunt said 'It's just a thing that happened and we reported it the way it happened at the time, which you know is about all you can do, I guess.'

NAME GREAT NORTH-EASTERN BLACKOUT

DATE 9 NOVEMBER 1965

PLACE NORTH-EASTERN UNITED STATES/
CANADA
MAP REF: N15

EVENT GREAT NORTH-EASTERN BLACKOUT

There have been many connections made between the appearance of UFOs and disruption of electrical circuits, particularly in cars approached by low-flying UFOs. There have also been several claims made that UFOs in the vicinity of major cities have caused power blackouts affecting many thousands of people. Such claims were particularly common in the 1960s. The most dramatic of all claims was that of the great North-East blackout which covered an area of 80,000 square miles (207,199 m²) and affected 26 million people.

Just after power failed at Syracuse, Deputy Aviation Commissioner Robert Walsh sighted a round fiery UFO ascending at moderate speed from a fairly low altitude. A second fireball is also reported. The objects were over the Clay power substation, an automatic control unit which regulated power from Niagara Falls to New York.

Witnesses in the Time and Life building saw a UFO in the sky above blacked-out Manhattan. *Time* magazine photographers photographed this object. Many other reports of UFOs came in across New York, New Jersey and Pennsylvania. UFOs were reported over Pennsylvania by pilot Jerry Whitaker and passenger George Croniger who believe they saw them being chased by jet interceptors.

At the height of the blackout it had spread to six states other than

New York, and a section of Canada. New York City had 600 trains and 600,000 passengers trapped in the underground train system; many thousands were trapped in elevators; bridges and tunnels were jammed due to traffic-light breakdowns; airports were shut down and flights redirected. The enormous north-eastern power grid was thought to have been invulnerable to accident or attack having hundreds of automatic controls and safety cut-outs. Congress had been told that a serious breakdown was quite impossible. Various heads of power plants indicated they had no explanation for the blackout, no severed transmission lines, faulty circuits or defective generators. One stated that it appeared that vast amounts of electricity had simply been 'lost' but without explanation.

New York and 80,000 square miles (207,199 m²) of the surrounding area was blacked out in 1965.

Because of the potential for panic, with people trapped in elevators and underground in the dark for many hours on end, calming and reassuring statements were broadcast by those radio stations that could transmit on emergency generators and certainly no mention was made of any UFO connection for fear of the panic it would cause. However, the press picked up the UFO reports (and indeed Air Force official denials) and by the end of the day it was already being speculated that UFOs had caused the blackout. No proof of this connection has ever been forthcoming though one Air Force Major made the point that 'The evidence was too strong to be ignored or debunked . . .

[particularly] . . . along with the reports of previous UFO-caused blackouts.'

Whether UFOs were the cause of the great North-Eastern blackout or not remains open to speculation. At least they cannot be blamed for one of the effects of the enforced hours of darkness and quiet. Nine months after the blackout New York experienced a baby boom.

NAME SWAMP GAS DEBACLE

DATE 18 MARCH 1966

PLACE ANN ARBOR, MICHIGAN
MAP REF: M15

EVENT THE 'SWAMP GAS' DEBACLE

Over forty witnesses including several police officers saw a UFO with blue and white lights, antennae and a pilot's cabin, in the marshlands near Ann Arbor, Michigan on 18 March 1966. Four other craft apparently travelled with it. Some witnesses claimed to reach to within 1,500 ft (457 m) of it, and described it as football shaped and pulsating.

Police patrolman Robert Hunawill agreed that he had watched the object together with other local citizens. Sheriff's deputies Stanley McFadden and David Fitzpatrick observed it flying over the area. The state Police Commissioner, Frederick Davids, commented 'I used to discount these reports too but now I am not so sure.'

The following evening the craft was again observed by other witnesses and it became apparent that the Air Force should send in an investigator if only to be seen to be doing something. They sent in their scientific adviser to Project Blue Book, Dr J. Allen Hynek. Hynek made an investigation of the area but was virtually assaulted by the press to make some kind of preliminary statement, although he always

stated since that time that he had had no wish to do so and believed it was premature at the time when he made his comment. His statement included the comment that some people in the area might have seen ignited swamp gas.

The press immediately pilloried him for the comment, and assaulted him for attacking the credibility of local witnesses. They completely ignored his further comment that a fuller investigation was required and that a thorough investigation of all phenomena was needed before comment should be made definitively.

Hynek always said afterwards that it showed how even the most experienced people can fall prey to the excesses of the press, it also shows how the excesses of the press can affect public perception of the UFO phenomenon.

Any analysis of the UFO phenomenon reveals how media coverage often creates a mythology around a truth. Insubstantial stories can easily become sensational.

NAME CATALINA ISLAND FILM

DATE APRIL 1966

PLACE CATALINA ISLAND, CALIFORNIA
MAP REF: E18

EVENT PHOTOGRAPHIC CASE

The Catalina Island film shot by professional cameraman Lee Hansen is important in UFO research not because it is a mystery but because it is not. Shot in April 1966 the film showed a silver, disc shaped object moving in the mountains on Catalina Island and casting a shadow below. For twenty years the object remained a mystery.

It was only the development of modern photographic analysis which gave final identification to the object on the film. Image enhancement techniques were employed by Dr Robert Nathan of the Jet Propulsion Laboratory in Pasadena; the film was scanned, enlarged and displayed on a television screen and broken down into individual pixels. Each frame of the film was similarly digitized and each overlaid on the earlier image causing an averaging of the lighting effects in the picture. Gradually the grain in the picture diminished and the image was able to be seen more clearly.

In fact the cameraman had filmed, out of focus, a light aircraft that had been manoeuvring in the mountains. By the time the image enhancement was completed it was possible even to see the outline of the pilot sitting in the cockpit. Because the aircraft had been filmed from its own flight level it had eliminated the image of wings and indeed the image of the tail fin.

Many UFO cases are solved in the first investigation, indeed some 90-95 per cent of cases are identified quite quickly but positive identification twenty years after an event is rare and this was an important breakthrough.

NAME BETTY ANDREASSON

DATE 25 JANUARY 1967

PLACE ASHBURNHAM, MASSACHUSETTS
MAP REF: 015

EVENT ABDUCTION

Perhaps the most remarkable case of imagery in a UFO abduction comes from the claims of Betty Andreasson.

On 25 January 1967 she was at home with her parents and her seven children in the early evening (her husband was in hospital having been injured in a car accident). Suddenly, she saw a pulsating light through the kitchen window and Betty's father saw entities outside who Betty then saw entering the house *through the walls*.

This was all Betty remembered for many years. Some eight years later she wrote to the tabloid newspaper *National Enquirer* about her experience, this was a paper noted for its interest in UFOs and for its $5,000 reward given annually to the best UFO story. However, they apparently took little interest in her case.

It was not until 1977, more than ten years after the event that Betty Andreasson underwent a series of hypnotic regression sessions suggested by MUFON investigator, Raymond Fowler. Her story was extraordinary.

The aliens that had entered her kitchen apparently lined up before her and stated they needed food for their minds. Their leader, Quazgaa, accepted a bible from Betty. She then left the house with them and entered an oval object hovering a few inches off the ground in her back garden.

She underwent a medical examination in a brilliantly lit 'operating room' on board the object and suffered a probe pushed into her nose and another through her navel.

These experiences have been commonly reported in America, but what was to follow is unique.

She was taken through various chambers inside the UFO, was covered in fluids and fed fluids through her mouth; she met reptilian creatures and flew over a crystal city. Inside one of the crystal buildings she was brought face to face with a bird like being and heard the voice of God.

Quazgaa told her that 'Secrets have been locked in her mind' and she was then returned to her home finding her family apparently paralyzed and unconscious.

To the present day there has probably been more written about this case than any other and the full case history is rich in detail, much of which may well be symbolic but all of which appears to have deep meaning for the witness.

NAME STEPHEN MICHALAQ

DATE 20 MAY 1967

PLACE FALCON LAKE, ONTARIO/MANITOBA
BORDER
MAP REF: K12

EVENT CLOSE ENCOUNTER OF THE SECOND
KIND

If Canada comes a poor second to the United States on the North American continent in terms of quantity of UFO events, then it goes a long way to making up for it in quality with the extraordinary close encounter of Stephen Michalaq which is recorded here.

Just after noon on 20 May, at Falcon Lake between Manitoba and Ontario, Michalaq witnessed the landing of a cigar shaped UFO. Two such red objects descended, one landing and the other silently flying back into the sky. The landed UFO appeared to 'cool down'; its red glow diminishing to a silver gold. The

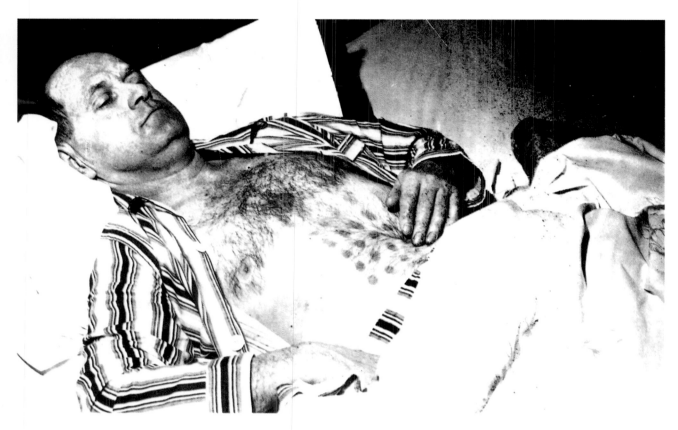

object was approximately 30 ft (9 m) wide and 12 ft (3½ m) high.

Michalaq was an amateur prospector and carried goggles normally worn to protect his eyes when hammering into rock. Through these goggles he observed the object from close range over the next half an hour, also making sketches. He noticed a bright purple light emanating from inside the object, detected the warm smell of sulphur and heard motor noises from within.

Michalaq was approaching closer when a door opened in the UFO and he could hear voices coming from inside. He called to the craft in several languages but received no responses. He peered inside, observing multi-coloured patterns of light. Eventually the opening was covered and Michalaq took some time to examine the outside of the object, discovering it to be hot enough to melt his glove.

At this point he found himself in front of a grid-type vent in the side

of the object. From it, a blast of warm air struck him causing him not only surprise but pain and fear as it set his clothes alight.

The object departed. Shortly afterwards Michalaq observed ground traces in the form of charred earth where the object had been. There were physiological effects from the encounter; Michalaq suffered nausea and vomiting as well as feeling a severe pain in his head. After returning home he went to the Misericordia Hospital where he was treated for first degree burns.

In the following week he was examined by his family doctor. Over those few days Michalaq lost considerable weight being unable to eat, suffered blood infection, skin infections, diarrhoea and nausea. He complained of burning sensations and stiff joints. Of particular interest was a pattern of burn marks on Michalaq's chest which corresponded to the exhaust vent on the object, where hot air had blasted him.

Stephen Michalaq, victim of a very close encounter, displays the extraordinary pattern of burn marks which appeared on his body following a blast of heat from a landed UFO.

Organizations such as the Whiteshell Nuclear Research Establishment, the US Navy Hospital and the National Research Council in addition to 27 doctors examined Michalaq over a period.

Michalaq appears to have received a dose of radiation which would have been lethal had it not been of slight duration.

The view of the Royal Canadian Air Force was that the case was a hoax though a Freedom of Information Act request some years later yielded a file 113 pages long, and this was acknowledged to be considerably abridged.

The Royal Canadian Air Force should be congratulated on the amount of work it is prepared to invest in a hoax!

NAME PATROLMAN SCHIRMER

DATE 3 DECEMBER 1967

PLACE ASHLAND, NEBRASKA
      MAP REF: J16

EVENT CONTACTEE ENCOUNTER

'Saw a flying saucer at the junction of highways 6 and 63. Believe it or not!' This was the brief report made by patrolman Herb Schirmer in Ashland, Nebraska following a UFO sighting in December of 1967. Shortly after the event, and after a short stint as Chief of Police, he resigned from the force. There has been a great deal of speculation that official pressure was brought to bear but Schirmer is adamant that his resignation came from him alone because he was no longer able to do his job properly.

The suggestion of a brief period of missing time, some twenty minutes, and a red weal on his neck was sufficient for regression hypnosis to be used to find out whether or not there was a more detailed story locked in Schirmer's mind. There was!

The former Chief of Police had apparently had an experience of contact with extraterrestrials that was somewhere between a contactee and abduction experience. Having approached the landed object on the highway and suffered vehicle interference cutting out the engine and lights of his car Schirmer, now under regression hypnosis, revealed that the car was apparently surrounded by entities from the globular UFO. He was prevented from drawing his revolver to defend himself by a mental block and was paralyzed by the entities who fired a green gas gun at his car. It was at this time that Schirmer apparently suffered the injury to his neck when, having been forced to wind down the window of the car, he was forcibly removed from it and taken on board the UFO.

The UFO is described as having been shaped something like a football, glowing silver, with a bright flashing light beneath. It apparently landed on tripod legs and later conversation with the aliens indicated that it required electricity to power it.

Indeed at the time Schirmer interrupted them they were busy stealing electricity from the overhead power lines with a device which the entities obligingly explained and went on to demonstrate to Schirmer.

The entities themselves were approximately 5 ft (152 cm) high and muscular with larger chests than on the normal human frame. Apparently their head was thinner and taller than an ordinary human head; they wore tight fitting silver grey suits and boots. Schirmer described their eyes as 'like cat's eyes', the nose was flatter and they had almost lipless mouths. Schirmer was informed that he would be given a cover story which would be all he would remember of the event; that he would recall seeing the craft land and watch it fly away; and that he would experience two return visits from the aliens.

Of particular interest to the investigators was the emblem seen by Schirmer on the uniform of the entities which he drew and described as that of a winged serpent. Much has been made of the connection between this and the ancient historical stories of winged serpent sightings and gods.

The aliens apparently told Schirmer that their mission was because the 'Earth people do not do things in the right way.' They also informed Schirmer that they had bases in the Bermuda Triangle, at the polar regions and in other locations around the world.

This case is probably more influential than any other in pointing to genetic manipulation as an explanation for the alien visitations. Schirmer said 'Maybe I asked if they kidnapped people. I don't remember, except he said they had a programme known as "breeding analysis" and some humans had been used in these experiments.'

EDWARD UHLER CONDON

In 1966, at the age of 64, Condon was appointed to head up the University of Colorado's study into UFOs – usually known subsequently as the Condon Committee. A friend of Dr J Robert Oppenheimer, Condon was one of North America's foremost theoretical nuclear physicists. He was also known for 'taking on' the establishment when the need arose. He must have seemed the ideal man to lead the impartial study. However it seems that the whole project was an Air Force publicity trick; its negative conclusions simply did not tally with the unsolved case on its files.

NAME SHANE KURZ

DATE 2 MAY 1968

PLACE NEW YORK STATE
      MAP REF: N15

EVENT ABDUCTION

Shane Kurz's experiences came during the early months of 1968 when there were a number of UFO sightings in the area around her home in New York State and the first of her own experiences was in mid-April. For several nights Miss Kurz and her mother had used a telescope to observe a bright cigar shaped object near their home and reported that they had a strange feeling of being observed. On 15 April Shane Kurz's mother awoke her at 2 o'clock in the morning because of a bright flashing light flooding her bedroom and it was only when Shane opened her eyes that she saw an intense light coming from outside her bedroom. Shane's sisters shared the room with her and corroborated the sighting of the light. Silently the light moved upwards and then vanished. A report was made to Griffis Air Base and the Oneida County airport.

The 2 May produced the puzzling experience which most concerned Shane. She had been outside her house for some time watching the sky when the cigar shaped UFO appeared at great speed, stopped, then shot upwards and turned red in colour. Shane went to bed and fell into a deep sleep.

Shane was awoken by her mother whose first question was 'Where have you been?' She was apparently lying on top of her bedspread with her slippers and dressing-gown on, her clothes and her legs covered in dried mud. There were muddy footprints leading from the porch to the bedroom.

In the days following, Shane experienced several physical and mental difficulties; red marks on the lower abdomen, pain and nausea and migraines, loss of menstruation, loss of weight and an irrational fear of being examined by the doctors. She became convinced that she had to know more about what happened to her on 2 May.

In January 1975 she appears to have had a 'follow-up' abduction, waking up to find a burn on her upper chest, spots on her cheeks and a purple mark on her right arm with a pinhole in the middle.

Subsequent investigation revealed there may have been a strange contact a year before her first UFO sightings, in 1967. It was her last year of high school and as she approached the school entrance one morning a figure came up alongside her and asked to share her umbrella. She thought he was a stranger but he was obviously very human and dressed in a very human fashion. She described his eyes as slightly slanted towards the back. He apparently knew her name but evaded her question as to how. During his conversation with Shane he had her explain what volleyball and basketball were as he was apparently unfamiliar with these terms, a fact which she quite rightly found surprising and he offered her a ride during her lunch hour in his 'vehicle'. She questioned him about his car but he only stressed that his *vehicle* was white and kept pointing towards a field. Reasonably enough she declined the offer, dismissed him, turned around and took just three steps, turned to look back to see where he was going and he wasn't there. She was stunned as there was no possible way he could have left the scene in that time. Other schoolgirls at the time were able to corroborate that she had been with him.

Hypnosis sessions conducted on Shane to further investigate the events of 2 May apparently filled in the details of the missing hours of that date. She was drawn to the window by a voice, perhaps telepathically, calling to her. She dressed, went downstairs through the kitchen and outside into the cold. Outside, she found herself looking at a landed UFO which was apparently 'powering down', its lights dimming. She saw windows and a revolving rim and in walking towards the UFO recalled being stuck in wet mud. The UFO was hovering in the corner of a field and Shane began to try to resist, wanting to return to her home. At one point she was kneeling on the ground, trying to hide. Somehow, and the details are unclear, she was drawn inside the UFO, into a room like a hospital operating room. In the room a medical examination took place where body samples were taken. It becomes clear to her that she is to be used to produce a hybrid human/alien baby. She resists this with great fear but the examination goes on.

In a recall strikingly similar to that of Betty Hill and Betty Andreasson she describes a long needle probed through her navel, apparently part of a gynaecological operation. Unlike the recall of many abductees it seems that Shane was not artificially inseminated but raped by the leader of the aliens who she describes as having an apparently human like body though generally slender. She apparently enjoyed the sexual experience though she attributes this to a jelly like substance smeared on her before the act commenced; a fact which predominates in the claims of Antonio Villas Boas (see page 181) a decade or more earlier.

Many of Shane's worst apprehensions about the encounter ceased – precisely nine months after the event.

1970s

NAME CALLERY CHEMICAL PLANT

DATE 14 APRIL 1971

PLACE BUTLER, PENNSYLVANIA
MAP REF: N16

EVENT CLOSE ENCOUNTER OF THE THIRD
KIND

The case of Dennis and Marion (pseudonyms adopted at the witnesses' request for anonymity) is important because of the similarities between this case and that of Betty and Barney Hill (see page 42) in the early events and for the dissimilarity of the way the encounter ended. Comparison of the two may result in a better understanding of both.

At approximately 8 o'clock in the evening the couple were driving from Evans City to Pittsburgh on an unlighted road through the farmlands. They had just passed the Callery chemical plant heading towards Butler when Marion noticed a UFO to the right of the car. The object was apparently pacing the car at much the same speed, it was glowing yellow-white and was silent. She estimated the object to be approximately 100 yds (92 m) from them. Dennis slowed down to approximately 10 miles (16 km) an hour and then also saw the object.

As in the case of the Hills the Butlers did not experience electrical difficulties with the car but pulled the car off the road for the purpose of properly observing and listening for sound from the object. They watched as it flew away becoming just a bright point of light and then returned to the same point where it had been before. It was a classic saucer shape, glowing luminescent and apparently the size of a small house as they watched it disappear over a large hill.

Marion was very concerned and somewhat frightened by the incident but Dennis was keen to investigate further, turning off the road and onto a dirt track near the chemical plant. (It is speculated that Betty and Barney Hill also turned off their main road onto a subsidiary road where they were abducted by the occupants of a UFO that had been pacing their car.) As they drove over the brow of a hill they could see the object hovering just above the ground of a ploughed field some 80 yds (73 m) away.

Dennis drove along to the farmhouse hoping to find further witnesses to the event but nobody was at home. Looking across the field towards a small wood they could see the UFO hovering near the trees. Shortly after this a shaft of white light beamed up from the top of the object. Several windows were observed in the upper section of the saucer and portholes below. From within the windows flickering lights could be seen which gave the impression of lights flickering across a computer screen.

Marion then saw two giant humanoid figures in the windows. Prudently both witnesses leapt back into the car very quickly and 'beat it out of there'. As they drove rapidly down the dirt road they could see the UFO remaining in the same position.

On investigation the next day researchers recorded that Marion was white as a sheet and shaking and had undoubtedly been alarmed by what she had seen. Researchers also confirmed that they were straightforward and respectable people.

The case shows that the opening events were very similar to that of Betty and Barney Hill, i.e. a bright light apparently pacing the car and proving itself to be a structured craft of some kind. It should be noted that the witnesses in this case did not necessarily believe the object was deliberately pacing their car but rather moving at the same speed and at the same place, possibly by coincidence, whereas there is some speculation that the Hills' car was under deliberate scrutiny. However, the outcome was very different; in the Hills' case the object apparently either guided the Hills off the main road and its occupants then abducted them or took advantage of their own decision to drive off the main road, which was subsequently forgotten during the amnesiac block apparently placed on them. In Marion and Dennis's case, although confronted with an opportunity for abduction, the UFO appears to have ignored the witnesses and allowed them to 'escape'. Having said that, it has been further speculated that possibly in both cases the UFOs scanned the occupants of the cars and in the Hills' case decided they were of use whereas in the case of Marion and Dennis decided they would not be suitable for their purposes.

Ignored or rejected? Either way Marion and Dennis seemed to have been spared the frightening ordeal which many abductees have undergone.

NAME DAPPLE GREY LANE

DATE AUGUST 1971

PLACE DAPPLE GREY LANE, LOS ANGELES, CALIFORNIA
MAP REF: E18

EVENT NON-HUMANOID CONTACTEE EXPERIENCE

By far the most common description of UFO-related entities is that of the humanoid form, i.e. two arms, two legs and a head containing the primary sensory organs raised to the highest point. Given the variety of non-humanoid forms on earth alone, this is in itself a matter for

some consideration. However, occasionally cases occur which have anything but humanoid entities and the encounter in Dapple Grey Lane in August 1971 is just one such case.

John Hodges and Peter Rodriguez had been visiting the apartment of a third friend in Dapple Grey Lane, Los Angeles and they left in the early hours of the morning. As they were getting into their car they noticed two seemingly alive brain-like objects on the road ahead of them, each some 3 ft (91 cm) high. Hodges drove past the objects, dropped his friend off and then drove to his own home arriving back some two hours later than he should have done.

Under regressive hypnosis it appears that the brain-like entities telepathically projected a message into Hodges' mind telling him that 'We will meet again.' When he arrived at his own apartment – but before he left the car – he apparently encountered the entities again and seems to have been projected into a control room where humanoid entities were manipulating the machinery.

There was a great deal of imagery in the encounter and it appears that the aliens were concerned about our lack of environmental awareness and the damage we were doing to our planet.

In 1978, during the period of the regressive hypnosis sessions, Hodges apparently encountered the entities yet again and was given a warning about a coming world war.

Hodges believes that both he and Rodriguez, along with thousands of other people, have implants in their brains which are designed to enhance psychic powers and the purpose of the creatures' interference is to help in developing the human race.

NAME	ST CATHERINE'S
DATE	16 OCTOBER 1971
PLACE	ST CATHERINE'S, ONTARIO
	MAP REF: M15
EVENT	ABDUCTION

Six members of a rock group including the principal witness of the case, known only as 'Jack', were pulled off the road by the appearance of a bright lighted UFO in the early hours of the morning when returning from a party.

Three members of the group were taken aboard the flying saucer and subjected to various medical examinations and interrogations while the other three remained in a tranced state in their van.

The aliens apparently showed an interest in both a recorder and drum kit, asking for detailed explanations of how they work and in fact retained one of the recorders as a souvenir.

Regression hypnosis by psychiatrist Dr Aphrodite Clamar and therapist Dr Susan Schulman seemed to indicate that Jack had been the subject of many abductions during his life: first a medical examination following an abduction from his pushchair at the age of two by creatures with big black eyes; then a joint abduction of himself and his father when Jack was six, which was apparently corroborated by regression hypnosis on the father; next an abduction at the age of ten; and finally the multiple abduction of the group when Jack was sixteen.

A scene from the 1929 film *Mysterious Island*. Although it shows an image created decades before aliens were being reported by UFO abductees, many features are remarkably similar: the dwarf shapes, prominent eyes, bald domed heads and webbed fingers. Can reported abductions and science fiction imagery be arising from a common source?

NAME THE DELPHOS RING

DATE 2 NOVEMBER 1971

PLACE DELPHOS RING, KANSAS
MAP REF: J17

EVENT CLOSE ENCOUNTER OF THE SECOND
KIND

The Johnson farm, Delphos, Kansas. At 7 o'clock in the evening Durel Johnson and his wife had just finished supper when their son Ronnie returned from feeding the sheep. Ronnie reported that he had heard a rumbling noise and had seen a mushroom shaped UFO hovering just above the ground some 70 ft (21 m) away from him in a group of trees near the farmhouse. He described it as glowing with every colour of the rainbow and beaming a shaft of brilliant white light towards the ground. Ronnie reported that he was blinded and paralyzed by the event which lasted about five minutes until the object flew away towards the town of Delphos. It was some fifteen minutes before he was able to focus his vision and to move and he immediately ran to the farmhouse to report the event to his parents.

His parents were disbelieving but accompanied him outside, both witnessing the UFO moving towards the south. Erma, his mother, described it as looking 'like a giant washtub'.

At the site where the UFO had been hovering the witnesses saw a circle glowing in the dark and noticed that the nearby trees were also glowing. The soil appeared to have been dusted with a white powder which was touched by Mr and Mrs Johnson who both stated that their fingertips had become numb shortly afterwards. Mrs Johnson also took photographs of the ring while Mr Johnson drove his son into Delphos to report the event to the local newspaper.

Considering the medical implications of the state their son was in and the possibilities suggested by having touched the glowing white powder and then suffered partial paralysis, the decision to visit the town to see the reporters of a local paper rather than any member of the medical profession has been one factor in reducing the credibility of the case. There have been many suspicions surrounding this event: the Johnsons refused to report the incident to the police; they seemed to greatly enjoy the fame and attention which their report brought to them; they were recipients of the much criticized $5,000 award from the *National Enquirer* for outstanding UFO reports; and just when the extraordinary reports of the next two years looked like overshadowing their story the UFO returned yet again, involving the Johnson farm in yet more strange events. Not the least of these was that sheep that had not been serviced by rams suddenly gave birth, though the young died shortly afterwards. The witnesses were invited to take a lie detector test but refused.

Analysis of the ground traces on the farm revealed some unusual component but there was nothing which demanded a non-terrestrial explanation. The possibility remains that the witnesses invented some of the details on the back of a sighting of extraordinary ground traces for reasons of their own. It is only because of the lack of hard physical evidence which UFO events generally offer that the Delphos ring has become so famous in the past twenty years.

Most modern research concentrates not only on the testimony but also on the credibility of the witnesses and on that basis this particular case might not be rated highly.

The Delphos ring appeared to have been dusted with a white powder which caused numbness in the fingers of those who touched it.

NAME MICHEL IMBEAULT

DATE 5 AUGUST 1973

PLACE MONTREAL, CANADA
MAP REF: N14

EVENT ANOMALOUS LIGHTS

At 5.30 in the morning, Michel Imbeault and a friend were walking near the St Lawrence river when they saw a string of lights across the sky. The lights moved quickly but he took one photograph.

Michel Imbeault's remarkable photograph of a string of unidentified lights in the sky.

NAME PASCAGOULA ENCOUNTER

DATE 12 OCTOBER 1973

PLACE PASCAGOULA, MISSISSIPPI
MAP REF: L19

EVENT ABDUCTION

During October of 1973 America underwent an extensive wave of UFO sightings; an extraordinary case during that period was the abduction of shipyard workers Charles Hickson and Calvin Parker.

At 7 o'clock in the evening the pair were fishing from a pier at the Shaupeter Shipyard in Pascagoula. At about that time, witnesses in the area sighted a blue light circling in the vicinity of the shipyard. Hickson and Parker did not see a light but, sensing something behind them, turned to see a UFO some 25-30 yds (23-27 m) away from them and just 2-3 ft (61-91 cm) above the ground. The machine was making a buzzing sound and caused some consternation amongst the witnesses. As Hickson stated under hypnosis 'And I started to hit the river, man. And Calvin just – he went hysterical.'

The witnesses watched as a hatchway opened in the object and three entities floated out. As Hickson went on 'They didn't have

toes. But they had feet shape . . . it was more or less a round like thing on a leg, if you'd call it a leg . . . I was scared to death. And me with the spinning reel out there – it's all I had. I couldn't, well I was so scared, well you can't imagine. Calvin done went hysterical on me.'

The entities apparently glided up to the witnesses continuing to make a buzzing noise, sounding something like a machine. They were vaguely humanoid in shape though apart from strange feet they also had most bizarre facial features long conical rods where nose and ears would normally be. Their long arms ended in crab like pincers and their skin was ghostly and pale, possibly wrinkled. Worse was yet to come.

Parker apparently fainted and Hickson was lifted off the ground by the entities and floated into the UFO. Inside, the entities apparently kept Hickson floating weightlessly while they moved him around and while an eye like scanning object looked all over him. Even though the entities left the room at one point Hickson could not move and does not even know if he remained conscious, though he believes he did. Recovering his senses somewhat Hickson tried to talk to the entities but could only get a

buzzing sound in reply.

Presumably, and understandably, near to hysteria Hickson cannot remember being removed from the craft and his first memory is of seeing Parker standing on the ground outside with a look on his face 'I've never seen that sort of fear on a man's face as I saw on Calvin's. It took me a while to get him back to his senses and the first thing I told him was, "Son, nobody gonna believe this."

Hickson's description of the craft is indistinct, he recalls it being approximately 8 ft (244 cm) tall and oblong with an opening at one end and exhibiting a blue light outside. Inside the craft it was very bright but there was no apparent source of the light.

Following the interview between Hickson and Parker and Sheriff Diamond and Captain Ryder, events occurred which give extraordinary authenticity to the claim. When the police left Parker and Hickson alone they quite deliberately left a tape recorder running, presumably in the hope that they would reveal their hoax, if that is what it was. Instead of that the two of them virtually rambled on, apparently still in a state of shock but both confirmed their impressions of the sighting. Hickson

Charles Hickson (RIGHT) photographed in 1990 with the author.

left the room at one point and Calvin was left alone and the tape recorder picked up almost inaudible words as he prayed 'It's hard to believe . . . oh God, it's awful . . . I know there is a God up there . . .'

In 1987 Charles Hickson summed up his feelings about the experience 'I make my living with my hands. I had a chance to make a million dollars like Whitley Strieber back in 1973. I was offered all kinds of money to let them do a movie. I declined. I am still declining. Making money is not what this experience is all about.'

NAME JEFF GREENHAW

DATE 17 OCTOBER 1973

PLACE FALKVILLE, ALABAMA
 MAP REF: L18

EVENT ENTITY PHOTOGRAPHS

At approximately 10 o'clock in the evening police chief Jeff Greenhaw of Falkville, Alabama received a telephone call at his home from a woman reporting a UFO landing in a field near the town. Coming as it did amid the October 1973 United States flap there had been some publicity regarding UFOs and Greenhaw reacted positively enough to take a Polaroid camera to the scene.

Outside the town he apparently encountered a tall, silver suited creature standing in the middle of the road. With extraordinary composure Greenhaw got out of the car and welcomed the entity 'Howdy stranger' and started taking pictures of him. When Greenhaw got back in the car and turned on the flashing blue police lights the creature turned and ran ahead.

Despite the fact that Greenhaw chased him in the car at up to 35 miles (56 km) per hour the entity outran him and indeed the chase ended when Greenhaw spun off the gravel road.

Greenhaw is perhaps the classic case so often mentioned in UFO lore when considering the effect of reporting on witnesses' life styles. After relating his experience on national television he received threatening phone calls, his wife left him, his home was burnt down and he was forced to resign his job.

NAME CAPTAIN COYNE

DATE 18 OCTOBER 1973

PLACE MANSFIELD, OHIO
 MAP REF: M16

EVENT CLOSE ENCOUNTER OF THE FIRST
 KIND

During the night of 18 October 1973 Captain Laurence Coyne and three colleagues, Lieutenant Jezzy, and Sergeants Healey and Yanacsek were flying a Bell UH-1H helicopter from Columbus, Ohio to Hopkins Air Force Base, Cleveland.

Around 12 miles (19 km) from Mansfield, Healey noticed a single red light to the left. He paid little attention to it. Just a few minutes later Yanacsek saw a red light to the right and he believed it was pacing the helicopter. Coyne told him to keep monitoring it and was shortly told that it seemed to be closing in on them. The witnesses were now paying some attention to the object as it approached.

The object was so accurately following a collision course that Coyne was forced to descend at increasing speed. The light apparently stopped and hovered over the helicopter.

Three of the witnesses who had a clear view of the object, Coyne, Healey and Yanacsek, stated that a cigar shaped metallic grey object filled the front of the windshield of the helicopter. The nose of the object contained the red light, a white light at the tail and from its underside shone a sweeping green pyramid shaped searchlight which at one point flooded the helicopter before the object accelerated away. The remainder of the flight was uneventful.

The following day Coyne wanted to report the incident and impressed the flight controller at Cleveland Hopkins Air Force Base with the degree to which he was obviously

disturbed by his sighting. Coyne eventually filed an operational hazard form confirming a military person exposed to danger during flight. Subsequent investigation showed that the magnetic compass of the helicopter had been rendered useless and it had to be replaced.

When the story was published by a news journal five witnesses on the ground reported seeing the steady bright light above them and witnessed the encounter between the light and the helicopter. Their observations confirmed the statements made by the crew.

The *National Enquirer* awarded the men a substantial prize of $5,000 for 'the most scientifically valuable report of 1973.'

NAME FLATTER/DONATHAN

DATE 22 OCTOBER 1973

PLACE BLACKFORD COUNTY, INDIANA
MAP REF: L16

EVENT CLOSE ENCOUNTER OF THE THIRD KIND

DeWayne Donathan and his wife were travelling home around 10 o'clock in the evening when they encountered on the road what appeared to be two figures dancing to music. As the car approached they continued dancing, apparently unable to leave the road. Donathan believed that they looked as if they were skipping but could not quite determine how they were holding their feet or arms. The Donathans passed the couple and looking back DeWayne saw they were just standing along the side of the road. They turned the car round and returned to the spot but the silver suited entities were gone. In the sky two separate bright lights were waving up and down in an extremely odd motion.

The Donathans may have been troubled by their sighting, but can only have been more so when they heard the next day that another witness, Gary Flatter, had also seen the creatures some three hours earlier on the same stretch of road. His sighting had been more dramatic. It confirmed the general descriptions given by Donathan but Flatter, who watched the pair for some five minutes and turned his spotlight on them, indicated that they kicked their feet which were covered in a box-like arrangement and just drifted away into the air at approximately 20-25 miles (32-40 km) per hour.

Whether this sighting truly belongs in a category of UFO sightings or whether other witnesses would more easily have referred to it as a ghost sighting or some other paranormal event is unclear. Certainly there are enough parallels to make it a valid inclusion in any UFO catalogue and it shows very clearly that at least some aspects of UFO encounters interface with other paranormal activity more closely than is often appreciated.

NAME POLASKI ENCOUNTER

DATE 25 OCTOBER 1973

PLACE GREENSBURG, PENNSYLVANIA
MAP REF: N16

EVENT CLOSE ENCOUNTER OF THE THIRD KIND

At 9 o'clock in the evening farmer Stephen Polaski and fifteen other witnesses saw a bright red UFO hovering high over a field. Stephen together with two ten-year-old boys decided to go towards the field to investigate.

As they approached, the car headlights dimmed and they watched the object descending. They left the car and walked up the hill towards the place where the object had either been parked or was hovering; now it was apparently approaching them and it was bright and illuminating the whole area and disturbing dogs in the house. Apparently it was making a sound like 'a lawn mower'.

While they were observing the object one of the boys saw two bear like figures walking along the side of a fence. Both the entities were tall, over 7 ft (213 cm), covered in dark hair and had green-yellow eyes. They were making baby like whining sounds and emitting the smell of burning rubber. Stephen instantly opened fire above their heads.

Undeterred by the shot the entities continued walking towards the trio and finally Stephen fired three bullets directly into the largest of them. One of the boys ran back to the house very scared, the entity that was shot apparently reacted mildly to the incident and the UFO's lights disappeared. The creatures walked back towards the woods.

The area of the ground where the object had been was glowing white and for some time afterwards animals would not go near the place.

Three-quarters of an hour after the beginning of the incident State Trooper Byrne assisted Stephen in an investigation of the site and as they were examining the glowing ring they heard the sound of something large walking towards them through the woods; they could hear the destruction of trees and foliage. As they moved so the sound followed them. When they stopped, uncannily the sound would stop. In a small field nearby they could see an illuminated area.

Although somewhat scared the trooper was all for investigating the incident but Stephen commented 'I don't get paid for being brave. I'm not going any further.' The trooper commenced on his own but called off

the investigation, ostensibly because he was afraid that Stephen in his excited state might mistake him for one of the entities and shoot at him. Although perfectly feasible it might be fair to say that the trooper had decided on discretion being the better part of valour and few people in that situation could blame him. However, prudent this action the behaviour that followed was less than cool and calculating: when Stephen noticed a brown object coming towards them he requested of the trooper that he use his last bullet to shoot at it and the trooper agreed to this. Undoubtedly the two of them were both panicking to some degree by this time. With the

entity coming towards them they both jumped in the car and drove some 50 yds (46 m) out of the field before they realized that they were probably safe inside the vehicle.

Investigation of the event was followed up within about four hours, by a local UFO study group. Ground traces and radiation were not evident and the only suggestion of something abnormal was a bull in a nearby field acting as if it were scared of something during the time they were watching.

During questioning Stephen apparently began to shake and looked as if he was going to faint. He was rubbing his face, breathing heavily and growling like an animal.

He then appears to have attacked his own father and the investigator and chased his dog. Finally he collapsed onto the ground growling before coming back to his senses.

However, whether in a state of shock or suffering some other difficulty, Stephen then became convinced that something was in the field and said he saw 'A man in a black hat and cloak carrying a sickle'.

Stephen also became obsessed that he was receiving contactee messages warning us of terrible catastrophe on Earth.

The interpretation of the meaning of this encounter has been the subject of speculation ever since; whether or not the effect on Stephen was an external event or something internally generated cannot easily be determined. The fact that there appears to have been corroborative evidence of the UFO sighting and even of some ground traces does not itself give evidence to Stephen's state being caused directly by the UFO but rather possibly merely triggered by it. Stephen himself has a history of violence; subjected to bullying by his father, beating up a boy at his school so badly he was off school for three weeks, stopping a car and joining in a fight between two people he had no connection with and breaking into a neighbour's house, doing $1,700 worth of damage and then making elaborate plans to kill the person.

Whatever the truth his state of mind was a reaction to a UFO event, and possibly one of quite high strangeness. For this reason alone it would be reasonable to expect the authorities to take the UFO phenomenon seriously, either by providing citizens with an appropriate defence or response or at least by ensuring that people's most fearful expectations are not heightened by unnecessary mystery.

PROFESSOR ALVIN LAWSON

Professor Alvin Lawson made a valuable contribution to the understanding of UFO abductions when he and his colleagues set up the imaginary abductee experiments in California during the 1970s. He took a group of test subjects who had not reported UFO close encounters and asked them each to create a false story. He wanted to discover the degree to which deliberately false stories might vary from real reports. In fact, there was very little variation, except in terms of emotional involvement. Perhaps the test subjects had read some background UFO stories, but the same would be true of those filing reports.

NAME TSUTOMU NAKAYAMA	
DATE 25 APRIL 1974	
PLACE HAWAII	
MAP REF: A17	
EVENT SURPRISE PHOTOGRAPH	

When Japanese news photographer Tsutomu Nakayama shot the picture below he had not noticed the UFO in the sky above the heads of the dancers. That fact, and the fact that the UFO did not appear in other shots on the film, suggest that the UFO is a photographic flaw, perhaps a lens flare. It is interesting to compare Nakayama's photograph with the one taken at Salem on 16 July 1952 (see page 27). Photographic surprises continue to occur.

Tsutomu Nakayama's Hawaiian surprise.

NAME CARL HIGDON ABDUCTION	
DATE 25 OCTOBER 1974	
PLACE MEDICINE BOW NATIONAL FOREST, WYOMING	
MAP REF: H16	
EVENT CLOSE ENCOUNTER/ABDUCTION	

When out on a day's hunting trip, Carl Higdon, an oil driller for A. M. Well Service of Riverton, Wyoming parked his company pick-up truck. It was 4 o'clock in the afternoon; Higdon took time to drink some coffee from a flask he was carrying. At this point he met a friend, Gary Eaton, and they discussed hunting elk.

The two separated and Higdon found a suitable target elk in a nearby clearing. Higdon took aim and fired. In the next second he could not believe his eyes! The bullet silently and slowly floated out of the end of his gun and fell gently to the ground some 50 ft (15 m) away. Higdon became aware of 'a cone of silence' surrounding the forest and a tingling feeling crawling up his spine. To his left a man approached who Higdon first thought was a hunter like himself. He was wrong.

Although humanoid, the man did not appear human. He had no chin or jaw and his face simply extended down to his throat. He was wearing a one piece suit with a metal belt. He had a yellow skin, a mouth but no lips and very large teeth, his eyes were small with no eyebrows and Higdon could not see any sign of ears. Almost unbelievably, the entity also had two antennae protruding out of his forehead.

Behind the entity was a cube-like object some 6 ft (183 cm) along each edge. In some strange way Higdon believes he was 'teleported' into the object and he believes his natural fears were being suppressed by pills the entity had given him to take. On board, Higdon may have been

somewhat alarmed to have seen that the five elk he had been previously attempting to shoot were now also in a compartment alongside him. Higdon makes no particular attempt to explain the obvious dimensional problems, accepting the quite extraordinary strangeness of the event.

Instantly, an entity appeared in the room beside him and wired Higdon up to machinery via a helmet placed over his head. Somehow he believes he was either transported to, or made to feel as though he was transported to, the home planet of the aliens where he saw tall platforms and bright lights before being returned to Earth.

When Higdon was found by a search party he was resting in his truck, exhausted, the vehicle axle was stuck deep in the middle of a ravine and it took a tow truck to pull it out.

During regression hypnosis sessions following the event one particular detail gives some cause for alarm; Higdon apparently saw – on the aliens' home planet – ordinary adult and child humans possibly prisoners of the aliens or possibly bred on their home world. Higdon reported that he was unable to talk with them.

Higdon has speculated that he was in effect rejected by the aliens as unsuitable for their purpose because he had had a vasectomy. This would seem to give support to the now current theory that the aliens are visiting the Earth on a programme of genetic breeding experimentation.

There appears to be some corroboration of the event; members of the search party looking for Higdon saw strange glowing lights in the trees around the area. There were also other reports of UFO lights around Wyoming at the same time.

NAME TRAVIS WALTON ABDUCTION	
DATE 5 NOVEMBER 1975	
PLACE SNOWFLAKE, ARIZONA MAP REF: G18	
EVENT ABDUCTION	

When the American government issued a contract to clear trees in the Sitgraves National Park in Arizona they could have had no idea of the extraordinary story they were about to unleash. The contract was awarded to a seven-man woodcutting team which included the case's principal witness Travis Walton and his brother Duane.

After the day's work was over they were driving back to their base when all the witnesses saw a large golden UFO hovering over the trees. It seemed to be solid, with windows and a fairly classical flying saucer shape complete with cupola on top. Travis Walton jumped from the truck and ran towards the object while the other six shouted for him to come back. Little could they know that it would be some days before he would heed their cries!

A blue ray shot from the object, hitting Walton and knocking him back into the trees. Perhaps understandably the remaining members of the gang fled the area in the truck and drove straight to the local police who instigated a search.

Walton was nowhere to be found. It is significant that three of the gang refused to join the search party or to go back into the woods at night and according to Sheriff Ellison who headed the search party 'One of the men was weeping. If they were lying, they were damned good actors.'

The search went on for five days at the end of which the witnesses took polygraph tests at the Arizona State Office of Public Safety. They were apparently concerned that it was rumoured that they had

The cover of Travis Walton's book which relates his incredible five-day abduction.

murdered Walton and they sought to clear their name. One of the six was apparently too agitated to take the test but the other five did and the administrator of the test, Cy Gilson, stated 'I gotta say they passed the test.' Fortunately for them, and indeed for Walton, the missing man turned up late that night.

His story was that he had been abducted by the UFO and found himself in a room being examined by aliens very familiar on the North American continent, i.e. pale hairless skin, large domed heads, large eyes and reduced physical features. Walton also recalls seeing a very human like person on board the saucer and recalls the image of what appeared to be either a space flight or the holographic projection of one. Walton also took a polygraph test under Dr Gene Rosenbaum of Durango, Colorado who stated 'This young man is not lying . . . he really believes these things.'

The Walton case was one that became a 'boxing ring' for various American UFO groups. One group claimed that he had failed polygraph tests, that his previous criminal record and interest in the subject of UFOs was against him and that the whole story had been fabricated to explain why he was late in delivering on the contract which would have incurred him financial penalty. The fact that the gang also received a $5,000 prize for their story has been regarded as a motive for the claims. Other groups have 'adopted' him believing him to be sincere.

While the passing of time makes it unlikely that any conclusion will ever be drawn about this case the fact that none of the many witnesses has ever come forward to denounce the story, although any one of them could probably make substantial sums of money by doing so, speaks greatly in its favour.

NAME FALCONBRIDGE

DATE 11 NOVEMBER 1975

PLACE FALCONBRIDGE, ONTARIO
MAP REF: N14

EVENT RADAR/VISUAL ENCOUNTER

Following a period of UFO sightings near the USA/Canadian border in autumn 1975, the 11 November brought a radar tracked UFO, confirmed by visual sighting, at the radar sites at Falconbridge, Ontario.

Radar detected a UFO some 30 miles (48 km) south of the site at a height somewhere between 25,000 and 70,000 ft (7,620-21,336 m). The UFO appeared as a large globe with porthole or crater like formations around the outside.

Two F-106 fighters from the Air National Guard's squadron at Selfridge Air Force Base in Michigan were sent aloft to intercept the UFO, but no contact was made.

1980s

NAME CASH/LANDRUM ENCOUNTER

DATE 29 DECEMBER 1980

PLACE DAYTON, TEXAS
MAP REF: K19

EVENT CLOSE ENCOUNTER OF THE SECOND KIND

Vickie Landrum, her grandson Colby Landrum and their friend Betty Cash were driving in the late evening/early night towards Dayton in Texas when they witnessed a huge glowing object descend to treetop height above the road in front of them.

The witnesses were frightened by the encounter but left the car to see what was happening although young Colby Landrum begged them to get back inside which they eventually did. It was Betty Cash who remained outside the car for the longest period of time. The UFO appeared to be indistinct though generally diamond shaped with long flames bursting down from below.

Of most interest is that the witnesses also identified some twenty-four Chinook twin blade helicopters escorting the UFO at a distance. They followed it in their car for a period of time before reaching home less than an hour after the encounter. The after-effects of the sighting have been horrific!

Vickie Landrum suffered a temporary loss of hair and inflamed eyes for a time, Colby appears to have suffered similar effects.

Betty Cash, who spent the majority of the time outside the car, suffered vomiting and diarrhoea, impaired vision, various aches and pains across her body and blistering to the scalp. She suffered temporary hair loss and developed breast cancer which required a mastectomy.

It appears certain that the three witnesses were subjected to some form of radiation and, even more alarming, the presence of the military helicopters suggests that the UFO – on this occasion at least – was terrestrial: some form of unshielded nuclear source was being transported across the Texas skies. Even if the object were a crash-retrieved extraterrestrial craft then at the time of the encounter it was in terrestrial hands.

Believing the object to have been American in design the two adult witnesses sued the United States government for $20 million but the case was dismissed on the grounds that the Americans did not have such an object in their possession. Senior officials of the Air Force, the Army, the Navy and the civilian space agency all testified categorically that the object was not of their making.

The final stories on this case cannot yet have been written because the American government now appears to have a serious alternative to face; if the object *was* American then the law suit should succeed and a few prominent heads may well have to roll. It appears that those heads are resisting that alternative. However, the only other option is that the object *was not* American. Be it terrestrial or extraterrestrial this means that someone other than Americans were toting an unshielded nuclear source over Texas that night and since it clearly has not yet been identified then it must rate as a UFO. If this is the course they continue to take, the American government can therefore never again state – as they have done so often in the past – that UFOs have no national security implications. Which course the American government will choose to take only time will tell.

NAME 'KATHIE DAVIS' ABDUCTIONS

DATE 30 JUNE 1983

PLACE 'COPLEY WOODS', INDIANA
MAP REF: L16

EVENT MULTIPLE LIFETIME ABDUCTIONS

The Kathie Davis case, investigated by top American abduction researcher Budd Hopkins, can probably be regarded as the current 'state of the art' in abduction lore.

On 30 June 1983 Kathie Davis (a pseudonym used to protect the identity of the witness) saw lights apparently searching the garden of her house and she went out to see them. It appears that because she drew attention to herself she received a blast of radiation, was abducted, and then possibly had a device implanted into her by means of a probe.

However, the June 1983 encounter appears to be one of many throughout her life.

There are vague suggestions of abductions in her very early years; Kathie has a dream of her mother protecting her from a threat in the sky by hiding her in a wardrobe. On another occasion she recalls going to a strange house and meeting a 'little boy'. Hopkins believes this is a false memory implanted by an alien to disguise her abduction. They took a sample of her skin; Kathie has a scar on her leg which is regarded as evidence of this event.

In December 1977, Kathie was abducted from a car, the other occupants were apparently 'switched off' to isolate them from the incident. She was taken aboard a flying saucer and given the first of many gynaecological operations. Hopkins believes that time she was artificially inseminated by the aliens.

A further abduction occurred in March 1978 and Hopkins believes that during this event the unborn foetus was removed from Kathie's

The face of an alien abductor, drawn by 'Kathie Davis'.

body. In 1979 Kathie was abducted again and a probe inserted into her nose possibly implanting some sort of monitoring device.

1983 begins with the incident of the lights in her garden which inspired her to contact Budd Hopkins. Some months later it would appear that she was abducted again and subjected to a gruelling medical examination, which left her bleeding and when she reawakened she was in her own backyard in her nightgown. Most incredibly of all she believes that during this abduction she met a child which was her hybrid alien daughter.

In a further abduction in November 1983, it appears that Kathie was subjected to medical examination and her ova contents were removed by aliens. There is some suggestion that her son Tommy was also abducted at this time. It appears that Tommy was abducted again in February 1986 and Kathie accidentally witnessed the alien emerging from his bedroom.

A further abduction takes place from Kathie's home in April 1986. She is shown two babies and allowed to name them and 'bond' with them though she is told that there is a

total of nine babies, the implication being that they are hers.

The case continues and Hopkins, who carried out the regression hypnosis sessions in the presence of a doctor, believes that the aliens are undergoing a series of examinations and that her son Robbie is now the subject of abductions.

The case is heavily dependent on regression hypnosis with very little of the detail being remembered consciously. Hopkins has also stated that there are many facts he has not yet made public hoping they will be corroborated in other cases.

NAME JAPAN AIR LINES

DATE 17 NOVEMBER 1986

PLACE ANCHORAGE AIRPORT, ALASKA
MAP REF: C8

EVENT CLOSE ENCOUNTER OF THE FIRST
KIND

Notable mainly for the sheer size of the UFO involved, the encounter of the crew of Japan Air Lines cargo flight No. JAL 1628 on 17 November 1986 attracted considerable interest.

The plane was flying from France to Japan and was making a stopover at Anchorage airport. At 39,000 ft (11,887 m) and preparing for descent, Captain Kenju Terauchi and his crew noticed lights near the jumbo jet. They were flying parallel and pacing the aircraft and Terauchi briefly saw the object carrying the lights, which he described as 'walnut shaped' and twice the size of an aircraft carrier.

The UFO apparently paced the plane for over half an hour and was radar-tracked by air traffic control.

Captain Terauchi had his own rather unique interpretation of the interest of the aliens, if that is what they were. 'We were carrying Beaujolais from France to Japan. Maybe they wanted to drink it.'

NAME GULF BREEZE CASE

DATE 11 NOVEMBER 1987 (TO THE PRESENT DAY)

PLACE GULF BREEZE, FLORIDA
MAP REF: M19

EVENT MULTIPLE PHOTOGRAPHIC CASE

In 1987, Gulf Breeze, the offshore area of Pensacola, Florida became the site of the most extraordinary photographic case and one which has caused considerable controversy in the United States ever since.

This is the first case in which a large number of photographs were used to support an abduction. At the same time that the events were occurring, the case was being studied by an investigation team. It is also alleged that there were multiple witnesses. The photographs taken have been subjected to a thorough investigation using modern photographic techniques.

On 11 November 1987 the witness (known generally as 'Mr Ed') took five Polaroid photographs of a UFO seen in the sky beyond his home at Gulf Breeze in Florida. While taking the last picture Mr Ed was apparently 'attacked' by the flying saucer which paralyzed him with a blue beam of light and lifted him into the air, nearly choking him. During this incident Mr Ed reported a very bizarre image which appeared in his mind and seemed similar to flicking through pages of pictures of dogs in a book. Mr Ed sent his pictures to the local *Florida Sentinel* newspaper and by coincidence the mother of the editor and her husband, a former editor, also spotted a similar UFO in the sky at the same time that Mr Ed had been taking his photographs. In response to the article a further witness Mrs Zammit also reported seeing the same blue beam.

From then until 1 May 1988

Mr Ed experienced a considerable number of sightings, each one preceded by a peculiar buzzing sound in his head. The investigators believe this may have been the product of an implant placed in his head at the time of an abduction early in his life and designed to give him warning of the impending arrival of the saucers.

Over the five to six month period Mr Ed took dozens of photographs, to some extent under controlled conditions. Optical physicist Bruce Maccabee, the chairman of the Fund for UFO Research, set up a system of stereo photography, to give an almost three-dimensional effect, by attaching two Polaroid cameras to each side of a wooden pole and with a further pole extending between them as a reference point. Later, controlled experiments included giving Mr Ed a sealed Nimslo three-dimensional camera which also produced pictures of the craft, which was also picked up on video.

Mr Ed also claims that on 2 December, having been roused out of bed by noises in his garden, he pulled back the curtains of his French doors and was 'eyeball to eyeball' with an alien entity who, extraordinarily, he chased – although it apparently got away.

Unfortunately Mr Ed was not able to take photographs of the humanoid but his description of it gives some indication that it matches the claims of many American witnesses. His drawing of the creature indicates that it had the same eyes as those recently made famous by the front cover of Whitley Strieber's book *Communion*.

On 12 January Mr Ed was driving from his home when he encountered the same UFO hovering over the road ahead of him and he was paralyzed by the blast of a white beam from it. As he hid under his truck he witnessed the UFO

depositing aliens onto the road which then appeared to come after him. Apparently he was able to get into his truck and drive off to escape capture.

In February 1988 Mr Ed had a lie detector test and the examiner was firmly persuaded that Mr Ed 'truly believes that the photographs and personal sightings are true and factual to the best of his ability.'

The 1 May 1988 date is important as it was then that Mr Ed had an encounter which he believes may have been an abduction during which the implant which forewarned him of his sightings was removed. It is further speculated that the reason that this was removed was because UFO investigators were 'closing the net' and had suggested that he have a CAT scan to identify the object implanted in his brain.

A provisional summary of the case issued by MUFON suggested that they believed the case to be genuine. More recently the investigating team have made a public statement that they believe that it was indeed a genuine case and not the fraud or hoax which many other investigators had suggested.

Other investigators have been less generous and believe that their own analysis of the photographs indicates that the object is a small model supported by struts and that therefore the whole case is a complete fabrication. Such is the controversy in the United States that investigators who have successfully worked together for many years are now at loggerheads with each other. Some appear to be disseminating virtually slanderous comments about each other's capabilities or personal characteristics in order to promote or discredit the case.

Mr Ed has his own story to tell, and indeed has told it in his own bestselling book.

FROM
SAUCERS TO
CONSPIRACIES

North America, and particularly the United States, is – as the scope and size of the database suggests – the home of the UFO phenomenon. It was born on that continent, on 24 June 1947, when pilot Kenneth Arnold reported that he had witnessed nine objects in flight while flying in the Cascade mountains of Washington State (see page 15). Although by today's standards, it was a very unimpressive sighting – of short duration by a single witness, of indistinct objects, and seen at some considerable distance – it had enormous social significance. When Arnold told reporters afterwards that the objects had moved 'like a saucer would if you skipped it across the water', one reporter coined the phrase 'flying saucer'. It was the perfect term for the mood of the times, a name that the public was instantly drawn to. It was also the most powerful advertising slogan ever coined.

The UFO has continued to live in the US ever since. Certainly the phenomenon has siblings and cousins in every country in the world; as this book shows it is far from a solely North American experience. However, the public acceptance of UFOs is far higher there, particularly in the United States, than anywhere else in the world. The uncritical acceptance of the more extraordinary theories regarding UFOs is also wider there. The media in the US have helped to make the subject there respectable, though also one of raging controversy. Only Britain comes close to the American response to UFOs, and this is largely America-driven.

The UFO has matured in North America, indeed there more than anywhere else it has evolved, and mutated. Some aspects of the subject have undergone a complete metamorphosis. In the early days UFO (or 'flying saucer') reports consisted of night-time lights in the sky, or discs and egg shaped objects seen in the

daylight. Until 1952 these reports seemed to satisfy the American need. In that year, however, the subject underwent its first major change which viewed with hindsight was inevitable. George Adamski (see page 28), reported not only seeing flying saucers at close quarters, but also claimed to meet with the extra-terrestrial pilots, in the desert in California. In subsequent adventures Adamski claimed he was taken on tours of the planets of the solar system. It is a claim that has not stood the test of time; the planets Adamski apparently visited have been shown in recent years to be quite incapable of supporting anything like humanoid life. Adamski's books sold well though, a fact which may have encouraged others to follow him in the next few years.

In 1961, less than a decade later, the phenomenon changed again. While driving from Canada to their home in New Hampshire state, a married couple, Betty and Barney Hill (see page 42), claimed that they were 'abducted' by the alien pilots of a flying saucer. These were not the graceful, gentle aliens Adamski had met who had shown such concern for the well-being of human kind; these were dwarf, alien forms, and their interest seems to have been virtually clinical. During their two-hour captivity the Hills were subjected to a medical examination of the most frightening nature. Such abductions have continued to be reported up to the present day, but the sequels have been increasingly frightening. Probably the 'state of the art' abduction at the present time is the 'Kathie Davis' case (see page 66) where the witness is claimed to have undergone a series of abductions throughout her life. It appears that she was artificially inseminated during one abduction, in a later abduction the foetus was stolen from her womb and – in a still further event – she was allowed to meet with her hybrid alien offspring.

LEFT Major Donald E Keyhoe was a prominent and vociferous opponet to UFO cover-up by the military, and took every opportunity to challenge the official line. He put a great deal of pressure on the establishment with such books as *The Flying Saucers Are Real* (RIGHT).

The UFO phenomenon had changed from being fascinating, to being fascinating *and* disturbing. It was like science fiction, but a science fiction that could happen to *you*, or *you*. It does not matter if you think the whole phenomenon to be one of wish-fulfilment or fantasy; whereas before it might have been a pleasure to be so affected, now it would be immensely frightening.

Both the Arnold case and the Hill case raise an interesting point about North American ufology. In neither case were the claims the first to be made in the world, but they were the first to gain media recognition. Prior to both these cases Europe had undergone the 'Foo Fighters' (see page 79) of the World War Two aerial combat arena, Scandinavia had experienced the Ghost Rocket sightings (see page 80) and South America had seen the first abduction claim in the case of Antonio Villas Boas (see page 181). However, these new and – for the times – innovative claims seemed unable to gain an acceptance outside America until they had first become acknowledged there. It is as if the world prefers either for America to sanction extraordinary claims before it will consider them, or to avoid being the first to look foolish, even if America is prepared to jump in with both feet.

There are other mutations of the phenomenon that seem uniquely American; perhaps the most obvious is the appearance of the 'men in black'. It has never been very clear precisely who these characters were supposed to be; they were repressive individuals who rode around in squeaky-clean Cadillacs and threatened UFO witnesses with Mafia style 'hints', suggesting strongly that they keep silent about their sightings. Obvious candidates would seem to be agents of the CIA or the FBI either on a very strange and non-productive mission, or just having a laugh at the expense of a 'fringe' subject. Other suggestions are that they were born in the Maury Island case (see page 14), and were agents of the Atomic Energy Commission. Eventually, the claims were made – inevitably – that the 'men in black' had a vested interest in silencing witnesses – they were themselves the aliens! One report suggested that they were trying to blend in with the human community by, for example, using heavy make-up and lip-stick. Unfortunately they got it all wrong – the men wore the make up, *proving* [!] their extraterrestrial lack of earthly knowledge . . .

No-one has ever successfully explained these very marked differences between America and the rest of the world, though Dennis Stacy's opening comments are enlightening coming as they do direct from within the USA.

One fact that might have coloured the development of the subject is the 'prize' offered by the *National Enquirer* – a tabloid publication – of $5,000 per year for the best UFO story. Certainly some of the most extraordinary claims have been awarded the sum – many are included in the database in this book – the Travis Walton case (see page 64), the Delphos ring (see page 58), the Coyne encounter (see page 60), and so on. But if this led witnesses to make false claims, and if some of those claims were regarded as 'real', then surely that alone would not account for the subject, after all the *Enquirer* was not paying for claims from South America and Africa, and so on, yet they came in too. It must be said though that a $5,000 reward for extraordinary stories would be totally irresponsible if ufology had offered it; we cannot blame the *Enquirer* for 'doing what comes naturally' but perhaps must take account of the effect it had.

One other suggestion made is that the US is both a more 'open' society able to accept new concepts and at the same time a xenophobic one, fearing outside invasion. It is a country that has never had its mainland borders attacked and the two famous situations where it appeared that this might be happening provoked remarkable responses. In 1938 Orson Welles broadcast a radio version of *The War of the Worlds* as if it were genuinely happening; there was extraordinary panic in the population including evacuation of homes. In 1941 it was feared that the coast of Los Angeles was being invaded by Japanese fighter planes, which was quite unfounded, but the resulting chaos caused several deaths and destruction of property.

The average American's relationship with his or her government has also affected the direction of ufology in recent years, and again in a way that seems to have been more extreme than that caused by similar situations in other countries. There has been great distrust of the government's honesty with regard to UFOs; claims abound that the government is covering up its knowledge of UFOs. Indeed, documents released under the Freedom Of Information Act have revealed that there has been some cover up. Claims by the FBI and the CIA that they had no interest in UFOs and were not investigating them have also been shown to be quite false. Unfortunately, this cover up has helped colour in a conspiratorial picture. As a result many in America believe that the government has retrieved crashed flying saucers, and dead alien bodies. Others believe that aliens work alongside human counterparts inside the Pentagon. Others still fear a worse scenario: that the government knows something so horrific that the public must not be told.

In fact, the cover up is most likely to be a cover up of ignorance rather than knowledge. The United States does not appear to be a country that maintains 'major' cover ups successfully in the long term, and the holding of crashed flying saucers and dead aliens is 'major' by any standards. Such a cover up is alleged to have gone on for over forty years and would have involved hundreds if not thousands of people; yet the American President could not cover up his own actions and the actions of his aides for the two more years needed to see out his last term of office in the 1970s.

Such crash retrieval stories are also uniquely American; although other countries, such as Australia, have the wide open spaces and military installations that seem to be favoured by the more clumsy of the extraterrestrial spaceships. No other country has produced this rash of such stories. A recent claim that a similar event had happened in Africa has proved to be a ludicrous fraud. We must assume that the Russians, for example, also benefit from these downed saucers, or that they are being very generous in allowing America the advantage of learning from this incredibly advanced technology. In any other circumstance we might have expected Russian espionage, if not a full scale Russian attack, on Wright Patterson Air Base, where – it is speculated – all UFOs are sent and stored, to equalize the balance of power as with atomic secrets, space technology and so on. Yet the Russians seem happy to let the Americans get on with this one.

Unfortunately America must also be said to be the home of the fraudulent claim. It is quite likely that some of the more extraordinary documents seeming to support crash retrievals were created by ufologists in support of their beliefs (and their lecture circuit income!). Since, in the past few years, ufology has become 'big bucks', fraudulent claims are increasing.

These negative considerations apart, America is responsible for much of the very significant effort that has gone into UFO research in the past four decades and more. The private research organizations there are more active than similar groups anywhere else in the world. Notable amongst them is MUFON – the Mutual UFO Network in Texas, and CUFOS – the J. Allen Hynek Center for UFO Studies.

Of private individuals that country has produced more informed researchers than any other. Jacques Vallée and John Keel have consistently shown the way to radical thinking into the phenomenon, and their

books have had a great effect well beyond the American borders.

In the early years there was much high level involvement in UFO study; Major Donald Keyhoe became a most vociferous exponent of the extra-terrestrial theory, and wrote many books trying to highlight his own government's apparent lack of proper commitment to the subject. He also suggested the idea of a 'lure' designed to attract and capture visiting extraterrestrials – the hunted turning hunter – based on a Canadian idea of the 1950s of offering UFOs a specified 'landing field' from which contact might be mutually arranged.

One name that cannot go unmentioned in this introduction is that of Dr J. Allen Hynek, who gave his name to the Center for UFO Studies on his death in 1986. A professional astronomer, he was engaged by the United States Air Force to investigate and debunk the flying saucer stories, to produce a final investigation of the subject that would rid the Air Force of what they perceived to be their problem. Far from succeeding, Hynek became convinced that there was indeed something extraordinary that needed to be investigated properly. When the Air Force's final official investigation, Project Blue Book, was closed down in 1969 Hynek formed the Center for UFO Studies from the hard core of scientists he had worked with over the years. They had been known as the 'Invisible College', now they were becoming visible. Throughout the remainder of his life Hynek doggedly pursued the UFO phenomenon through its many evolutions, always exhibiting the very best efforts; an emphasis on the scientific style of study and a determination to be rational in his thinking and leadership. It was he who talked of the 'escalation of hypotheses', warning that it was improper to assume the extraordinary before the ordinary had first been successfully eliminated. Hynek's death has left a void in ufology that has not yet been filled, and it is a void that reaches across the world. If other countries took their lead from America in the early years, it was at least a strong, if sometimes a headstrong lead. Today, it is both confused and leaderless. Hynek's death and the attempts to replace him have left a very violent power struggle in America which is damaging ufology the world over. Those who 'would-be-Hynek' are insubstantial shadows of the real man.

That leaderless lead has produced one very damaging effect, to which Dennis Stacy refers in his commentary; that of litigation by Americans, mostly in pursuit of their more absurd theories. As one of the nations affected by this new trend, Britain now looks with more suspicion at the American continent, and – it must be admitted – with more suspicion at the very foundation of ufology. Has it always been just a game of extremists pursuing the great American dollar? Surely not. The sheer weight of substantial evidence in support of some extraordinary phenomenon is too great to be dismissed that simply. Nonetheless, we must trust that authoritative UFO groups strive to avoid a situation which could result in the USA losing its well-respected lead position in world ufology.

Project Blue Book was the last UFO Air Force investigation. ABOVE Dr J Allen Hynek, who was engaged by Project Blue Book to debunk UFOs; he became convinced of their reality and went on to become the most famous ufologist of all time. RIGHT Seated is Major Hector Quintinilla, head of Project Blue Book.

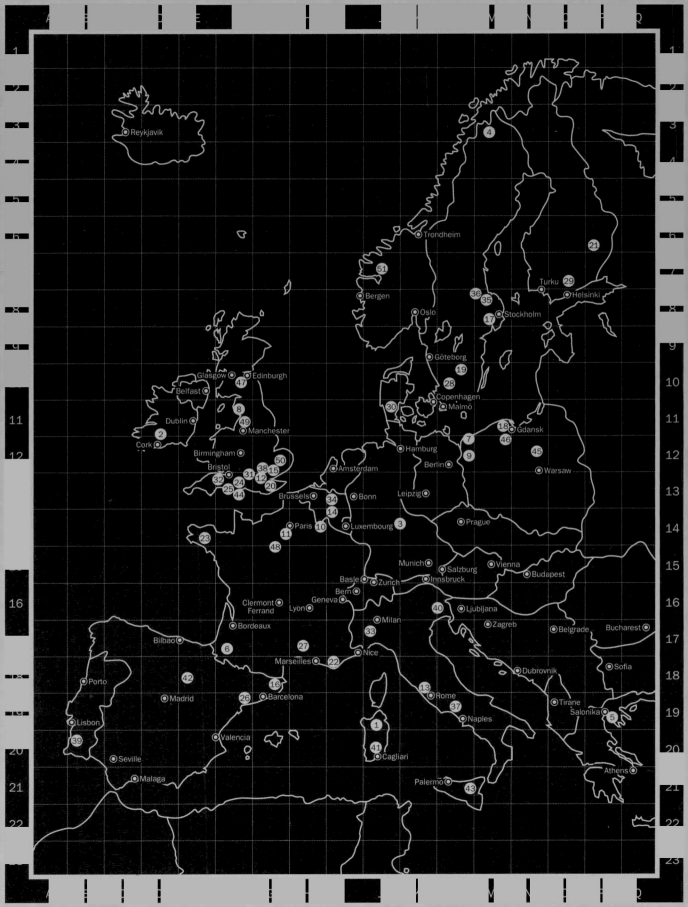

EUROPE

PUBLIC AWARENESS OF FLYING SAUCERS WAS

THUS WIDESPREAD IN EUROPE AT THE SAME TIME

AS CHEWING-GUM, COCA-COLA AND THE OTHER

AMERICANA THAT THE 'MARSHALL' PLAN TOOK TO

EUROPE AFTER WORLD WAR II.

KEY TO MAP OF EUROPE

① Historical Perspective, Sardinia, Roman Mediterranean
② The Irish Airship, Cloera, Ireland
③ The Birth of the 'Foo Fighters', Schweinfurt, Germany
④ Swedish Ghost Rockets, Lake Kölmjärv, North Sweden
⑤ Greek Ghost Rockets, Salonika, Thessalía, Greece
⑥ Oloron, Oloron-Ste Marie, Pays Basques, France
⑦ Wolin Island Sighting, Wolin Island, Szczecin, Poland
⑧ The Stephen Darbishire Photographs, Coniston, Cumbria, England
⑨ Węgierska Górka Encounter, Węgierska Górka, Poland
⑩ The Dewilde Encounter, Quarouble, France
⑪ Sinceny Misjudgement, Sinceny, Aisne, France
⑫ Flight Lieutenant Salandin's Encounter, Thames Estuary, England
⑬ The UFO Fleet, Rome, Italy
⑭ Namur Photographic Case, Namur, Belgium
⑮ Bentwaters/Lakenheath, Suffolk, England
⑯ Angelu Encounter, Figueras, Catalonia, Spain
⑰ Väddö Retrieval, Väddö, Roslagen, Sweden
⑱ Gydnia Humanoid, Gydnia Harbour, Gdánsk, Poland
⑲ The Jelly Entities of Sweden, Domsten, Southern Sweden
⑳ The Batman Encounter, Saltwood, Kent, England
㉑ Kallavesi Lake, Kuopio, Finland
㉒ Valensole Sighting, Valensole, Southern France
㉓ Coquil Encounter, Bolazec, France
㉔ The Hook Vehicle Interference, Hook, Hampshire, England
㉕ The Moigne Downs Encounter, Moigne Downs, Dorset, England
㉖ Serra de Almos Encounter, Serra de Almos, Spain

㉗ Dr 'X', Southern France
㉘ Kathryn Howard, Southern Sweden
㉙ The Imjärvi Encounter, Imjärvi, Southern Finland
㉚ The Maarup Encounters, Hadersley, Jylland, Denmark
㉛ The Peter Day Film, Long Crendon, Oxfordshire, England
㉜ Langford Budville Encounter, Langford Budville, Somerset, England
㉝ Torino Sighting, Caselle Airport, Torino, Italy
㉞ The Vilvorde Humanoid, Vilvorde, Brussels, Belgium
㉟ The Anders Encounter, Gustavslund, Sweden
㊱ Mrs Andersson's Encounter, Söderby, Gustavslund, Sweden
㊲ The Bellingeri Sighting, Piedmont, Alessandria, Italy
㊳ The Aveley Abduction, Aveley, Essex, England
㊴ The Trident Sighting, Portuguese Coast, 40 miles (64 km) south of Lisbon, Portugal
㊵ The Aviano Blackout, Aviano NATO Base, North-east Italy
㊶ The Sardinia Helicopter Encounter, Cagliari, Sardinia, Italy
㊷ Medinaceli Abduction, Medinaceli, Soria, Spain
㊸ The Mount Etna Encounter, Mount Etna, Sicily, Italy
㊹ The Flying Elephant, Southampton, England
㊺ Piastów Encounter, Piastów, Near Warsaw, Poland
㊻ Czluchów Sighting, Czluchów, Poland
㊼ The Livingston Encounter, Livingston, Lothian, Scotland
㊽ Cergy-Pontoise Abduction, Cergy-Pontoise, France
㊾ Godfrey Encounter, Todmorden, West Yorkshire, England
㊿ Rendlesham Forest, RAF/USAF Woodbridge, Suffolk, England
51 Hessdalen Lights, Hessdalen Valley, Norway

A COMMON EUROPEAN UFOLOGY?

I t will be no surprise that as Europe is only a geographical expression, a unified 'European ufology' does not exist. The language barrier has long been an obstacle in developing a common framework of any kind in Europe – let alone in the field of ufology. Indeed, even if we limit ourselves to the eighteen countries of Western Europe, as many as fourteen different languages are spoken, and local ufologists are often unable to understand any language other than their own.

As a consequence, those countries with languages other than English and French have had fewer exchanges with other nations, both in terms of input and output and it is possible that as many national ufologies as there are European languages have developed over the past forty-odd years.

European 'flying saucer' sightings were already taking place in 1947 and even earlier than that: suffice it to mention the 'foo fighters' of World War II, on the German front in 1944-45 (see page 79) and the Scandinavian 'ghost rockets' scare of 1946 (see page 80). We should distinguish between the phenomenon (UFO sightings and reports) and its study (ufology). While anomalous aerial phenomena reports in Europe were contemporary with (if not older than) the American ones, they were not always labelled as flying saucers in those early years.

Since there were no ufologists at that time, we have to rely on the press coverage of such events in order to learn of the social impressions UFOs made when it all began. It is easy to see that saucers were at first regarded as nothing more than 'another of those American follies', and even those (few) local reports published in the media were not seriously considered. The year UFOs really arrived in Europe was 1950: the spring of that year saw the first real waves of UFO reports in Europe (France, Italy, Spain, the UK),

closely following news of sightings from the USA. Public awareness of flying saucers was thus widespread in Europe at the same time as chewing-gum, Coca-Cola and the other Americana that the 'Marshall' plan took to Europe after World War II. In the autumn of 1954 a second widespread 'great wave' of flying saucer sightings and landings took place throughout all the countries of Europe, and as a consequence more and more people began to take an interest in the subject in the following years.

It should be repeated that two different levels of national ufologies may be considered, according to the spoken language: as English and French are widely read and spoken, the early British and French ufologists were able to reach a wider audience within ufology, while those speaking other languages could not. Indeed just about every history of ufology (even the American-centered ones) mentions Frenchmen Aimé Michel or Jimmy Guieu, whose books were also translated into English. This often resulted in more being known about some small, local English groups than of important, say, Spanish or Swedish researchers.

It is also important to remember that no European country ever had anything similar to the US Air Force involvement or equivalent to its Project Blue Book. This situation did not change very much even when the first organized national ufologies surfaced in most European countries, mainly in the 1960s: the British UFO Research Association (BUFORA) in the United Kingdom; the Centro de Estudios Interplanetarios (CEI) in Spain; the Centro Unico Nazionale (CUN) in Italy, and so on.

The only journal of truly international stature in Europe has been the British *Flying Saucer Review* (*FSR*) published since 1955. It has often been in its pages that UFO events and research from the

non-English-speaking European countries could be found. Nonetheless, the very first attempt at a rationalistic approach to UFOs came from France as early as 1958, when Aimé Michel published his book on 'orthoteny' (straight line theory), attempting to show that UFO sightings in the French wave of 1954 were aligned along straight lines.

The birth of scientific ufology may also be traced back to Europe. It was a young French-born scientist, astronomer Jacques Vallée (who later moved to the USA), who published the first scientific UFO books in the mid-sixties. We have to acknowledge that European ufologies as a whole retained only a minor role in

Silbury Hill in southern England. This huge man-made hill is the focus of much attention by those concerned with the powers of ancient man, and paranormal activity. It is also close to Warminster, the centre of much UFO activity in Wiltshire.

the history of ufology through the 1960s and 1970s, mostly following the impulse from North America.

It was during this period that the first real differences in interpretation between North America and Europe occurred. The schism was caused by the so-called 'new ufology', which was initiated by American researchers as early as 1969 but soon abandoned in the USA. It made a big impact in some European

UFO circles, and the effect may still be seen in the 1990s. Once again, it all began in the USA, when two similar books were published by journalist John A. Keel and scientist Jacques Vallée. They both considered a non-extra-terrestrial explanation for the origin of UFOs which, they suggested, might instead be derived from a form of intelligence in a 'parallel reality' which had always existed beside our own reality.

In the USA these ideas never found great favour, the majority of ufologists still preferring the simple Extra-terrestrial Theory (ETH), and by the second half of the 1970s these notions were virtually forgotten. However, they stimulated at least three different lines of thought in Europe, mainly in Great Britain and France. The first was the literally 'paraphysical' current, hinting at 'parallel realities', mostly diffused in the UK in the pages of *Flying Saucer Review*. It has gradually lost ground in favour of the next two lines of thought. The second was the 'humanistic ufology' heralded by the *Magonia* magazine's editorial team in the UK; greater emphasis is placed upon the 'human factor' in the UFO experience, both at an individual (i.e. psychological) level and at a collective (i.e. sociological) level.

The third concept was typical of French ufology in the mid-1970s, where 'paranormal' aspects openly bordered with psychical (i.e. parapsychological) overtones. It was stimulated by the French edition of yet another of Jacques Vallée's books, *The Invisible College* (1975). Several French UFO writers were heavily influenced by that, and 'parapsychological ufology' prevailed in the French UFO journals between 1975 and 1979. Among the most interesting authors are Jean Giraud, Jean-Jacques Jaillat and Pierre Viéroudy.

Such a line of thought is no longer prevalent in France, because in turn it stimulated a totally different current, called 'the new wave', also known as 'nouveaux ufologues', or 'neo-skepticism'. It all began when Michel Monnerie, co-editor of the French UFO journal *Lumières dans la nuit* (*LDLN*) realized that the 'psycho-ufology' was demonstrating that a genuine, concrete phenomenon was no longer needed to account for the sightings: the witness was enough. He presented his thesis in a book, provocatively titled *What if UFOs did not exist?* But if it were so, why call for such exotic mechanisms as psychic powers?

Monnerie's book had the same effect as a bomb: fierce attacks on his own somewhat naïve suggestion of an 'open-eye dream' as an explanation for the strangeness of some UFO sightings forced him to a more and more inflexible attitude. He published a second book on the *Shipwreck of the Extra-terrestrials* (1979) where he tried to demolish the whole ufological building, openly becoming a true skeptic and finally leaving ufology. This first generation of 'new skeptics'

For centuries man has pondered over the origins of the huge stone circle known as Stonehenge on the plains near Salisbury. It is built at a point reputed to be a centre of major energy lines (leys), and is of great mystic importance. The area is also a focus of UFO activity. Why our ancestors went to the enormous trouble they did to create this monument remains unknown but UFO-related worship has often been suggested, perhaps because of the circular shape of the monument. The coincidence of modern UFO activity near this ancient site has suggested to many researchers that the UFO phenomenon may only be a modern version of something very ancient, something that has perhaps been a part of the Earth for longer than Man.

(including a re-writing and debunking of the great French UFO wave of 1954 by G. Barthel and J. Brucker) virtually ended in 1980, because these 'disillusioned ufologists' abandoned the UFO field.

The lesson of doubt was taught and, after a severe crisis due also to the lack of UFO sightings in the early 1980s, a new generation of French ufologists has emerged. They keep a skeptical but open mind, try to re-define the scope of ufology and consider psycho-sociological hypotheses to be as valid as the ETH, until data arises to prove or disprove either theory. Claude Maugé, Bertrand Meheust, Jacques Scornaux and Thierry Pinvidic are the best known names. Interestingly, a somewhat similar position is now shared by most active European UFO researchers, in countries other than France.

In Great Britain Jenny Randles's writings parallel the Monnerie/Hendry evolution of thought although they never negate the physical reality of UFOs. She has moved from paraphysical reasonings to Hendry-like texts such as *UFO Study* (1981) and *UFO Reality* (1983), finally considering natural unexplained aerial phenomena as good candidates for some UFOs. In this context, we see Paul Devereux's *Earthlights*, Hilary Evans's Ball Of Light International Data Exchange (*BOLIDE*) or the very responsible position BUFORA has been holding vis-à-vis the corn circle phenomenon and the plasma vortex hypothesis.

Europe has come of age: there is a collective movement towards a less critical attitude towards the ETH origin of UFOs, a greater attention not only to identifying IFOs but also to studying them, and a re-definition of the aims and scopes of ufology.

In Spain the sound, scientific-oriented work of Vicente-Juan Ballester Olmos has greatly contributed to the new breed of researchers presently collected around the journal *Cuadernos de Ufologia*. In Italy 'revisionists' like Paolo Toselli and Maurizio Verga have become the core of a national ufology. German ufology is presently represented by either cultists or the skeptical CENAP and mildly skeptical GEP groups. The same may be said – to a lesser degree – of the Belgian SOBEPS, the Swedish AFU or the Danish SUFOI.

The so called 'revisionists' are all former 'classic' believers who gradually developed a critical attitude based on their on-field experience. They do not refuse 'exotic' hypotheses but minimize their importance.

Europe has also had two major breakthroughs concerning science and UFO study. As early as 1976, the very first scientific journal on UFOs was launched as an international venture by a group of Italian ufologists (Renzo Cabassi, Roberto Parabone, Francesco Izzo): *UFO Phenomena – International Annual Review* (*UPIAR*). It was a refereed journal whose editorial board looked like the who's who of the world's scientific ufology, and in 1981 UPIAR was granted a Science Achievement Award by the Fund for UFO Research, based in America. The second breakthrough was in France, where in 1977 physicist Claude Poher succeeded in getting a UFO study group formed within the *Centre National d'Etudes Spatiales* (the French equivalent to NASA): *Groupement d'Etudes des Phénomènes Aérospatiaux Non-identifés* (*GEPAN*).

Specific national areas of interest may be found for single nations and given periods of time. For example, sky-watching was popular in the UK in the 1960s, in France and Italy in the 1970s, and in Scandinavia in the 1980s. The series of cosmic messages known collectively as the 'UMMO' affair is virtually confined to Spanish-speaking countries. The earthlights debate has barely passed the British boundaries. Even specific UFO/IFO types may be found: lighted toy balloons (miniature hot air balloons) cause as many as 30 per cent of sightings in Germany, where virtually no landing has been reported; Italy is plagued by 'laser beams' in concerts, circuses and the like; and the abduction scene occurs in a different way in each European country.

A unifying pattern has begun to appear in the last few years. A common European framework is visible when considered against the background of American ufology – characterized, in particular, by the greater attention to uniformity of research, investigation methodology and definition of terms. The role of human sciences, in the case of both individual reports and of the development of a 'UFO myth' parallel to the UFO phenomenon, is a further characteristic of the cohesive European framework.

We only need to overcome practical difficulties, such as the language barrier, in order to get better and more stable exchanges. International Congresses held in the last few years have increased cooperation. May we hope that by 1993 we will also have a European Community of ufology?

EDOARDO RUSSO is a 'director' of the Italian group the Centro Italiano Studi Ufologici (CISU). This group has an integrated Italian network and many international associations. In 1988 it formally joined the International Committee for UFO Research (ICUR).

DATABASE

PRE 1900

NAME HISTORICAL PERSPECTIVE

DATE 216 B.C.

PLACE SARDINIA, ROMAN MEDITERRANEAN
MAP REF: J19

EVENT EARLY 'UFO REPORT'

'Things that looked like ships were
seen in the sky over Italy . . . in
Sardinia, a knight was making his
rounds inspecting the posts guarding
the ramparts when a stick in his
hand burst into flames. The same
thing happened to Roman soldiers in
Sicily who saw their javelins start
burning in their hands. . . . at Apri a
round shield was seen in the sky. It
seemed as if the moon was fighting
with the sun . . . at Capua, the sky
was all on fire and people saw
figures above them that looked like
ships.'

NAME THE IRISH AIRSHIP

DATE 1211 A.D.

PLACE CLOERA, IRELAND
MAP REF: D11

EVENT CLOSE ENCOUNTER OF THE SECOND
KIND

Airship style encounters have been
common enough with the panics of
1897 in America and 1909 in
Europe. Many of these sightings
were of terrestrial prototypes; they
were seen only a few years before
they were openly admitted to, and
some even had inventors' names
attributed to them. Some of the
accounts were very strange and
deserved further investigation, but
one particular airship account is
remarkable if only because it
certainly cannot have been an early
prototype of a terrestrial airship . . .
coming as it did in the year 1211.

During a Sunday mass, witnesses
saw an anchor drop from the sky and
attach itself to the arch above the
church door. As they rushed out of
the church the witnesses saw in the
sky a ship with men on board. They
watched as a man appeared to leap
off the ship and 'swim' through the
air down towards the anchor to
release it. The witnesses apparently
attempted to capture the entity but
the bishop forbade them to do so.
The man was allowed to return to
the ship which then cut its anchor
rope and sailed away. According to
the report the anchor was preserved
in the church.

Clearly, investigation of a case
nearly 800 years old is out of the
question but, if nothing else, it
serves to emphasize that there were
extraordinary events occurring in
the sky long before the birth of the
UFO phenomenon in 1947.

BASEL

This illustration is taken from the Basel
Broadsheet of 1566 and depicts fleets
of huge globes seen over Basel on 7
August in that year. Whether we can
rightly regard the image as an early
UFO report or not is subject to
question, but the drawing is thought-
provoking and one of many from earlier
centuries that suggest the UFO
phenomenon is far older than its
'official' start date of 1947.

1940s

NAME THE BIRTH OF THE 'FOO FIGHTERS'

DATE 14 OCTOBER 1943

PLACE SCHWEINFURT, GERMANY
MAP REF: K14

EVENT FOO FIGHTERS

Foo fighters were part of the UFO phenomenon that occurred during World War II in both the European and Pacific battle arenas. For the most part they consisted of bright lights which paced aircraft, occasionally even moving inside them, but they were also sometimes identified as small discs just a few inches across, some of which were felt clattering across the wings of the planes. 'Foo' incidentally is thought to derive either from the french word for fire – *feu* – or from a cartoon character, popular in England at the time, who went by the name of Foo.

The British believed that they might be an Axis power's secret weapon. However, following the end of the war documents revealed that the Axis powers had themselves encountered foo fighters and believed that they might have been Allied weapons. There were also sightings reported from the Japanese aircraft in the Pacific.

The foo fighters made their first appearance, at least officially, on 14 October 1943 when the 384 Bomb Group was making its final run over the industrial complex at Schweinfurt in Germany, coded Mission 115. The German fighter planes disappeared from the air and the bomb group's pilots confirmed that 'there were no enemy aircraft above.' Ahead of them a cluster of tiny discs some 3 in (8 cm) across were reported and discussed by the crews of the aircraft over the radio.

B-17 bomber number 026 attempted to evade the objects but was unsuccessful and reported that one wing cut directly through the cluster but did not damage the plane. It is possible that this case represented an early experiment with 'window' (a device which attempted to confuse radar return signals).

Later foo fighter reports told mainly of fireball like lights and glowing spheres. Because the UFO phenomenon had not yet been officially born (see Kenneth Arnold in the North American section, page 15) and because these reports came in soon after the first foo fighter reports, they were understood at the time to be further examples of the same phenomenon – in retrospect this seems less likely to have been the case than was thought initially.

The foo fighter mystery was never solved. They are much less frequently reported nowadays, though of course many current ball-of-light and night-light phenomena may well have been called foo fighters had they been seen in those early years when the phenomenon was common over Germany.

The picture is alleged to show the mysterious 'foo fighters' that buzzed aircraft during World War II. It was taken over Germany in 1944. No definitive explanation for these bright light sources has been found.

ABOVE An early photograph of a Swedish ghost rocket taken in 1946. RIGHT Karl Gosta Bartoll examining Lake Kölmjärv for debris following a crash on 19 July 1946.

NAME SWEDISH GHOST ROCKETS

DATE 19 JULY 1946

PLACE LAKE KÖLMJÄRV, NORTH SWEDEN
MAP REF: M3

EVENT GHOST ROCKET SIGHTING

Throughout the early 1930s and into the late 1940s Scandinavia, and particularly Sweden, was the setting for a particular form of UFO sighting known as the 'ghost rockets'. They first occurred around the Arctic Circle near the Swedish/Norwegian border at Västerbotten in the last months of 1933 when distant lights in the valleys were sighted by local people. The assumption made was that the lights were made by smugglers but customs action found no support for this claim. Perhaps the most substantial of the ghost rocket claims was that of 19 July 1946 when two witnesses observed a small object crash into Lake Kölmjärv.

Just before noon, farmer Knut Lindbäck and his maid Beda Persson were working at the lake shore when they heard a sound above them. They looked up and saw what

they first thought was an aeroplane but then realized was a rocket like device crashing towards the lake surface. As it hit the water an enormous column of water cascaded out proving beyond doubt that the object was physical. They described it as approximately 6 ft (183 cm) long with small wings on either side. On another shore of the lake a further witness, Frideborg Tagebo, heard the crash and described it as being like a bomb detonating.

The following morning a company of soldiers blockaded the area and searched the lake for the next two weeks. No debris was apparently recovered, although even with an explosion of this intensity there should have been some material left.

The ghost rocket saga continued and eventually became the subject of an official 'ghost rocket' investigation committee. Erik Malmberg of the committee summed up: 'If the observations are correct, many details suggest that it was some kind of a cruise missile that was fired on Sweden. But nobody had that kind of sophisticated technology in 1946.'

NAME GREEK GHOST ROCKETS

DATE 1 SEPTEMBER 1946

PLACE SALONIKA, THESSALÍA, GREECE
MAP REF: P19

EVENT GHOST ROCKETS

During the ghost rocket wave which occurred across Europe in the latter half of the 1940s, a number of such objects were seen over Macedonia and Salonika. One report of these came from the highest possible source – an interview on 5 September in London with the Greek Prime Minister, M. Tsaldaris. One of the principal scientists of the country, professor Paul Santorini, investigated the sightings and 'soon established that they were not missiles'.

However, the investigation into the sightings was stopped by the Army. The professor believed that a blanket of security had been placed over the question of the origin of UFOs because of the alarming defence significance of the subject. This is particularly plausible in view of Erik Malmberg's summing up of the subject (above).

1950s

NAME OLORON

DATE 17 OCTOBER 1952

PLACE OLORON-STE-MARIE, PAYS BASQUES, FRANCE
MAP REF: F17

EVENT ANGEL HAIR PRECIPITATION

Shortly after noon on 17 October 1952, headmaster Monsieur Prigent and his wife and children observed a strangely shaped cloud and behind it a long, cylindrical, luminous object emitting puffs of smoke. Ahead of the object were some thirty UFOs shaped like the planet Saturn: red globes surrounded by a yellow ring which were travelling in a zigzagging motion across the sky.

The sighting left physical traces: long trails of angel hair (filaments reportedly dropped from UFOs and similar to spider's webs), which covered trees, houses and electric lines in the area. Analysis of angel hair from this and other cases has proved inconclusive. It has been suggested that it is a natural substance unnaturally affected by certain properties of the UFO, possibly super-ionization of the air. Any such speculation must remain only that as angel hair does not last long enough for in-depth analysis.

An artist's impression of UFOs seen over Oloron-Ste-Marie, France in October 1952. The Saturn-like UFOs were accompanying a huge cylindrical object. Thin filaments of material known as 'angel hair' were reported dropping from the objects, one of several such cases.

NAME WOLIN ISLAND SIGHTING

DATE 31 JULY 1953

PLACE WOLIN ISLAND, SZCZECIN, POLAND
MAP REF: L12

EVENT CLOSE ENCOUNTER OF THE FIRST KIND

One of the earliest 'modern' UFO reports from Poland originates from Wolin Island. At 7 o'clock in the evening of 31 July 1953, five Polish nationals together with two Germans witnessed a saucer shaped object landing next to a railroad. It appears to have been some 60-70 ft (18.3-21.3 m) wide with a series of what may have been portholes around its edge.

The sighting lasted only a few minutes and the object took off at remarkable speed.

NAME THE STEPHEN DARBISHIRE
PHOTOGRAPHS

DATE 15 FEBRUARY 1954

PLACE CONISTON, CUMBRIA, ENGLAND
MAP REF: F11

EVENT PHOTOGRAPHIC CASE

Just over a year after George Adamski's celebrated encounters in California (see page 28), in which he took several photographs of the aleged Venusian scout ship, 13-year-old Stephen Darbishire photogaphed a very similar craft at Coniston in the Lake District.

The main doubts about the authenticity of these photographs mirror the suspicions which surround the Adamski case itself, but no definite conclusion has been reached with regard to the veracity of the case despite considerable publicity and circulation at the time.

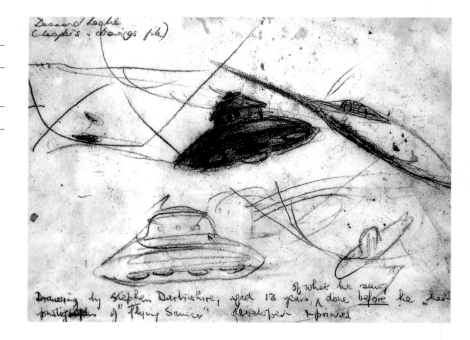

ABOVE At the age of thirteen, Stephen Darbishire drew these pictures of a UFO he had seen and photographed just half an hour earlier.

BELOW The photograph Stephen Darbishire took at Coniston on 15 February 1954, shortly *before* he drew the above sketches.

NAME WĘGIERSKA GÓRKA ENCOUNTER

DATE JULY 1954

PLACE WĘGIERSKA GÓRKA, POLAND
MAP REF: L12

EVENT ABDUCTION

In 1986 a conversation took place involving the witness (name with-held) in this case, which suddenly awoke in her memories of a strange event that had taken place when she was a child of eleven, in July 1954.

She had been on holiday at Węgierska Górka when she and her friends had gone to the woods to pick mushrooms. While walking alone near a cliff, she saw a glowing, oval-shaped light near the ground. She walked to it. A figure approached her from a door in the object, then seemed to draw her into the object in a way she cannot recall; she just walked up a small flight of stairs and then stepped in through the door.

Inside the object there were four other entities; they were of average height and with many human features such as skin colour and hand shape. However, they were wearing close fitting clothes, were surrounded by a mist and had on the back of their bodies something resembling a hump. It is interesting to compare this description with the one in the Czluchów sighting (see page 110), a case which occurred after the Węgierska Górka encounter but before the recall. Their eyes were small, there was no nose and the mouth was just like a crack. The girl was 'instructed' to lie down, and she fell asleep.

Her next memory is of being found by her friends, sitting near the cliff. She had been missing for seven hours. While they had full baskets of mushrooms, her's was empty. What had she been doing in all that time, they asked? All she could recall was a vague memory of flying . . .

NAME THE DEWILDE ENCOUNTER

DATE 10 SEPTEMBER 1954

PLACE QUAROUBLE, FRANCE
MAP REF: H14

EVENT CLOSE ENCOUNTER OF THE THIRD KIND

Marius Dewilde and his family at the scene of the UFO encounter of 10 September 1954, at Quarouble in France. The railway track over which the object landed can be seen. Dewilde was not intimidated by the encounter, and pressed home a vigorous assault, met by a paralyzing beam.

When entities chose to visit Quarouble in France they may have recognized that they had superior technology on their side. They were certainly going to need it because they came up against one of the most tenacious responses – from a single individual – on record.

Alerted by the sound of his dog howling outside, Marius Dewilde, at approximately 10.30 in the evening on 10 September 1954, opened his door and saw two strange humanoids just a few feet away from him. They were wearing one piece diving style suits and their heads were enclosed in enormous globular glass helmets. They were short and very stocky and the witness does not recall seeing any arms.

Dewilde's reaction was immediate; he tried to grab the entities but was blinded by a beam of light from an object resting on nearby rail tracks. As he tried to move he discovered that he was paralyzed in his legs.

That would be enough for many men but Dewilde was not finished yet. Having been shocked by the appearance of the entities and prevented from grabbing them and having been paralyzed by a beam from their craft, once he had regained the use of his limbs he apparently ran towards the UFO in an attempt to catch up with it. He failed to do so and the object lifted off and flew away.

Dewilde alerted the police and the subsequent investigation involved the French intelligence services and its scientists. One of the scientists indicated, from the ground traces left at the site of the encounter, that the object resting over the rail tracks must have weighed at least 35 tons.

NAME SINCENY MISJUDGMENT

DATE OCTOBER 1954

PLACE SINCENY, AISNE, FRANCE
MAP REF: G14

EVENT SLIGHT ERROR OF MISJUDGMENT

'Seeing a silhouette moving in the light of two lamps, I thought I was in the presence of a Martian in the process of repairing his flying saucer. I went to get my gun and I fired at him.'

A perfectly reasonable assumption you might think (and a charming gesture of greeting), but one which was unfortunately a bit wide of the mark. In this case the target turned out to be the witness's own neighbour repairing his motor car. Fortunately his aim was no better than his judgment and the shot only damaged the car, presumably leaving his neighbour somewhat startled.

Our witness might have had even more trouble explaining himself if he had offered the explanation 'I'm sorry. I thought you were someone else . . .!'

NAME FLIGHT LIEUTENANT SALANDIN'S
ENCOUNTER

DATE 14 OCTOBER 1954

PLACE THAMES ESTUARY, ENGLAND
MAP REF: G13

EVENT CLOSE ENCOUNTER OF THE FIRST
KIND

Flight Lieutenant James R. Salandin of the 604th County of Middlesex Squadron, Royal Auxiliary Air Force, took off at 4.15 in the afternoon from RAF North Weald in Essex in a Meteor Mark 8 jet fighter. It was a cloudless deep blue sky and Salandin was able to see the vapour trails of two Meteors in formation high above him. At 16,000 ft (4,877 m) – as he approached Southend on the Thames estuary – he saw three objects heading towards him.

As they approached one gold and one silver object flew to his left side and the third came directly at him almost filling his windscreen. He described it as saucer shaped with a bun shaped top and a bun underneath. Salandin was shaken at the tremendous speed at which it had been travelling. He reported the sighting to his base and after landing made a report both to Derek Dempster, an intelligence officer who was later to become the editor of *Flying Saucer Review,* and also the Air Ministry.

Of the sightings Salandin said 'I haven't found a satisfactory explanation for what I saw but I know what I saw.' Earlier he had already expressed one disappointment 'The thing was right in my sights, next time I will be on the ball.'

NAME THE UFO FLEET

DATE 6 NOVEMBER 1954

PLACE ROME, ITALY
MAP REF: K18

EVENT CLOSE ENCOUNTER OF THE FIRST
KIND

The Italian politician Dr Alberto Perego was one of over a hundred people who, on several occasions during October and November of 1954, saw fleets of UFOs in the skies above Rome. Most noticeable of these sightings was on 6 November when dozens of white dots appeared, occasionally leaving short vapour trails. They were estimated as moving at approximately 800 miles (1,300 km) per hour and flying at a height of approximately 20,000 ft (6,096 m). Occasionally they grouped into formations of diamond or V shapes.

During the encounter a considerable amount of angel hair (filaments reportedly dropped from UFOs and resembling spider's webs in texture) dropped towards the witnesses and evaporated in a few hours.

Dr Perego had a similar sighting on 12 November, again with other witnesses, and was soon to become a devotee of the extraterrestrial hypothesis and supporter of flying saucer research.

NAME NAMUR PHOTOGRAPHIC CASE

DATE 5 JUNE 1955

PLACE NAMUR, BELGIUM
MAP REF: I14

EVENT PHOTOGRAPHIC CASE

At approximately 7.30 in the evening, postman and amateur photographer, Monsieur Muyldermans was able to take three photographs of a disc shaped object flying low near his car near Namur in Belgium.

Meteorological study of the photographs suggested that the altitude of the objects was some 4,921 ft (1,500 m) and the size was approximately 39 ft (12 m) in diameter. Though unremarkable by the standards of what was to follow in subsequent years, these photographs became world famous. German investigator Gerald Mosbleck used them as the basis of his own deliberate fakes to prove the ease with which such photographs could be faked, and to demonstrate, correctly, that photographs alone do not prove much unless there is other substantial evidence (see photographic evidence page 27).

The sequence of photographs taken by Monsieur Muyldermans in Namur on 5 June 1955.

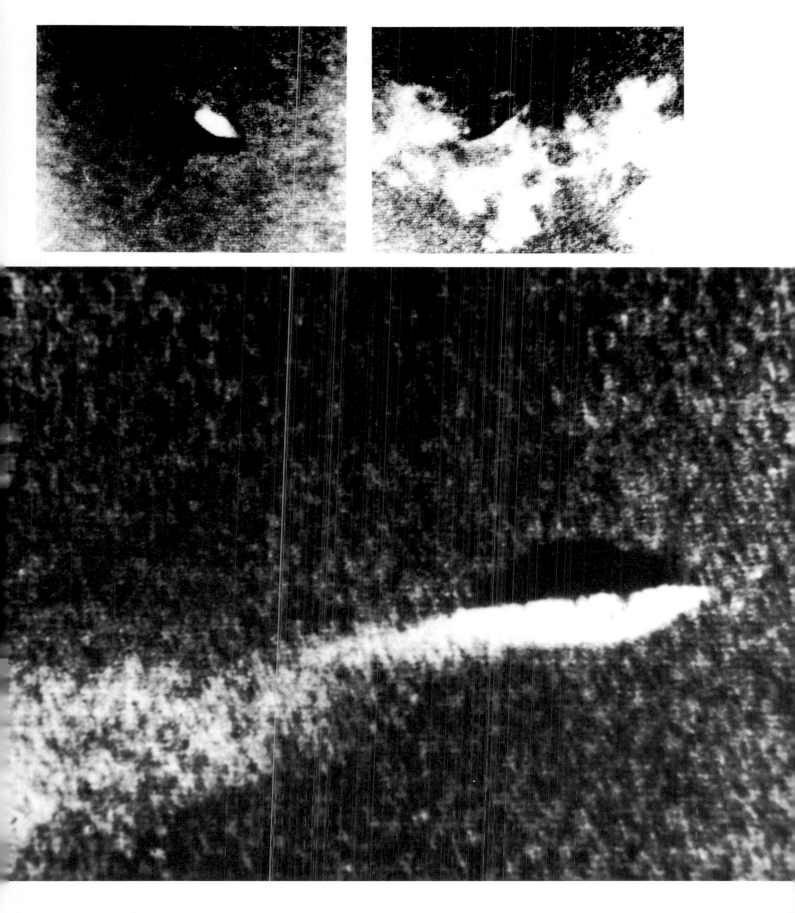

NAME BENTWATERS/LAKENHEATH

DATE 13 AUGUST 1956

PLACE SUFFOLK, ENGLAND
MAP REF: G12

EVENT RADAR VISUAL ENCOUNTER

Radar operators at USAF/RAF Bentwaters, at 9.30 in the evening of 13 August 1956, tracked a UFO return incoming from the North Sea some 25-30 miles (40-48 km) off the coast. According to the radar it was travelling at approximately 5,000 miles (8,047 km) per hour, certainly far faster than any aircraft of the time. Radar also tracked another group of targets moving towards Bentwaters from approximately 8 miles (13 km) out at the more reasonable speed of some 80-125 miles (130-200 km) per hour.

Checks on the radar could not determine any malfunctions and therefore a T-33 interceptor from the 512 Fighter Interceptor Squadron, which was returning to Bentwaters from a training flight, was diverted to search for visual confirmation of the radar targets. The plane could not verify the sightings but was searching blind having no airborne radar of its own.

Approximately an hour later radar reported another target moving at between 2,000-4,000 miles (3,200-6,400 km) per hour. This object was also seen by control tower personnel and described by them as a bright light passing over the airfield at terrific speed. At the same time the pilot of a C-47 transport aircraft reported a bright light streaking beneath him. Bentwaters sounded the alert!

Other radar stations in the area were alerted; the 7th Air Division Command Post and the 3rd Air Force Command Post were contacted and RAF coastal air defence also became involved. At Neatished a de Havilland Venom

night fighter was scrambled to intercept the objects. At midnight the pilot gained visual contact with the object and shortly afterwards also confirmed radar contact.

It is believed that gun camera film was taken. Indeed the former head of the Ministry of Defence department which studies UFOs, Ralph Noyes (now an active UFO investigator) stated that at the time he watched the film but admitted that 'the film clips were very brief, rather fuzzy and not particularly spectacular.' However, the independent radar corroboration and the visual sightings, despite unclear gun camera film, suggest very strongly that something physical was in the air over Suffolk on that night in 1956.

NAME ANGELU ENCOUNTER

DATE OCTOBER 1958

PLACE FIGUERAS, CATALONIA, SPAIN
MAP REF: G18

EVENT CLOSE ENCOUNTER OF THE FIRST KIND

At approximately 7 o'clock in the evening Señor Angelu, riding his motorcycle near Figueras in Spain, saw what appeared to be an object crash in a nearby wood. Wanting to help, he went towards the site but saw that it was not a crashed plane but a landed UFO of traditional saucer shape, a transparent dome on top and standing on landing legs. It was approximately 25 ft (7.62 m) wide.

The witness saw two dwarf like entities with large heads moving around the craft and collecting samples from nearby terrain. Aboard the saucer, in the dome, he could see a third figure. The witness watched for some 15 minutes until the entities reboarded the ship which took off quickly.

NAME VÄDDÖ RETRIEVAL

DATE 9 NOVEMBER 1958

PLACE VÄDDÖ, ROSLAGEN, SWEDEN
MAP REF: M8

EVENT ALLEGED CRASH RETRIEVAL

Physical traces from UFOs are rare and usually confined to ambiguous ground marks, burn marks, etc. Occasionally, however, solid artefacts alleged to be part of UFOs are recovered though it has to be admitted that there has not yet been a recovery of anything made of a substance which has definitely been confirmed as extra-terrestrial in origin.

On 9 November 1958 two witnesses to the landing of a UFO near Väddö in Sweden investigated the area following its departure and recovered a small metallic artefact. Analysis indicated that it was made of tungsten carbide, cobalt and titanium.

According to the witnesses, when recovered, shortly after the UFO had departed, the object was warm to the touch. Whether it was heated up by the action of the descent of the UFO or whether it truly dropped from it is not certain.

NAME GDYNIA HUMANOID

DATE 21 JANUARY 1959

PLACE GDYNIA HARBOUR, GDAŃSK, POLAND
MAP REF: M11

EVENT CLOSE ENCOUNTER OF THE THIRD KIND/HUMANOID RETRIEVAL

An abnormal number of fingers, a one piece suit that required metal shears to remove it, a strange arrangement of internal organs and a circulatory system following a spiral path around the body. This was the remarkable conclusion of a post mortem examination which is alleged to have taken place in a

BELIEVE IT . . . OR NOT.

There are very few photographs of UFO entities, and no reliable ones. There have, however, been some very spectacular hoaxes, or suspected hoaxes. The photograph below allegedly depicts an alien taken alive from a UFO that crashed near Mexico City in the 1950s. The alien died shortly afterwards and was sent to Germany for analysis. (Most modern day reports suggest that recovered cadavers were sent to Wright Patterson in Ohio.) There have been several similar photographs from Germany and it has been suggested that at one time faking outrageous UFO stories was a favourite pastime of the American troops stationed there. There is no supportive evidence for this photograph.

hospital at Gdynia following the recovery of a humanoid from the seafront there.

It must be said that this legendary tale is of doubtful authenticity; it appears without reference in Arthur Shuttlewood's book *The Flying Saucerers* and also without reference in *UFOs in the Soviet Union* (although dated 21 February 1959 in that article). None of our researchers in Poland were able to produce documentary evidence for the alleged event.

As the legend has it . . . A UFO apparently crashed into Gdynia Harbour and shortly afterwards a small humanoid in a space suit was found wandering along the seafront in a confused state. He was taken to the local clinic for observation where

it was noted he had an abnormal number of fingers. The hospital staff attempted to remove the one piece suit that he was wearing but it was of an extremely hard material and it took metal shears to cut it from him. The staff also removed a bracelet from his wrist which may or may not have led to his dying immediately afterwards.

A post mortem examination at Gdynia Hospital showed a strange arrangement of internal organs and a different form of circulatory system spiralling around the body. The hospital was apparently sealed off by guards and the body removed in a refrigerated container under heavy security. According to one report the lorry was destined for a research institute in Moscow.

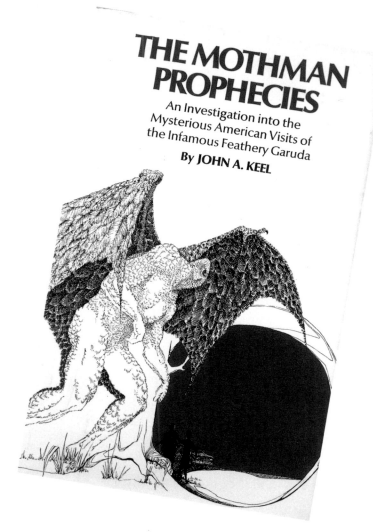

THE MOTHMAN PROPHECIES

An Investigation into the Mysterious American Visits of the Infamous Feathery Garuda

By JOHN A. KEEL

NAME	THE JELLY ENTITIES OF SWEDEN
DATE	20 DECEMBER 1959
PLACE	DOMSTEN, SOUTHERN SWEDEN MAP REF: L10
EVENT	CLOSE ENCOUNTER OF THE THIRD KIND

Returning from a dance two witnesses, Stig Rydberg and Hans Gustavsson, stopped to examine a light in a glade near to the road on which they were driving in their car. They saw a disc shaped object some 15 ft (4.5 m) across standing on three landing legs.

Incredibly, they were attacked by several tiny jelly like creatures that tried to drag them towards the saucer and a fight broke out. One of the two witnesses reached the car and sounded the horn, the second was then released and the entities scampered back to their craft which took off.

Hypnotic regression undertaken by doctors seemed to indicate that the witnesses were telling the truth. However, the allegation was rejected by an Air Defence Department official investigation because of the unreliability of the witnesses.

1960s

NAME	THE BATMAN ENCOUNTER
DATE	16 NOVEMBER 1963
PLACE	SALTWOOD, KENT, ENGLAND MAP REF: G13
EVENT	ENTITY ENCOUNTER

In the 1960s there were many reports in West Virginia, United States of America, of the so called 'Moth Men' which were red-eyed, moth- and bat-like creatures,

In *The Mothmen Prophecies*, Keel describes bat-like entities reported in West Virginia, USA during the 1960s.

occasionally the size of small light aircraft, which terrorized local inhabitants.

England was never plagued by the Moth Men to this extent but there was one report from Kent in November of 1963. Two courting couples watched a star-like UFO hover near some trees as they paused from their amorous activities. Those amorous activities came to a startling end when the witnesses suddenly saw, coming towards them, a grotesque, headless, black entity with webbed feet and wings like a bat.

No other coherent information is available as the couples, understandably, beat a hasty retreat leaving researchers with only this outline report.

NAME KALLAVESI LAKE

DATE AUGUST 1964

PLACE KALLAVESI LAKE, KUOFIO, FINLAND
MAP REF: P6

EVENT ALLEGED CRASH RETRIEVAL

Raimo Blomqvist witnessed a UFO hovering near him above Kallavesi Lake, Finland in August 1964. The case became more interesting when, shortly before speeding off, the UFO dropped a small chunk of material into the lake's edge.

Blomqvist retrieved it; analysis indicated that it was made out of iron oxide and trace elements.

At Akademi University, Professor Edelman X-rayed the object and determined it was not a geological entity although it resembled materials that are found near the site of active volcanoes in certain sections of the world. Turku University also examined the object and their Professor Papunen ruled out the possibility that it could be a meteor, at least of known composition, because of trace

elements present which are not generally found in such objects.

In the end, the findings were inconclusive with many suggestions as to what it could not be, but none as to what it might have been.

NAME VALENSOLE SIGHTING

DATE 1 JULY 1965

PLACE VALENSOLE, SOUTHERN FRANCE
MAP REF: I18

EVENT CLOSE ENCOUNTER OF THE THIRD KIND

Farmer Maurice Masse grew lavender for use in the perfume industry and on 1 July 1965 he left his house very early in the morning to walk to the fields to begin work. He had stopped in the shade to smoke a cigarette before starting when he heard the sound of an object above him which he thought might be a military helicopter. He walked towards the field to see it.

Some 100 yds (92 m) away he saw an object unlike anything he had seen before. It was oval shaped with a small dome on top and about the size of a car. It stood on six legs radiating out from a central spike.

Slightly in front of the object Masse saw two entities who were examining the plants in the field. He thought at first they were young boys and believed he had caught the vandals who had been damaging his plantations in the weeks before the encounter. But as he put it 'From the moment I started out . . . I knew that it wasn't with men that I had to deal.'

The two entities were dressed in green one piece suits; they had huge bald heads, large slanting eyes and lipless mouths. Their skin was chalk white. On their belts they carried small cylinders which Masse would have been well advised to take more notice of!

When Masse was around 20 yds (18.3 m) away from the entities one of them spotted him, took the cylinder from his belt and fired a beam at Masse who was paralyzed immediately. Despite the nature of the encounter, however, Masse said he never felt fear and believed that the entities had no animosity towards him.

Approximately a minute passed and the entities boarded their craft which then took off at an incredible speed. It took something like fifteen minutes for the paralysis to wear off and Masse returned to Valensole where he discussed the story with his friends. They were impressed by Masse's state of mind and did not doubt that he was telling the truth.

Subsequent investigation found traces in the soil where the craft had landed; the soil was hard and crumbly with a high calcium content. Lavender on the site died and even future crops were affected until the field had been thoroughly ploughed.

There is an as yet unknown detail to the story. Masse has admitted that there was something else of importance which he has kept to himself ever since.

For ufologists the importance of the encounter is its similarity to many cases that occurred earlier in France during the 1954 wave of entity reports. Masse himself was also impressed by the similarity between the object he described and the one seen by officer Lonnie Zamora in Socorro, New Mexico in the United States only one year earlier (see page 46).

Of the mysterious truth yet to be revealed we can only presume that it is some form of contactee message or perception. Masse has stated the immovability of his stance indicating the seriousness of his reaction to the experience: 'I have not told anybody, not even my wife, and nobody will make me tell it.'

Artist's impression of the entities and object seen by Maurice Masse; they have been drawn over a photograph of the site.

NAME COQUIL ENCOUNTER

DATE 16 JANUARY 1966

PLACE BOLAZEC, FRANCE
MAP REF: E14

EVENT CLOSE ENCOUNTER OF THE FIRST KIND

At 4 o'clock in the morning of 16 January 1966 carpenter Eugene Coquil was driving in Brittany when he saw lights in the middle of a field. He stopped his car, believing there may have been an accident, and walked across the field towards the light. As he did so he noticed that the lights were on an object. And it was moving silently towards him!

Only when he got to within approximately 30 ft (9.14 m) of it did he realize that it was not moving along the ground but was in fact flying some 15 ft (4.5 m) above it. That was enough for him, he ran back to his car and got in but the object followed and hovered above him.

He had difficulty starting the car which may have been due to his own panic or may have been a vehicle interference by the UFO (this is commonly reported). Eventually it started and he drove off, leaving the object behind.

NAME THE HOOK VEHICLE INTERFERENCE

DATE 26 OCTOBER 1967

PLACE HOOK, HAMPSHIRE, ENGLAND
MAP REF: F13

EVENT VEHICLE INTERFERENCE

Mr W. Collett was driving his Ford Transit bus along the A32 towards Reading in the early hours of Thursday, 26 October 1967. He was transporting machine casings produced by his engineering company. The prompt delivery of the casings was crucial to an important contract. Mainly for that reason Collett was very concerned when the electrical system of the bus cut out, causing the lights, radio and engine to go dead.

Collett got out of the vehicle, opened the bonnet and examined the engine but found nothing amiss. He returned to the vehicle and while doing so noticed a dark, unlit form hovering motionless over the road ahead of him. After a short pause the engine fired, the lights and radio came alive and Collett drove off – only to have the same breakdown occur just a few hundred yards down the road.

Again the witness got out of his vehicle; this time he felt an extreme pressure change which caused pain in his ear drums, similar to that which can be experienced in an aircraft. He also noticed the smell of burning electrics but this was obviously not coming from his vehicle as it was still in good order although not functioning. Once again he saw the object in the sky just a hundred yards away and perhaps 50 ft (15 m) high – dark and suspended above the road.

Collett believes that he watched the object for a few minutes until it moved away at reasonable speed over the trees. When he returned to the driving seat the engine restarted, the vehicle was back to normal and he again drove off.

There were certain other effects noted by Mr Collett which are reminiscent of many cases of vehicles stopping, including abductions. He apparently completed his journey without reference to his road map although it was a new route for him (he had, however, studied the planned route before setting out). He described a certain lack of co-ordination when driving off almost as if he had to re-learn how to use the controls of the bus. On returning home he noticed a throbbing in his fingers. Perhaps connected to the encounter he also found that he now remembered his dreams, which he was not able to do before.

Dr Bernard Finch, a London doctor, examined Mr Collett for physiological effects and suggested that there was a possibility that the UFO had emitted a force field which had interfered with the witness's nerves and spinal cord, damaging his normal reflexes. It appears from the doctor's report that he believes Mr Collett was only mildly 'washed' by the force field, if that is what it was, because the craft was emitting only low power. Had it been emitting a more radiant energy, if perhaps it had been preparing to perform a rapid manoeuvre, then Mr Collett might well have been hit by a much more powerful backwash which could have had a more serious effect on his nervous system.

No attempts to analyze the potential time lapses during this incident have been made, and indeed none are probably appropriate. However, it is interesting to note the aspects of this case which are similar to other reported abductions. Of further interest is the idea that the interference with the nervous system could in some circumstances also create hallucinations.

Cases such as this may hold some of the answers to much more elaborate claims.

NAME	THE MOIGNE DOWNS ENCOUNTER
DATE	26 OCTOBER 1967
PLACE	MOIGNE DOWNS, DORSET, ENGLAND MAP REF: F13
EVENT	CLOSE ENCOUNTER OF THE FIRST KIND

One of the most credible UFO reports and certainly one of the best documented by the witness himself, comes from the wave of British sightings in 1967. The witness was Mr J. B. W. (Angus) Brooks, a former Comet flight administration officer for the British Overseas Aircraft Corporation (now part of British Airways) and a former RAF intelligence officer. Every analysis of the case by UFO investigators has concluded that Mr Brooks was a very reliable witness who exhibited considerable common sense in coming to terms with his sighting. Of great use was the fact that Mr Brooks prepared his own report which reflected his detailed grasp of administration and intelligence work. Indeed the opening lines even indicated the ordnance survey grid reference of the encounter and an estimate of wind force and direction.

At 11.25 in the morning Mr Brooks, who had been walking his dogs, was lying on his back in a shallow trough in the hills to shelter from a force 8 wind. He placed his hands behind his head to rest himself and saw what he at first believed was a fine vapour trail over the town of Portland coming from a high flying aircraft. Very quickly Mr Brooks realized that it was no such thing; it was not growing in length or disintegrating. Indeed, it had all the appearance of a craft rushing headlong towards him!

It descended rapidly, 'put the brakes on' with remarkable tenacity and at a height of some 200-300 ft (61-94 m) hovered motionless some 400 yds (366 m) away from where Mr Brooks was watching it. It was a unique UFO, never reported before nor since. It was a circular disc shape with a long girder-like fuselage reaching forward and three girder-like fuselages reaching backwards. However, as it went into hover mode the fuselages spread out into the shape of a cross. The craft while hovering rotated slowly but remained in a stationary position, apparently unaffected by the extremely strong wind blowing.

Mr Brooks noted that the object seemed to be made of some translucent material, was approximately 175 ft (53 m) in diameter and he could see no portholes or windows. The sighting lasted 22 minutes, then the object resumed its original shape – realigning its fuselages – and shot away towards Winfrith.

One of Mr Brooks's dogs, usually at ease with him on the downs, was agitated and pawed him as if urging him to leave the area. His other dog had gone off hunting. Mr Brooks's own analysis of the event is clear: 'Before the Moigne Downs sighting I was only mildly interested in unidentified flying objects but now I am convinced there is something to be investigated and the sooner we

find out what is going on the better it will be.'

Mr Brooks circulated his report to many flying saucer research organizations across the world and has expressed no doubt that what he saw was an alien spacecraft. He commented 'To begin with I was apprehensive, wondering if I had been spotted. It even crossed my mind that I might be captured and I planned, if there seemed any danger of that, to leave my walking stick in the ground as a clue to where I had been. But after a bit I felt easier, even content, and it has since occurred to me that the green anorak I was wearing may have camouflaged me.'

The sighting came at a time when the 'flying star' or 'flying cross' was the much reported UFO of the period. Indeed only days apart from the Moigne Downs sighting, two police constables in a police car had chased a flying cross along the edge of Dartmoor. Other police officers were reporting such sightings in other parts of the country. Obviously it was speculated that what Mr Brooks had seen was the flying cross.

The case was investigated by a Ministry of Defence team: Dr John Dickison from the Royal Aircraft Establishment at Farnborough; Alec Cassie, a psychologist with the RAF and Leslie Akhurst from S4 at the Ministry of Defence (S4 is the section of the Ministry of Defence which investigates UFO reports). They came up with an explanation which was imaginative, and indeed plausible and not unreasonable, but it was not one which was ever going to satisfy Mr Brooks.

They suggested that Mr Brooks had lain down to rest from the wind and had fallen asleep or entered a near sleep state. This was the reason why his dog was agitated and trying to wake him. During the near

sleep state he had seen a vitreous floater in his eyeball (a loose piece of dead cell matter frequently seen when looking at a clear background such as the sky). Mr Brooks had had an eye injury some years previously which was repaired by corneal transplant and this may have led to him seeing larger floaters than usual. This explanation is believed to account for the fact that the object would have remained motionless despite the wind and why it moved very rapidly and decelerated quickly to a standstill; it is a characteristic of 'floaters' as the eyeball moves and then stops.

The Ministry of Defence further concluded that Mr Brooks had attributed an extraordinary nature to the incident because of publicity relating to the flying cross sightings in the national newspapers at the time.

With perhaps only the slightest irony Mr Akhurst's letter to Mr Brooks setting out their conclusions stated 'I recognise that you may find our conclusions unsatisfactory.' They also pointed out that 'Our radar cover is such that we are also quite satisfied there is no clandestine aerial activity over the United Kingdom under terrestrial control.'

It must be said that Mr Brooks replied with equal precision to the Ministry, critical of their conclusion: 'The fact that the gale was howling and my Alsatian was painfully clawing me to leave the spot was hardly conducive to "dropping off".'

The fact that Mr Brooks's sighting has remained unique and that no similar object has been seen since need not weigh heavily against the report since most UFO sightings are unique in some detail or the other. We are left only to decide whether the craft was an external event or indeed in the eye of the beholder.

NAME SERRA DE ALMOS ENCOUNTER

DATE 16 AUGUST 1968

PLACE SERRA DE ALMOS, SPAIN
MAP REF: F19

EVENT UNUSUAL ENTITY ENCOUNTER

One of the main aspects of UFO entity claims is that the vast majority – by far – are of humanoid entities, i.e. aliens which resemble human form in having two legs, two arms and a head carrying the sensory organs at the highest position. However, not all cases are of this nature, for example the brain-like entities in the Dapple Grey Lane encounter in the United States (see page 56).

In August 1968 at Serra de Almos, Spain, a chicken farmer was to report one such rather frightening variation. It was approximately 6 o'clock in the morning when he saw a dome shaped object hovering a few feet above the ground. As he approached, two entities ran back to and into the object which then took off. The entities he reported were octopus like, approximately 3 ft (91 cm) tall and had several legs each. He also described them as being light in colour and disgusting in appearance.

For me, there was an amusing side to this story. Although it had happened in 1968 it was not a widely reported case and I was unaware of it when I was editing a book, *Phenomenon*, for the British UFO Research Association (BUFORA). As an experiment for the book I asked top British special effects modelmaker to the film industry, Martin Bower, to fake a UFO encounter solely for the purposes of proving how easily it could be done. In the book the whole story is clearly described so that there is no doubt that the resulting photograph is a deliberate fake. In order to further emphasize that fact I asked

Martin to produce an octopoidal type alien which I believed had never been reported and would therefore not confuse the issue by looking as if it could be real. (The last thing I wanted was to produce a picture that would one day turn up in the literature as 'real' and unnecessarily add to the mythology that surrounds the UFO phenomenon.' The resulting picture proved the point and was suitably amusing, but the book had only been out a few months when the Serra de Almos case was drawn to my attention. Far from creating a fake UFO encounter so extraordinarily unbelievable that no-one could believe it to be real, I had hit on one that had been 'seen' already! It was around about this time that I discovered the true meaning of the expression 'The best-laid schemes o'Mice an' Men gang aft a'gley'.

FAKE PHOTOGRAPHS

RIGHT In 1962 Alex Birch claimed to have photographed five UFOs over Sheffield, England. Having impressed the Air Ministry and an inaugural meeting of BUFORA, he went on to confess that he had stuck the images on a pane of glass through which he took the photograph.

BELOW This fake UFO photograph, with the author as victim, would not pass many modern analysis tests but it shows clearly how easy it is to set up fake alien encounters. This whole image took less than thirty minutes to make, set up and photograph.

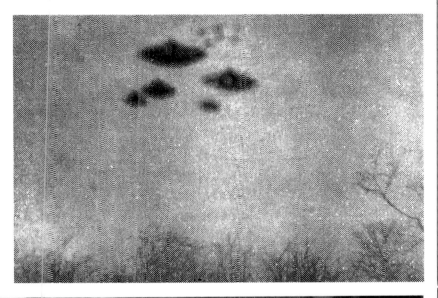

NAME DR 'X'

DATE 1 NOVEMBER 1968

PLACE SOUTHERN FRANCE
MAP REF: H17

EVENT CLOSE ENCOUNTER OF THE SECOND
KIND

Around 4 o'clock in the morning Dr X (his name and the precise location of the event are withheld to avoid unwanted publicity) was awoken by the cries of his toddler. When he reached the child, the boy was indicating that something was outside the window with great excitement. The doctor saw lights which he believed to be lightning and calmed his son.

Following this he then opened a window to look over the open landscape outside the house and observed two saucer shaped UFOs, white above and red beneath. He also noticed antennae on top and a beam of light reaching down from beneath the objects. The UFOs were moving towards the doctor and he saw with astonishment that, as they approached him, they appeared to merge into each other leaving just one single UFO.

The beam of light from underneath the UFO suddenly rotated round and illuminated the house, shining directly on the doctor. There was a loud bang and the UFO disappeared leaving behind just a glowing 'presence' which dispersed. But it seemed that the UFOs had taken something with them!

They had taken the doctor's pain and disabilities. Three days before the encounter the doctor had injured his leg while chopping wood and had a very painful bruise which still showed. Several years before he had also received wounds during the Algerian war. Astonishingly, both of these unpleasant injuries instantly disappeared.

However, the effect on the witness was not totally beneficial; he experienced cramps and stomach pains, he lost weight and there was a peculiar triangular shaped coloration around his navel. Even more extraordinary, the same triangle appeared on the baby's stomach a day or so later and the doctor dreamed that it was in some way connected to his sighting.

The triangle would appear and disappear on both the father and the son for days on end for some considerable time after the event and indeed was recorded on film in 1986, 18 years after the first sighting! The story continues.

For years since the event the family has been the subject of paranormal phenomena; telepathy frequently reported between members of the family, levitation, unusual effects on electrical instrumentation. Indeed the family seems to have undergone something of a change in mental attitude leaving them sensitive to all kinds of phenomena.

NAME KATHRYN HOWARD

DATE 6 APRIL 1969

PLACE SOUTHERN SWEDEN
MAP REF: L10

EVENT CLOSE ENCOUNTER OF THE THIRD
KIND

The Kathryn Howard case is one which clearly demonstrates the interface between the UFO phenomenon and other paranormal experiences. Because of the nature of her encounter Kathryn believes that she will not fully recall the events, nor feel able to openly relate to all of what she has recalled, until she has been able to emotionally feel as she did at the time. For that reason what follows is of necessity incomplete and no doubt the case

will reveal more as time passes.

It was an early spring in southern Sweden, in 1969, when Kathryn and two companions, Harvey and Martin (pseudonyms used), were sitting in a meadow relaxing and discussing the events of the time that were so important to the young; mainly the Vietnamese war and the Biafran famine. Kathryn felt emotionally upset by the violence and lack of compassion that seemed to be embracing the world; indeed she began to cry.

Suddenly above them an object appeared in the sky, oval shaped with what appeared to be legs protruding from it. Martin and Kathryn saw it, but they heard nothing. Without warning their very perception of normality turned inside out: the sky no longer seemed to exist and in front of them, both Martin and Kathryn saw the moon looking as it did in the photographs that were beamed back to the Earth by the Apollo astronauts. They saw space as an almost fluid-like grey endlessness.

Strangely, although Martin and Kathryn appear to have shared the same experience, Harvey saw nothing, either he was unable to face the sensory input or he was cut off from it. None of the trio could explain why that should be, nor indeed how it should have come about. Kathryn felt compelled to talk about what she was seeing or lose the image forever. 'I must talk. I will forget if I don't talk. Look at the sky. There is no sky. We are sitting in the Universe. This is the Universe.' Her perceptions were still changing!

The Earth itself seemed to be expanding around them and Kathryn said 'I feel like a puppet on strings.' She felt as if she were looking at the Earth from way above while at the same time standing on it. Both Martin and Kathryn were crying and they felt they could hear the slow

Kathryn Howard now lives in America, where this photograph was taken in 1990, but she had her abduction experience in Sweden over twenty years earlier. She believes that she will not fully understand her experiences until she is able to return to the surroundings of her earlier life.

deep beat that was the rhythm of the Universe itself.

The emotions overwhelmed them. A feeling of love and compassion gripped them and Kathryn said she felt the greatest joy she had ever known. But there were also less joyful impressions; images of great destruction, possibly the end of the human race and the end of time itself; there were many other images which Kathryn feels unable to talk about even now.

Of the three, only Kathryn has felt compelled to follow up the experience having been conscious even from an early age that her life had special meaning. She states 'Ever since that day, I have felt strongly that there is a message I have to get out, that I know how to get people to open their eyes in a way they have never done before,

that everyone wants to express their hidden desires and secrets with me, and on and on I could write about these things.' Neither Martin nor Harvey have felt able to follow up the experiences; Kathryn believes this is due to their submergence into a fundamentally materialistic world.

Of all the impressions she received the last was of great compassion and she said as she began to come around from the experience 'If Hitler was here now, I would put my arms around him and tell him that I loved him. He didn't know what he was doing. He was not alive yet. He was just a shell.'

There then appears to be a period of missing time. Although this event had happened during a bright day their next memory was of 11 o'clock in the evening at the house of one of them only an hour away from the meadow where they had been. There has been one attempt using regression hypnosis to fill in this missing time period; the recall of this mostly concerns the UFO itself.

The legs that had been sticking out underneath the UFO turned out to be cylinders, one of which pulled

Kathryn into the object. Looking down between her feet she could see the treetops and the Earth and at one time even the impression of her own body. Inside the object she felt as if she were free floating but nonetheless restrained at the wrists and ankles.

Apparently she became fearful that the abduction was to be permanent, that she would be removed from the Earth forever, and she screamed 'Please take me back. I am not ready to leave yet.' The only time she felt real fear was under the regression hypnosis, but whether this is a product of the technique or of her memory is debatable.

Under hypnosis Kathryn saw herself wearing a kind of crystal head-dress and since that time clairvoyants and others have seen a similar mass around her head. The entities she encountered were transparent, not a particularly frequently given description but, interestingly, one that has arisen in other cases from around the same area and the period of time (see the Anders case, page 103).

In the future, Kathryn feels that she must return from the United States, where she presently lives, to Sweden and to taste the sensations of her earlier life before she will be able to fully understand the true meaning of the experiences she has had. Both I and the other UFO researchers she is working with must leave her to rediscover these events in her own way rather than use the high pressure, almost interrogative, techniques so common in America. Kathryn's case will then almost certainly be a most valuable piece in the enormous global jigsaw that is the UFO phenomenon.

Only time will tell; and with Kathryn's spirit free, it will no doubt tell the truth.

7 January 1970, Imjärvi. A close encounter of the third kind was experienced by Aarno Heinonen and Esko Viljo who were out skiing in the snow-covered forests of Southern Finland.

1970s

NAME THE IMJÄRVI ENCOUNTER

DATE 7 JANUARY 1970

PLACE IMJÄRVI, SOUTHERN FINLAND
MAP REF: 07

EVENT CLOSE ENCOUNTER OF THE THIRD
KIND

'I felt ill. My back was aching and all my joints were painful. My head ached and after a while I had to vomit. When I went to pee the urine was nearly black, it was like pouring black coffee onto the snow. This continued for a couple of months.' These were the after effects reported by one of two witnesses involved in an incredible encounter in the snow-covered forests of southern Finland in 1970.

It was late afternoon on Wednesday, 7 January 1970 when countrymen Aarno Heinonen and Esko Viljo were out skiing. They paused in a small clearing to enjoy the few stars in the cold sunset. After a short time they heard a buzzing noise and saw a bright light moving through the sky towards them. As it neared them above treetop height, they saw a red-grey mist swirling around it and puffs of smoke emanating from it. Inside the cloud was a circular, saucer shaped object, metallic in appearance and some 9 ft (274 cm) wide. It had a dome above, and beneath were three spheres around the rim, reminiscent of the Adamski photographs of nearly twenty years earlier (page 28). From the base of the object a tube suddenly fired a sharp beam of light down towards the ground. By this time the object had lowered itself to around 10 ft (3 m) from the ground, almost within touching distance of the men.

If the witnesses were astonished now the next instant was to take what was left of their breath away.

As Heinonen related 'I was standing completely still. Suddenly I felt as if somebody has seized my waist from behind and pulled me backwards. I think I took a step backwards, and in the same second I caught sight of the creature. It was standing in the middle of the light beam with a black box in its hands. From around the opening in the box there came a yellow light, pulsating. The creature was about 35 in (90 cm) tall, with very thin arms and legs. Its face was pale like wax. I didn't notice the eyes, but the nose was very strange. It was a hook rather than a nose. The ears were very small and narrow towards the head. The creature wore some kind of overall in a light green material. On its feet were boots of a darker green colour, which stretched above the knee. There were also white gauntlets going up to the elbows, and the fingers were bent like claws around the black box.'

Viljo also described the creature as 'luminous like phosphorus' and wearing a conical, metallic like helmet. The creature was less then 3 ft (91 cm) tall.

Suddenly Heinonen was hit by the light from the box in the creature's hands. The forest became suddenly quiet, the red-grey mist drew down from the object and sparks could be seen flying into the snow. The mist hid the creature and surrounded both the witnesses. Suddenly the light beam disappeared and was sucked up into the craft apparently taking the entity with it. Then even the craft itself was gone! Heinonen was paralyzed on his right side and Viljo had to almost carry his friend the 2 miles (3 km) to their home.

Later, at the Heinola clinic they were examined and the doctor prescribed sleeping pills and sedatives. He believed that the symptoms of aching joints and

headache would disappear within ten days but for Heinonen they continued for some time. Some five months later he was still suffering from the same pains and although the paralysis of his right leg disappeared he could still not balance properly.

Heinonen's memory was also severely affected and it got so bad that whenever he left home he had to tell his family where he was going so that they could search for him and collect him if he didn't return! Viljo himself was not unaffected by the event; he had a red and swollen face and had become incoherent and absent-minded.

Dr Pauli Kajanoja stated 'The symptoms he described are like those after being exposed to radioactivity.' He added 'Both men seem sincere, I don't think they had made the thing up. I am sure they were in a state of shock when they came to me; something must have frightened them.'

The experience was corroborated by two other people who reported UFOs in the sky at the same time and in the same area as the Imjärvi encounter.

For Heinonen it was not at an end; between the time of the encounter and August 1972 he reported twenty-three other UFO contacts. Occasionally, he reported meeting with an extremely beautiful space woman and one entity very reminiscent of the Adamski Venusian who had progressed considerably beyond the mere telepathy of the Adamski encounter and was able to speak fluent Finnish.

These later claims have tended to create an atmosphere of disbelief even amongst hardened UFO researchers, but this is probably the failure of UFO researchers to understand the phenomenon for what it really is. (An understanding that I feel is still a long way off for us all.) Of those who knew the witnesses one farmer, Matti Haapaniemi, a neighbour, stated 'Many people in this neighbourhood have laughed at this story. But I don't think it's anything to joke about. I have known both Aarno and Esko since they were little boys. Both are quiet, rational fellows and moreover they are abstainers. I am sure their story is true!'

There were many other sightings of 'distant lights in the sky' in the area around the same time as this event, which also added to the credibility of the case.

NAME THE MAARUP ENCOUNTERS

DATE 13 AUGUST 1970/14 AUGUST 1973

PLACE HADERSLEY, JYLLAND, DENMARK
MAP REF: J11

EVENT CLOSE ENCOUNTERS OF THE FIRST
KIND

At almost 11 o'clock on Thursday, 13 August 1970 police officer Evald Maarup was driving home in his police car along a minor road when he suddenly encountered a bright white light. His car engine cut out immediately, and all its lights went out. Maarup was almost blinded by the power of the light and found difficulty even in finding the microphone of his radio to call his base; a fruitless search because when he did find it it was also dead.

The car heated up to the equivalent of a warm summer's day and Maarup watched as the light rose above him. Beyond it he could see that it emanated from a large grey object which made no sound whatsoever. To officer Maarup's astonishment he watched as over a five minute period the light seemed to be drawn up inside the object and as this was completed Maarup stepped out of the car and watched the thing move on swiftly and

silently. As the object left, the car systems returned to normal and Maarup reported the encounter to his base.

Maarup was particularly concerned over the strangeness of the light; it had not faded but had actually drawn upwards, as if it were solid. He had a Fujaxa camera in the car and took three photographs of the object as it departed, also taking three more photographs once the object was gone. Unfortunately they show very little, and nothing distinctly. While still outside the car Maarup investigated the area discovering that the metalwork of the car was warm, but he could find no other traces.

Of the object itself Maarup described it as being some 30 ft (9.14 m) in diameter with an opening in the base approximately 3 ft (91 cm) wide from which the light emanated. There were two domes on the underside (possibly reminiscent of the three seen in the Adamski craft, see page 28, and the Imjärvi encounter, see page 98).

On reporting the incident to his base he received the reply, almost tongue-in-cheek, that he should consider being committed to a mental hospital. However, following more serious questioning afterwards, all of his colleagues stated that they believed he was telling the truth. One of his colleagues informed the press and within a twenty-four hour period officer Maarup was being besieged by journalists not just from Denmark but from many other countries.

The official explanation given by the Air Force through Major Hellden of Air Tactical Command was that Maarup had seen the landing lights of a jet trainer (T-33) but Maarup replied to this that he had indeed seen the aircraft some ten minutes after the sighting and was quite adamant that the two were unalike.

It must be said that the Air Force were reasonably open and commented 'We have the greatest confidence in the police officer. He is a trained observer, and we do not seek in any way to dismiss this kind of observation.' Subsequent investigation showed that the pilots of the T-33 training jets had not seen anything unusual below them and other explanations were offered such as shooting stars and comets.

None of the explanations appeared to give credence to officer Maarup's statement that he had watched the object stationary for some five minutes and seem to dismiss rather than explain the event. Perhaps the encounter was not that extraordinary by UFO standards, but unlike many this one had a sequel!

Officer Maarup commented that the sighting had taught him one thing and that was to keep his mouth shut. However, he did admit to a second encounter on 14 August 1973 in almost exactly the same conditions and almost exactly the same time of evening and again he had taken some photographs.

On this occasion the light apparently came across fields, disturbing cattle and horses before bringing his car to a halt and extinguishing its lights. On this occasion he saw three domes protruding from the underside of the craft, exactly as in the Adamski claims of two decades earlier. As the object left it apparently scanned the road with its beam and also tilted towards him to show the solid superstructure and portholed windows.

Officer Maarup was left with the same questions we all are left with. Why? As he stated 'I have no doubt what I have seen, but why at almost exactly the same time? Why on no other day in the year? Why in almost exactly the same place?'

NAME THE PETER DAY FILM

DATE 11 JANUARY 1973

PLACE LONG CRENDON, OXFORDSHIRE,
ENGLAND
MAP REF: F13

EVENT DAYLIGHT SIGHTING/FILM

Driving through Oxfordshire towards Aylesbury, surveyor Peter Day watched an orange ball of light (possibly of the kind which in the early days of flying saucers used to be affectionately known by the nickname 'amber rambler') travelling at approximately treetop height less than a mile away from him and pulsating. Day was able to record

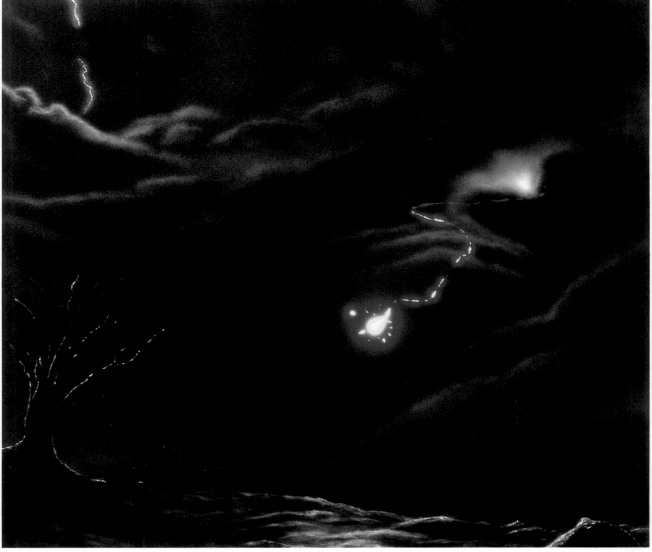

OPPOSITE ABOVE A still from Peter Day's cine film on 11 January 1973.
OPPOSITE BELOW Artist's impression of ball lightning, which may well be the phenomenon filmed by Peter Day. Ball lightning often gives rise to UFO reports.

the sighting on cine film which has been highly publicized since and indeed analyzed extensively by Kodak who have confirmed that it is genuine. The sighting was also corroborated by children and teachers at the Long Crendon School nearby.

Investigation suggested at first that the sighting could have been of a crashing jet aircraft and indeed one did crash on the day in question but without doubt not at the same time. The teacher and the school children were quite precise about when they had seen the object and it correlated exactly with Peter Day's own claims, thus ruling out the aircraft theory. Frame by frame analysis of the film shows that in the closing frame, at the point when the object disappears, all of the trees appear to bend fiercely away as if in response to an airborne explosion.

No confirmed identification has ever been made of the object but it has been speculated that Day may have captured elusive ball lightning phenomena on film for the first and possibly only time to date.

NAME LANGFORD BUDVILLE ENCOUNTER

DATE 16 OCTOBER 1973

PLACE LANGFORD BUDVILLE, SOMERSET, ENGLAND
MAP REF: F13

EVENT ABDUCTION

Mrs A. (identity withheld) was driving along a country road near Langford Budville in Somerset when her engine and lights cut out. When she got out of the vehicle to examine the engine she felt a touch and turned to see a robot like figure some 6 ft (183 cm) tall standing behind her. She fainted.

When she came around she found that she and the robot were standing next to a domed object some 18 ft (5.5 m) wide and 36 ft (10.9 m) high. She fainted again! When she next became conscious she found herself naked and tied on to a metallic table in a room where the walls were glowing in an eerie fashion. Three human like figures conducted a physical examination and when two of them left the third sexually assaulted her. Not surprisingly, Mrs A. fainted yet again. When she came to she was inside her own car and discovered that three hours had passed.

C3-PO from *Star Wars* – the classic science fiction idea of an alien robot.

Her subsequent report to her husband and the police suggested no question about her own belief in the event. It was impossible to determine whether or not this was an internally generated image or an external reality. There were of course many similarities to earlier cases which had by then become well known.

NAME TORINO SIGHTING

DATE 30 NOVEMBER 1973

PLACE CASELLE AIRPORT, TORINO, ITALY
MAP REF: J17

EVENT RADAR VISUAL ENCOUNTER

It was approximately 7 o'clock in the evening when Riccardo Marano approached Caselle Airport in his Piper Navajo. As he was about to land the control tower radioed

information of an unidentified flying object some 1,200 ft (365 m) over the runway. Marano aborted the landing and flew towards the object but it zigzagged away in a non-ballistic motion quite beyond the capabilities of any aircraft. Given the distance it covered Marano estimated it to be moving at approximately 3,100 miles (5,000 km) per hour.

There was no lack of corroboration for the sighting; it was detected on the airport radar, on military radar, and visually sighted by two other pilots and several civilians at the airport.

There has been some thought that the radar picked up the echo of a weather balloon, and that the visual sighting was of the planet Venus. However, the high number of corroborative witnesses suggests that there is more to the case than mere collective suggestion.

NAME	THE VILVORDE HUMANOID
DATE	19 DECEMBER 1973
PLACE	VILVORDE, BRUSSELS, BELGIUM MAP REF: 113
EVENT	CLOSE ENCOUNTER OF THE THIRD KIND

The Vilvorde humanoid of 1973 displayed some unusual characteristics which have made this case quite famous across Europe.

The witness, Mr V. (name withheld) and his wife were in bed asleep in their house at Vilvorde, some 7½ miles (12 km) to the north of Brussels, in Belgium, on the night in question. At approximately 2 o'clock in the morning Mr V. left his bed to go to the toilet which was in a small outside yard next to the kitchen.

As he reached the kitchen he heard a sound from outside as if someone was striking the ground with a metallic object and he looked through the kitchen curtain and saw a greenish light emanating from his garden. When he parted the curtain to get a better view he saw an astonishing sight in his small walled garden.

At the end of the garden was a small humanoid just over 3 ft. tall wearing a shiny one piece suit, and glowing green. On his head the humanoid had a transparent globular helmet with a tube running backwards to a backpack. On his stomach there was a bright red box which was luminous and sparkling. Even more remarkably, in his hands he was holding what appeared to be a vacuum cleaner or metal detector, which he was passing across the ground in front of him.

Mr V. flashed his torch at the humanoid who turned round. When he turned he had to rotate his whole body, apparently unable simply to turn his head, indeed all of his movements as observed by Mr V. were jerky and uncomfortable-looking.

As the humanoid turned to face him Mr V. can hardly have been any more comfortable at the sight. The ears were pointed, no nose or mouth was visible and the eyes were oval and yellow, very large and very bright. As Mr V. flashed his torch at the humanoid the entity raised his hand and stuck his fingers up in a V-sign (which perhaps doesn't have the same meaning wherever the entity came from as it might in Europe.) The entity then turned away and walked off towards the tall back garden wall.

If the sight of the creature or his gestures were a less than pleasant awakening for Mr V., what followed was even more astonishing.

The creature scaled the wall walking up and over it as if it were a continuation of a flat surface, and always remaining perpendicular to the surface he was walking on. When he reached the top he simply flipped over the top and presumably walked down the other side of the wall in the same way. Shortly afterwards a small round object making a muffled noise appeared beyond the wall, rising away from the scene of the event.

A drawing of the Vilvorde encounter shows the entity and the walled garden in which it was seen. It scaled the walls of the garden by walking up them at a 90° angle to the surface of the wall.

No ground traces were found of the event, and no other witnesses came forward. Our witness seems unaffected by the encounter himself, he continued the evening by making himself a light snack in the kitchen!

It is worthy of note that Mr V. had had a previous UFO sighting and went on to have yet another one in July 1974 though no humanoids were involved in either of these.

NAME THE ANDERS ENCOUNTER

DATE 23 MARCH 1974

PLACE SÖDERBY, GUSTAVSLUND, SWEDEN
MAP REF: M8

EVENT ABDUCTION

At around midnight on Saturday, 23 March 1974 Anders (pseudonym) left a party in a school hall near Hagalund near Malmhagen. Although he had been drinking alcohol he was not drunk and only stepped outside for a breath of fresh air. For some reason he then decided to walk home some 2½-3 miles (4-5 km) to Lindholmen. It has been a subject of debate, never reconciled, as to whether or not he was at this stage simply making a spontaneous decision or whether he was actually in the control of 'other' entities.

He took a 'backwoods' route towards his home avoiding a more major road in order to take a shortcut. It was a cold bright night with a full moon and the area was luminescent with a layer of snow across the ground. In this brightened darkness Anders passed a small cottage and a circle of runic stones, as he walked towards a bend in the road. Ahead of him on the side of a hillock Anders saw a bright light getting stronger and gained the impression that it might be a car approaching from behind. He left the road and walked onto the grass to

his right and threw himself to the ground. He missed!

Instead of hitting the ground he felt himself drawn upwards into what seemed to be a cone of light coming from an object above. His next conscious memory was of desperately ringing his doorbell to be confronted by his wife concerned about a bleeding wound on his forehead and an unpleasant burn on his cheek.

Anders contacted the division of the national defence known as 'The Cavalry' who put him on to the local Home Guard chief, Hardy Broström. The press interviewed Broström and were quick to catch on to the story, publicizing it locally and on radio. Alerted by the publicity Anders was contacted by local UFO investigator Sten Lindgren who set up regression hypnosis sessions at Danderyds Sjukhus (hospital) with Dr Ture Arvidsson. These took place on 1 April and 20 May 1974 and during these sessions Anders recalled some of the details of his abduction aboard the vehicle.

Having been sucked aboard, he was confronted by four semi-transparent beings. They were tall

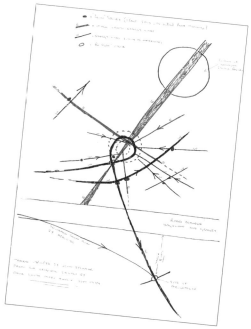

Above The Anders abduction took place at the centre of a concentration of energy lines, mapped out using the dowsing technique undertaken by investigator Arne Groth. This sketch was made by the author from Groth's original.

Below Looking towards the site of the Anders Encounter, this photograph was taken at the position from which an independent witness reported seeing the cone of light that allegedly abducted the witness.

and apparently wearing hoods, appeared to be slightly glowing and communicated by a series of musical tones. It appears that during the abduction the entities pierced his forehead with a probe like instrument which resulted in the bleeding wound his wife later saw. In a dream one year after the event Anders received a message 'You have had my sword within you for a year, but you don't know for what to use it.'

There are two major aspects to the case. First, Anders sought an alternative type of investigation to the usual regression hypnosis, which he found an unsuitable and unsatisfying technique. He approached investigator Arne Groth who searched for answers with Anders using the energy of crystallography and by studying Anders's biorhythms. Groth also used a divining rod to dowse the area of the site in a search for energy lines and studied Anders's enhanced 'aura'. According to Groth's analysis, the site of the abduction is the precise location of a 'crossroads' of major energy lines and the event happened at a particular peak in Anders's biorhythms which occurs only once every forty-six years. These two facts suggest that the encounter was pre-ordained and that Anders's decision to take a particular road or leave at a particular time could not have affected the outcome. It leads the investigators to believe that both of these decisions were involuntary on Anders's part.

Secondly, the event happened during a wave of encounters in the Vallentuna area with over thirty reports coming in within an approximately two-hour period of the Anders abduction and over a hundred within a two-month period. The wave caused significant concern and the Home Guard set up a 'sky watch' in the local area fielding fifty of their own personnel as well as the fifteen ufologists already present. During the course of that 'stake out' these groups also reported some unexplained night lights. One of the reports received also corroborated the Anders encounter, coming as it did from a witness who had seen the cone of light in exactly the same place at exactly the same time of the abduction from a site some 550 yds (500 m) away. Unfortunately, her precise location made it impossible to see Anders himself as he would have been behind a copse of trees from her point of vision.

The Anders abduction was not the only close encounter of the Vallentuna wave and one of the other important cases is that of Mrs H. Andersson the following evening (see below).

NAME	MRS ANDERSSON'S ENCOUNTER
DATE	24 MARCH 1974
PLACE	SÖDERBY, GUSTAVSLUND, SWEDEN MAP REF: M8
EVENT	CLOSE ENCOUNTER OF THE FIRST KIND

Less than 24 hours after the abduction of Anders (see page 103) and coming at the same time as some thirty independent close encounter reports in the same area, Mrs H. Andersson sighted an object in a small valley towards Söderby (which was also reported by an independent witness at Granby nearby). Mrs Andersson is a local UFO 'figure' and acts as the lynchpin of an informal support group for UFO witnesses where they can exchange their experiences without fear of ridicule.

Her first sighting of the object took place at 7.25 in the evening when she was driving towards Vasaskolan, a school north of Lindholmen. She thought at first that she was seeing a helicopter descending into the valley near Söderby, north of Granby and very close to the Anders abduction site. Mrs Andersson drove to the crossroads at Haga but could not see the object and she drove on to collect her parents at Malmhagen.

During her stay with her parents there was interference on the television and the telephone was out of order. They observed a large, bright UFO moving through the forest east of Malmhagen towards a nearby gravel pit. This was corroborated by a further independent report from a local 90-year-old retired blacksmith and also by a woman who watched the object travel between Skrattbacken and Malmhagen.

Mrs Andersson drove on to her brother's at Skrattbacken where they saw the object again. Later in the evening she left her brother's house to travel home with her brother and his daughter in the car behind. As they were driving along her brother noticed an object pass over the road shortly after his sister's car had cleared the spot, and he sounded his horn to attract her attention. He accelerated to catch her up and they watched the object disappear towards a nearby farm.

However, Mrs Andersson and her children left the area and found that they were paced by orange coloured objects high above them, one of which was apparently sweeping a torch like beam across them. There was an aftermath; the children suffered headaches and stomach aches and Mrs Andersson had severe pain in her kidneys for some days. She summed up the event 'It was so horrible I wish it had never happened. I got the impression that we were checked out by someone – like a big torch that swept the area.'

MARS – THE CLASSIC HOME OF ALIENS

RIGHT Close-up of one of Mars's two moons, Phobos. Phobos has intrigued astronomers for years, because its orbital movements seem to violate natural laws. There have been suggestions that Phobos could be an artificial, hollow, spaceship in orbit around Mars. Of even more interest, Jonathan Swift in the eighteenth century gave accurate details of both Phobos and the other Martian moon, Diemos. It took years for modern astronomers to catch up with him. BELOW The Red Planet. Ever since Schiaparelli wrote of 'canali' on the surface, Mars has been considered as a possible home for intelligent life.

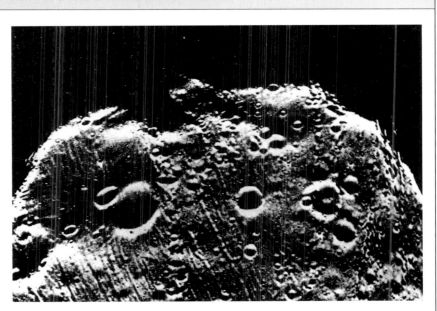

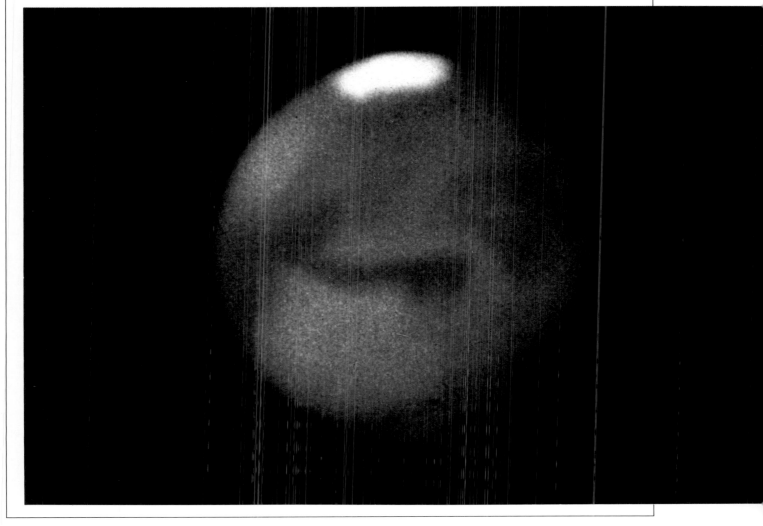

NAME THE BELLINGERI SIGHTING

DATE 16 APRIL 1974

PLACE PIEDMONT, ALESSANDRIA, ITALY
MAP REF: L19

EVENT CLOSE ENCOUNTER OF THE THIRD
KIND

A young married couple, Carla and Mauro Bellingeri were driving home from a festival in the early hours of 16 April 1974 when suddenly Mauro spotted a bright object flying to their left and he pointed it out to his wife. They saw the object dive to within 50 ft (15 m) of their own house.

As they drove up to their house, Mauro opened the garage door and then returned to the car where they stood together watching the object. It hovered soundlessly above the house and consisted of a dark ring surmounted by a transparent cockpit. The ring had a row of various lights around its edge. Inside the cockpit they believed they could see three humanoid shapes and at one point one of the humanoids appeared to look at them before the UFO turned, fired its jets and began to rotate fast before disappearing in a north-easterly direction.

Mauro's sister-in-law who lives in the same house heard the noise but did not see the object. There were many reports from the area over the next few days.

NAME THE AVELEY ABDUCTION

DATE 27 OCTOBER 1974

PLACE AVELEY, ESSEX, ENGLAND
MAP REF: G12

EVENT ABDUCTION

The Aveley event was the first British abduction to involve regression hypnosis. (The real names of the witnesses have been made public in many books and articles about this event, but Mr

Avis made clear at a public meeting of BUFORA that he had not found all of the attention caused by the event to have been very pleasant. For that reason I am reverting to the original pseudonyms that were used for the couple by the original investigators.) John and Elaine Avis together with their three young children were driving home to the village of Aveley in Essex after 10 o'clock in the evening of 27 October 1974.

Shortly after seeing a blue light in the sky, described as oval shaped and pale in colour which they occasionally glimpsed as they were driving, they rounded a bend in the road and encountered a green fog, which seemed to move across the road, obscuring it just outside their home village. They also appeared to enter a 'cone of silence', a commonly reported feature of UFO abductions where an unnatural stillness and quiet surrounds the witnesses. They were unable to stop driving into the fog. When they did so the car radio crackled and smoked, the engine went dead and the car jerked violently. Suddenly they were back driving towards their home!

On arriving home the couple switched on the television set keen to watch a programme for which they had raced back from Elaine's parents but they were disappointed to see a blank screen. In fact the television had shut down its broadcasts for the evening and on checking the time they were amazed to discover it was now one o'clock in the morning. They had lost two and a half hours!

Some three years after the encounter, when it was brought to the attention of the UFO investigators, regression hypnosis was carried out. From this came the suggestion that the couple were subjected to medical examination by tall silver suited figures and small bat like creatures.

Elaine related something similar to an out-of-body experience describing floating sensations and even looking back and seeing herself inside the car while being inside the UFO. John was apparently shown the power unit of the UFO and saw videos of the aliens' home planet. The aliens told them that genetic experimentation was part of their reason for being there, an element which features strongly in North American cases.

There has been some speculation about the direction of the Avis's life since the encounter, in particular John has undergone changes which have led him to be more ecologically concerned and more artistically inclined. He himself at a public meeting of UFO researchers denied that any change had been dramatic stating that he believed he had always been interested in these subjects anyway, and the interests would have surfaced at some stage.

Interestingly, many encounter cases in Sweden have left the witnesses with profound feelings of concern for the environment and it is speculated that this aspect was part of the meaning of these experiences.

NAME THE TRIDENT SIGHTING

DATE 30 JULY 1976

PLACE PORTUGUESE COAST, 40 MILES
(64 KM) SOUTH OF LISBON,
PORTUGAL
MAP REF: B20

EVENT DISTANT ENCOUNTER

One of the most impressive UFO sightings, which has been corroborated, comes from a trio of planes that witnessed a UFO over the Portuguese coast in 1976. The primary report was made by the crew of a British Airways Trident II. The captain, and the first and second

THE BILLY MEIER PHOTOGRAPHS

Swiss farmer Eduard 'Billy' Meier took well over a hundred clear photographs of UFOs including the one here. Controversy has raged over Meier's claims, with many believing him a true contactee and others claiming his story – and the photographs – are a fraud. Sceptics have pointed out that the photographs are usually taken with the camera facing into the sun, which would obscure such details as supporting wires. Further controversy raged when small models of the saucers were found in Meier's possession; he stated he had made them based on the objects he had seen. His case was investigated by writer Gary Kinder who has released the story to the world in the book *Light Years*.

officers were all interviewed and confirmed the story which was subsequently also confirmed by the crews of the other planes.

The Trident was about 40 miles (64 km) south of Lisbon when the captain heard Lisbon air traffic control radio to a Tristar, which was flying above them, saying 'We have reports of the UFO. Could you confirm the sighting?' The Tristar was already confirming to Lisbon air traffic control 'Yes we have this UFO in sight', when the crew of the Trident II also spotted the object. It was a very bright light, later described by one of the passengers of the plane, who had binoculars, as a bright light surrounding something like crumpled silver paper. As they were looking at it a long brown cigar shape appeared slightly below and to its right. The captain of the Trident also confirmed to Lisbon air traffic control that they had seen the UFO and stated 'There is no way that this

is a star or planet.' The captain also took the unusual step of radioing to the passenger cabin and telling the passengers 'If you look on the starboard side, you will see what we believe to be a UFO.'

The third corroboration came from a Portuguese State Airlines 727 whom they also heard radioing Lisbon air traffic control confirming the sighting. However, the story was not yet over.

After landing at Faro airport the aircraft 'turned around' and took off for the return flight to London. The captain decided to use the radar to scan the area where the sighting had been. As the plane was climbing towards 31,000 ft (9,450 m) with the radar tilted upwards he got an astonishing return. He stated afterwards it was 'much bigger than any ship I have ever seen.' The captain was specifically questioned about this reference to a ship in case he meant aircraft but he did indeed

mean a ship. It was customary to track ships on the English Channel which gave much more significant returns than the smaller aircraft. This return on the radar suggested something three times bigger than a 200,000 ton (203,200 tonne) tanker! Although they turned down the cabin lights they could see nothing in the direction of the radar return which may mean only that it was not illuminated.

No conclusion has been reached concerning this case though for a time the hoary old weather balloon explanation was trotted out but to nobody's satisfaction.

Just over two months later on 19 September 1976 a Portuguese State Airlines Boeing 707 taking off from Lisbon had a near mid-air collision with a UFO described as bright and glowing and with a row of red and white lights around it. This object was also seen by the air traffic controller.

NAME THE AVIANO BLACKOUT

DATE 1 JULY 1977

PLACE AVIANO NATO BASE, NORTH-EAST ITALY
MAP REF: L16

EVENT CLOSE ENCOUNTER OF THE SECOND KIND

In the early hours of 1 July 1977, US soldier James Blake at the NATO base at Aviano saw a very bright light hovering over the location of two military aircraft; this was corroborated by other personnel on the base. It was described as being some 150 ft (46 m) in diameter, spinning with a dome on top and varying in colours from green through to red.

During the one hour which the object remained at the base there was a total power blackout. This was corroborated by an independent witness living nearby who noticed that the base was in darkness which was something he had 'never seen before.' He also noticed a 'mass of light' low over the base. Just a few seconds after the object flew away beyond the mountains the base lights came back on in a mysterious fashion.

The official explanation of the encounter was that it was no more than the reflection of the moon on low cloud.

NAME THE SARDINIA HELICOPTER ENCOUNTER

DATE 27 OCTOBER 1977

PLACE CAGLIARI, SARDINIA, ITALY
MAP REF: J20

EVENT DISTANT ENCOUNTER

Major Francesco Zoppi of the 21st Helicopter Group of the Italian Air Corps and his co-pilot Lieutenant Riccardelli released a statement regarding a sighting confirmed by other witnesses including control tower personnel.

During a normal training flight they had encountered a bright, circular, orange-coloured object pacing the helicopters. The circle disappeared at an amazing speed quite beyond the capabilities of aircraft of the day.

Other helicopters in flight confirmed the sighting and on the ground several people had been watching it through binoculars.

Radar had detected nothing and the official explanation was that the helicopters had encountered 'an aircraft operating out of Sardinia in the course of an ordinary flight mission.'

NAME MEDINACELI ABDUCTION

DATE 5 FEBRUARY 1978

PLACE MEDINACELI, SORIA, SPAIN
MAP REF: E18

EVENT ABDUCTION

The witness, known only as Julio, was walking his dog in the early hours of 5 February 1978 when he realized he had experienced a time loss. In regression hypnosis sessions with psychologists, Julio recalled being blinded by a light, taken into a room and being confronted by tall, Nordic type aliens who were more concerned to examine his dog than himself. In fact, a full medical examination was undertaken of both and after a period of blackout he found himself returned to Earth with painful eyes.

Apparently during his encounter he discovered that our planet is regarded as a beautiful oasis in the Universe which attracts many visitors, suggesting an explanation for the astonishing variety of entities reported. Even more amazingly, and assuming that the case is not a prefabrication, the witness explained that there were two basic races visiting the Earth: the tall blond graceful people concerned for us and the short dwarf aliens interested in genetic engineering.

This latter claim, of course, mirrors the findings of many ufologists over the past thirty years and has been highly publicized since the Betty and Barney Hill encounter (see page 42).

Mount Etna, Sicily. The scene of an extraordinary encounter in July 1978.

NAME THE MOUNT ETNA ENCOUNTER

DATE 4 JULY 1978

PLACE MOUNT ETNA, SICILY, ITALY
MAP REF: L21

EVENT CLOSE ENCOUNTER OF THE THIRD
KIND

A group of four witnesses, two Italian Air Force personnel (F. Padellero and A. Di Salvatore), an Italian Navy officer (M. Esposito) and Signora Antonia Di Pietro saw a UFO consisting of a triangular pattern of three bright red lights pulsating in the sky while they were together on Mount Etna in Sicily. One of the lights headed down towards the group and disappeared some 1,000 ft (304 m) away behind the brow of a hill.

When the group drove towards the site they saw that resting on a rock was a saucer shaped UFO some 40 ft (12 m) across with a brilliantly lit plexiglass type canopy on top. Six tall entities were standing next to the object. They were described by the witnesses as beautiful. As two of the entities walked towards them, the group was paralyzed by some power. The entities, however, did nothing but returned to their saucer which took off. Shortly after the witnesses had recovered the use of their limbs.

They noticed one very interesting point; as another car had passed by the site, the UFO had dimmed and then brightened again when it was beyond them, apparently concealing itself.

NAME THE FLYING ELEPHANT

DATE APRIL 1979

PLACE 36,000 FT OVER SOUTHAMPTON
ENGLAND
MAP REF: F13

EVENT DUMBO RETURNS!

Occasionally a UFO mystery is
solved, as in the case of this report.

When the passengers of an
airliner flying at 36,000 ft.
(10,972 m) reported seeing an
orange, flying elephant outside the
aircraft every UFO researcher and
every psychologist must have
considered that here was proof of
mass hallucination if ever there was.
However, some extraordinary
claims turn out to have not so
extraordinary explanations; in this
case a huge advertizing balloon for a
circus had broken free of its
moorings and had risen to terrorize
the airlanes!

NAME PIASTÓW ENCOUNTER

DATE 22 MAY 1979

PLACE PIASTÓW, NEAR WARSAW, POLAND
MAP REF: O12

EVENT CLOSE ENCOUNTER OF THE SECOND
KIND

An event occurred near Warsaw in
May of 1979 which was reminiscent
of the film *Close Encounters of the
Third Kind*, and could well have
been an imaginative attempt at
communication.

The witness, W. R., was walking
in the local park at approximately 10
o'clock in the evening, when he saw
three bright lights on the path ahead
of him. He realized that the lights
were beaming down from a dark disc
shaped object hovering above the
path. The object was apparently
some 10 ft (3 m) wide and shaped
like an ice-hockey puck.

The witness walked to within

10 ft (3 m) of the object and watched
as geometric figures began to form
on its surface; triangles, squares,
trapezoids, circles, etc. He noticed
that other lights were apparently
flashing on other parts of the disc.
At one point the whole upper
surface of the disc illuminated a large
H-shape. In this respect it sounds
somewhat reminiscent of the UFO
once seen over San Jose de Valderas
in Spain. Suddenly the object
emitted a bright blue light and the
witness felt burning before he
turned and ran away.

The following morning he had a
form of oppressive headache, burns
and sore abcesses on his face.

NAME CZLUCHÓW SIGHTING

DATE AUGUST 1979

PLACE CZLUCHÓW, POLAND
MAP REF: M12

EVENT CLOSE ENCOUNTER OF THE THIRD
KIND

Mr Z. (name withheld) was rowing
on a lake at Czluchów in Poland in
August 1979 when he saw a dark
egg shaped object moving on the
surface. It was apparently making no
sound and causing no commotion in
the water and shortly after it was
first sighted, it moved behind a
peninsula and out of sight.

A second witness, Mr Y.,
verified this sighting but also lost
sight of the object from his position.
As Mr Y. approached the site he
saw two humanoids in dark clothing
moving into the nearby forest. Two
dogs owned by Mr Y. ran towards
the entities who faced them and
apparently forced them to run back
to their owner.

The witness noticed that the
entities were approximately
4-4 ft 6 in (122-137 cm) tall wearing
something resembling a diving suit
with shields across their eyes. The

entities appeared to have had
hunchbacks or at least some form of
enlarged growth between the back
of the neck and the shoulders, a
rarely reported observation. This is
a feature that occurred in the 1954
case in Węgierska Górka (see
page 83), which was not recalled by
the witness until 1986 by which time
the details of the Czluchów sighting
were generally known.

Even more extraordinarily, the
entities glided over the ground
rather than obviously walking on it,
aided, possibly, by the fact that their
legs apparently ended at the knees
with only an invisible gap between
the knees and the ground itself! The
witness shouted at them but they
glided away even faster and
vanished. He never saw them again
but he did see a brilliantly lit UFO fly
over the treetops approximately
100 yds (91 m) away from him.

The only physical trace that
appears to have been left of the
event was that the dogs' fore-paws
were paralyzed for six months
following the incident.

NAME THE LIVINGSTON ENCOUNTER

DATE 9 NOVEMBER 1979

PLACE LIVINGSTON, LOTHIAN, SCOTLAND
MAP REF: F10

EVENT CLOSE ENCOUNTER OF THE SECOND
KIND

At approximately 10.15 in the
morning on Friday, 9 November
1979 forester Robert Taylor, a 61-
year-old local inhabitant of
Livingston, Scotland, encountered a
UFO and entities of the most
extraordinary nature.

With his dog, Taylor drove in his
pick-up truck to inspect young forest
trees in an area just off the M8
motorway which connects
Edinburgh to Glasgow. He stopped
the pick-up and walked to the site he

Forester Robert Taylor witnessed a close encounter at Livingston in Scotland in November 1979. He was attacked by two mine-like objects.

wanted to inspect; as he rounded a corner he was astonished to see what was hovering in the clearing ahead of him.

The object was approximately 20 ft (6 m) wide and 12 ft (3.65 m) high, globular for the most part but surrounded by a flange similar to the brim of a hat. Protruding upward from the 'hat' were what appeared to be motionless propellers placed around the rim. Behind them and on the main body of the object appeared to be the outline of portholes or at least somewhat different coloured patches. Beneath the rim the object was slightly darker and the witness got the impression that the object

may have been trying to camouflage itself by hazing in and out of solidity. The witness was uncertain whether the object itself was transparent or reflective but got the impression that its normal colour was of a dull grey and had a texture of a rough sandpaper. The real shocks were yet to come!

Just seconds after first seeing the object, two small, spiked spheres either dropped down from it or rushed from behind it, rolling across the ground on extended spikes towards Taylor. They were approximately 3 ft (91 cm) wide and also a dull grey, similar to the main craft. As they reached him, the spheres, one on each side, attached themselves to his legs and he felt himself being dragged towards the object. He was overwhelmed by an acrid smell and lost consciousness.

When he came to, the objects were gone and his dog was racing around him in an agitated state. Taylor himself had apparently lost his voice and was unable to stand comfortably. He was forced to crawl some 90 yds (82 m) back to his pick-up truck but shortly ran it into soft mud in his desperation to leave the area and consequently had to walk home. For hours afterwards he had a headache and a thirst which lasted for two days.

Subsequent investigation of the site showed ground markings which correlated to the spikes on the small spherical objects where they had apparently churned up the grass. Of particular importance was the damage to his trousers; they were of a heavy blue serge but were torn on each leg where, apparently, the spherical objects had attached themselves. The tears were upwards, suggesting that they had been formed by dragging him forwards and were investigated by the British UFO Research Association who currently hold the

trousers for any further forensic examination that can be undertaken.

Of the witness himself, Taylor is described as honest and responsible and not the sort of person to play jokes. With perhaps some difficulty he now believes he saw an extraterrestrial craft and robots. For a while he carried a camera in case he should encounter them again. Investigation into his personal circumstances revealed a man who drank very little alcohol, was of generally good health and with no significant history of head injury or suffering from headaches or blackouts. According to the investigator his hearing is good and he wears glasses only for reading.

Whether the experience was an objectively real one or something created by Taylor is, as in many cases, always open to question. However, the very thorough investigation by Steuart Campbell suggests that the ground traces and physical evidence which was found gave little support to the contention that there were no physical objects present at all.

On the other hand, the investigation also suggested that it was unlikely that the object was man-made since there appeared to be no likely manufacturer in the proximity. In any case, flying such an object to the clearing would almost certainly have come to the attention of somebody on the M8 motorway which is a most frequently used one in Scotland. Although very close to the motorway the encounter itself could not have been seen since the trees would have obscured the view of the site. However, any flight path into the clearing would have been seen, yet there are no corroborative reports. Did the object emerge in the clearing in some other way or was it a natural phenomenon misperceived by Taylor?

9 November 1979. Just seconds after first seeing the object, two small spheres on extended spikes rolled across the ground towards Robert Taylor, a forester.

NAME CERGY-PONTOISE ABDUCTION

DATE 26 NOVEMBER 1979

PLACE CERGY-PONTOISE, FRANCE
MAP REF: G15

EVENT ABDUCTION

Some UFO cases are important for their mystery while others are important for their eventual solution. The abduction of Franck Fontaine belongs with the latter.

On 26 November 1979 Franck Fontaine, with two companions, was outside an apartment block in the suburbs of Paris early in the morning when they saw a UFO above them.

Fontaine got into his car to get a better look at it but when his companions found the car he had vanished. A week later he returned, apparently unaware of having been away. He gradually told his story of having been abducted aboard a UFO and taken to an alien planet. Franck said that the aliens were interested in one of his companions, Jean-Pierre Prévost, who they were selecting as one of their missionaries on Earth.

The three men apparently enjoyed the public appearances and notoriety which followed the encounter and the case split French

Frank Fontaine leaving police headquarters at Cergy-Pontoise after his abduction. French ufology was divided by the case; Fontaine later confessed it was a hoax.

ufologists into those who supported the claims and those who believed they were prefabricated. According to a report on the case sent to me by respected French researcher Claude Maugé, prominent ufologists such as Michel Piccin and investigators from the French-government-associated research group (GEPAN) concluded that the affair was a hoax. Fontaine later admitted that it was indeed a hoax.

1980s

NAME GODFREY ENCOUNTER

DATE 28 NOVEMBER 1980

PLACE TODMORDEN, WEST YORKSHIRE, ENGLAND

MAP REF: F11

EVENT ABDUCTION

UFOs frequently fall foul of the law and there is an impressive list of police officers across the world, and particularly in the United States, who report encounter experiences. England, too, has its share as in the case of police constable Alan Godfrey of Todmorden, West Yorkshire, who was interrupted towards the end of his night shift on 28 November 1980.

Driving onto a main road, heading towards a local estate to investigate reports of loose cattle, Godfrey saw what he thought to be a bus ahead of him. As he approached he was alarmed to discover that the bus seemed in fact to be an object some 20 ft (6 m) wide, 14 ft (4.2 m) high and hovering above the road. It was dome shaped and spinning. Godfrey could see what appeared to be windows around the top. When he tried to radio his base he found neither his car radio nor personal transmitter would work. While watching the object he sketched it. Godfrey was hesitant about making his report but did so when he heard that other police had been reporting UFOs around the same time.

Regression hypnosis sessions were undertaken and revealed that the constable appeared to experience fear and heightened emotion at his apparent experiences. He believed he was in a room faced by a man about 6 ft (183 cm) tall wearing a robe and skull cap. There were other creatures in the room, non-humanoid dwarf like objects, which apparently caused Godfrey, under hypnosis, to cry out 'They are horrible, horrible.' He even saw what appeared to be a large dog (a feature unique to this experience). The tall humanoid entity was apparently called Joseph, and he encouraged Godfrey to lie down on a bed where some form of examination took place.

Constable Godfrey (now no longer with the force) has always maintained a very level headed and sensible attitude towards the experience. He acknowledges that he does not know what the object was nor what the degree of reality was in relation to the regression hypnosis sessions but of course maintains his desire to find out.

PC Alan Godfrey displaying a sketch of the object that may have abducted him, together with one of the entities that he encountered. Godfrey maintains level-headedness in his search for answers.

NAME RENDLESHAM FOREST

DATE 29 DECEMBER 1980

PLACE RAF/USAF WOODBRIDGE, SUFFOLK,
ENGLAND
MAP REF: G12

EVENT CLOSE ENCOUNTER OF THE SECOND
KIND

The tranquil darkness of
Rendlesham forest was shattered in
the early hours of a late December
morning when a triangular shaped
UFO landed, or possibly crash
landed, amid trees to the rear of the
joint United States and United
Kingdom airbase at Woodbridge in
Suffolk.

According to a report by
Lieutenant Colonel Charles Halt, the
deputy base commander at the time,
two United States Air Force
security officers saw unusual lights
in the forest to the rear of the base.
They requested permission to
investigate on the basis that an
aircraft may have crashed into the
trees. It was to be the beginning of
an extraordinary night.

Three patrolmen tramped
through the forest towards the
glowing object and approached to
within a few feet of it. It was
described as triangular in shape
approximately 8 ft (244 cm) wide
and 6 ft (183 cm) high and emitting a
bright white light. There were
reports of a red light on top and a
bank of blue lights beneath which
seemed to indicate that the object
was sitting on short legs. Possibly
wishing to avoid direct contact as
the officers approached, the object
manoeuvred through the trees away
from them towards a nearby farm,
driving cattle there into an agitated
state before taking off at
extraordinary speed.

Investigation the following day
showed three small depressions in
the ground where the object had
been sighted. These strangely
formed indentations were believed
to be landing traces.

There were more extraordinary,
and more dubious, claims of silver
suited aliens, of communication
between the base commander and
the extraterrestrials, and of films
and photographs of the contact being
taken which were then confiscated.
There is little corroborative
evidence for these later claims.

Radar stations in the area,
including RAF/USAF Bentwaters
(itself the subject of an earlier radar
visual encounter in the late 1950s,
see page 86) tracked an unidentified
object on radar at the time.
According to USAF intelligence
officers, the radar indicated a
possible crash landing in the forest
near Woodbridge.

According to the book *Skycrash*,
by Jenny Randles, Brenda Butler
and Dot Street, the two security
officers, one given the pseudonym
James Archer and the other airman
John Burroughs, gave reports which
confirmed the report given by
Lieutenant Colonel Halt. They made
no comment about alien occupants
though did state that they believed
there were shapes inside the object.
'I don't know what, but the shapes
did not look human. Maybe they
were like robots.'

The mystery deepened further
when a tape recording alleged to
have been made by Lieutenant
Colonel Halt and others was
released, apparently describing, as
it happened, the search through the
woods and encounter with the
object. I have heard portions of the
tape and had the impression that it
was stage managed but whether it is
a total fabrication or whether the
tape is edited badly, falsely creating
a wrong impression, is difficult to
say. If it was fabricated then the
question remains as to who
fabricated it. Presumably it was
either a military or defence

establishment intent on
disinformation (feeding ludicrous
information to people with a view to
discrediting it) or by unprofessional
ufologists who by chance found
themselves involved in a major case.
If the tape is faked then the precise
identity of the person who did it may
never be known.

Perhaps the most telling part of
the encounter came in 1985 when
former Chief of Defence Staff,

Admiral of the Fleet Lord Hill-Norton, wrote to Michael Heseltine, the then Secretary of State for Defence, requesting details of the case. On behalf of Heseltine a reply was received from Lord Trefgarne stating that 'The events to which you refer were of no defence significance.'

Lord Hill-Norton pointed out that this was an extraordinary claim by any standards. If there had been an intrusion into British airspace around a United States/British airbase from a foreign or alien power then clearly there was a defence significance. The alternative was that the report by deputy base commander Lieutenant Colonel Halt was a hoax, a joke, or a symptom of him being 'out of his mind'. One could argue that any one of these surely also has defence significance!

'I don't know what [they were], but the shapes did not look human. Maybe they were like robots.' So said one of the security officers of USAF/RAF Woodbridge after seeing this object in the forest behind the Air Force base. It manoeuvred through the trees, and took off in spectacular fashion. Despite all this, and a written report by the deputy base commander (see database entry for details), the official British line was that there was no defence significance.

NAME HESSDALEN LIGHTS

DATE 1981 – 1985

PLACE HESSDALEN VALLEY, NORWAY
MAP REF: J7

EVENT LIGHT PHENOMENA

The problem for most ufologists studying reports of UFO activity is that they are invariably studying a historical claim, sometimes years old, and studying an event which seems never to repeat itself. Hessdalen provided one of very few opportunities for ufologists to undertake a long-term controlled study of repeating phenomena between 1981 and 1985.

In November 1981 local people in the area of the Hessdalen valley reported strange lights sweeping between the mountains and making extraordinary manoeuvres. Many witnesses described the objects as egg shaped, with porthole like features, but there were also spherical objects, cigar shaped objects and less distinct forms.

Over a four-year period many ufologists camped in semi-permanent bases in the Hessdalen valley and employed a variety of equipment to study the lights. Officers of one of the Norwegian defence divisions joined them for a period and Project Hessdalen received at least the approval if not the support of the authorities. Project Hessdalen was set up which included UFO Norway, UFO Sweden and the Society for Psychobiophysics, as well as independent ufologists from Finland. The project was able to obtain technical equipment from universities, and employed an Atlas 2000 radar, a seismograph, a magnetometer, a spectrum analyser, geiger counters, cameras and infrared analysis.

Few people studying the Hessdalen claims would attribute the events which occurred to extraterrestrials or their craft. It is far more likely that the lights are part of a natural phenomenon but not one which is fully understood by science. In one sighting it appeared that the lights were interactive with the witnesses; as they flashed torches at the lights so the lights flashed back. Some investigators have speculated that these represent some form of hitherto unknown intelligence on the Earth.

Support for a natural explanation seems to come from the fact that after 1985 the sightings died away. The earth lights theories proposed by Devereux and others (Paul Devereux's books *Earth Lights* and *Earth Lights Revelations*) indicate

that there must be some possibility that the sightings were the result of some underground seismic activity which then subsided. Certainly the whole of Scandinavia is subject to considerable seismic activity as a result of the isostatic readjustment (which is a movement of the earth's crust) caused by the last retreat of the ice age.

As with most UFO events, some of the explanations offered were most extraordinary. One suggestion was that too much inbreeding in the area had produced an entire local population of physically and mentally defective people whose problems included hallucination. There is more photographic evidence for this investigation than any other UFO event in history. It suggests that this explanation, to put it in the nicest possible way, is supported by everything except the facts!

OPPOSITE Professor J Allen Hynek (right) visits Project Hessdalen which gave ufologists a rare opportunity to study anomalous lights over an extended period of time between 1981 and 1985.

ABOVE AND BELOW Two of many photographs of lights in the Hessdalen valleys, seen over a four- to five-year period. A wide range of instrumentation was used in the course of the study.

BEYOND EXTRA-TERRESTRIALS

Europe is a ufologically rich continent, as the database demonstrates. In fact, in terms of ufological activity it is second only in the world to North America, and specifically the United States. The way in which UFOs are perceived and reported in these two continents, however, is very difficult.

Firstly, there is no United States of Europe; the different nations of Europe have distinctly individual characteristics. Indeed, ufology seems to be following the business world where the intensified pressure towards turning all nations into one European 'nation' are actually increasing nationalistic tendencies. In the field of UFO study these national characteristics have surfaced not in the *nature* of the UFO reports, which have a global uniformity within very wide parameters, but in the *interpretation* of those reports.

Within Europe, there are significant national differences in approach. Britain, Scandinavia (particularly Sweden) and France lead the field in the comparative study of modern day UFO claims with the folklore claims of earlier centuries and particularly the stories of the faerie folk and other Celtic legends. Germany, Sweden, Belgium and Spain have been strongly receptive to contactee claims (the claims of those who believe they are in contact with benevolent aliens seeking to guide and protect the Earth). Sweden and Britain are very strong in studying the connection between UFOs and the Earth mysteries and particularly the belief that the UFO phenomenon may represent something natural, but non-human, about the planet.

Seen against the background of North American ufology, the common ground which exists between European countries begins to emerge. Whereas in America there is a general, national acceptance of the extraterrestrial hypothesis (ETH), i.e. that UFOs represent a visitation to this Earth of alien spaceships, this theory is not as strongly held in most European countries. In America, the study of the psychological aspects of the UFO phenomena are broadly confined to treating them as a by-product of a physical event. In Europe, the study of psychological aspects has tended to concentrate on examining whether or not UFO events could themselves be the manifestations of psychological processes.

Sociological study of the UFO phenomenon is strong in Europe, with a great deal of emphasis placed on understanding the human background to witnesses and events. Again this is regarded as only incidental to the American study of ufology; and, broadly speaking, amounts to a study of the extent to which physical UFO events may affect sociological processes.

Mythological comparisons are heavily studied in Europe whereas they are totally rejected in America. It is recognized in Europe that the UFO phenomenon, whatever else it may be, is a modern mythology. This is not to say that it is totally mythological, but that a mythology has built up around real events to such a degree that it is probably masking the truth – which remains yet to be understood.

Another major difference between America and Europe is that the story of American ufology is told

through its cases each characterized by a firm acceptance of the ETH, whereas in Europe the story of ufology is told through its theories.

One example of this is the famous cornfield circle phenomenon, which occurs mainly in southern England. These formations appear in the late spring and summer, generally in crop fields. They are usually remarkably symmetrical in shape and represent swirling patterns of flattened crops. It is held that these represent a part of the UFO phenomenon arising originally from the theory that they were the landing nests of alien spacecraft. This was a theory that never held water since, for a start, it required space craft with specially rotating landing legs to form the patterns that emerged. In fact no such object had ever been reported and indeed very few UFOs were ever reported in the vicinity of cornfield circles. The British UFO Research Association (BUFORA) made a considerable study of the cornfield circles along with bodies such as the National Farmers Union and the Tornado and Storm Research Organisation. They were able to conclude that the cornfield circles were a form of hurricane vortex pattern caused by the touchdown of wind and pressure vortices. In short they were an extraordinary but nonetheless natural phenomenon.

Although corn circles are interesting in themselves, they should not be linked to UFOs. Unfortunately a great deal of the study that is being applied to cornfield circles is by amateurish, cultist devotees who have already decided what results they want from their examinations. Indeed cornfield circles have become a modern 'ink-blot' test for anyone to see almost anything they want to in them. It is also very obvious that many of the people involved in cornfield research are there because of the publishing prospects offered. In other words cornfield circles are the modern equivalent of the more extreme contactee claims of the 1950s in America.

Individual European countries have experienced waves of particular types of sighting, or at least interpretation of sighting: in 1954 France was subject to an extraordinary wave of UFO reports almost all of which involved entities and most of which were varied in description; in 1967 Britain was subject to a considerable wave but mostly of aerial sightings and – for one period – particularly of flying crosses. It seems that sightings, or at least interpretation of sightings, were governed by national rather than European characteristics at this time.

Britain was home to one of the world's great UFO concentrations at Warminster in Wiltshire. Warminster was far more than a series of UFO reports and cases, it was a sociological event. It really kicked off in 1965 when Gordon Faulkner photographed something resembling a child's spinning top which was highly publicized in the *Daily Mirror*, a tabloid newspaper, and gained the nickname of 'the thing'. Suddenly 'the

RIGHT The cornfield circles have been forced upon ufologists by a puzzled public hungry for answers. Apart from the glowing red ball which appears over their formation and is probably due to the ionization of air, their relevance to the subject of Unidentified Flying Objects is minimal. They are almost certainly a purely natural formation, though they are extraordinary enough to suggest that an understanding of their characteristics will add to an understanding of similar mysterious phenomena.

LEFT For those who thought cornfield circles were a new phenomenon this 1678 woodcut suggests otherwise; here 'the devil' mows circles in Hertfordshire.

thing' was being photographed and spotted all around the Warminster area. Sky-watches of devoted ufologists took place on Cradle Hill and Starr Hill which often had the appearance of being something like a UFO specialist's scout camp. Large groups of UFO devotees would flock to the area from all over the country to spend the night watching the skyline and the stars in the hopes of seeing one of Warminster's famous 'things'. There was a great camaraderie – a camp fire atmosphere without the camp fire – and it has to be admitted not all of the nocturnal activity was devoted exclusively to UFO-watching.

For the most part the sky-watches consisted of swapping UFO stories, of occasional dubious sightings that caused some excitement at the time and of the odd extraordinarily humorous episode. I recall being at one sky watch (not at Warminster, in fact, but at Horsenden Hills just outside London) where it became apparent to me that the leader of the sky-watch was a little over-enthusiastic about ETH to say the least. While the rest of us took only scant notice of the flickering lights coming from underground trains crossing the points as they entered stations next to the hills this particular individual logged each and every one as an incoming UFO. He did the same for every moving light in the sky despite the fact that we were on the main flight path into the world's busiest airport at Heathrow. I finally gave up in desperation when he ran off across the hills shouting that he had seen an entity which he was chasing, leaving the rest of us shouting 'Do you mean that rabbit?'

More seriously, the sky watches were a very useful source of UFO-related data, not about the UFOs but about the people involved in researching them. In the decades that have passed since, UFO research has much more come of age, at least in Europe, with far more critical and broad-minded analysis than in those early years.

Spain had its extraordinary UMMO affair which comprised a bizarre series of messages coming from 'The Cosmic Federation of Planets'. The messages gave full details of the origin and home of the visiting aliens which came from the planet UMMO, rotating around the star IUMMA, which we apparently call Wolf 424. There were extraordinary photographs of walnut shaped spacecraft with strange hieroglyphs on the underside.

In Wales there was the extraordinary Dyfed enigma: hundreds of UFO sightings which attracted remarkable local publicity and which became sociological events similar to Warminster. Undoubtedly they were some form of concentrated light phenomena perhaps similar to the phenomena at Hessdalen (see page 118), but other claims built on these – almost certainly mythologically – were incredible. One example was the claim that a UFO had an underground base in a rocky island off the coast despite the fact that every investigation indicated no secret UFO base whatsoever.

Europe, of course, has had its share of hoaxes. Six bleeping saucer shaped UFOs were found across the southern counties of England. They turned out to be part of an elaborate prank organized by students from Farnborough Technical College. There were also the very dubious assertions of one Cedric Allingham who claimed to have met a Martian in Scotland and photographed his craft, which was remarkably similar to the Adamski saucer photographed in America the year before (see page 28). Allingham seemed to have been overly protected from enquiries by his publishers and suddenly died making further analysis impossible. It was almost certainly someone playing a joke on ufologists though his identity has never been proven. Jenny Randles points out that one of the candidates for the role was none other than astronomer Patrick Moore, who has never shown any serious tolerance for UFOs.

UFOs became so popular that they could be used to explain almost anything. In 1963 farmer Roy Blanchard found a crater 8 ft (244 cm) wide in his potato field and apparently was in no doubt that the crater had been formed by a spaceship landing in the field. As he told reporters 'I didn't actually see it but what else could it have been? Obviously some craft from outer space since it sucked up my barley and potatoes when it took off.' The Charlton crater (the field was at Charlton in Wiltshire) became world famous. One Australian 'expert' calculated that the saucer that had

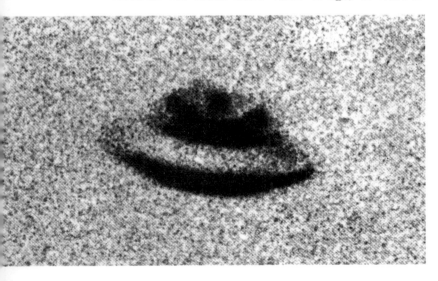

RIGHT A photograph taken by 'Cedric Allingham' at Lossiemouth, Scotland where he met a Martian in 1954. The similarity between this saucer and the ones photographed by George Adamski a year earlier are unlikely to be coincidental. Allingham is almost certainly a hoaxer who was playing on the publicity of the earlier claims, probably as an attack against gullible ufologists.

OPPOSITE 'The Thing' photographed by Gordon Faulkner in 1965. This photograph was highly publicized in the tabloid press at the time and started a wave of interest in flying saucer sightings in the Warminster area of England. Flying saucer spotting in Warminster became a social event.

done the damage was 500 ft (152 m) wide and weighed 600 tons (610 tonnes), probably having a fifty man crew. According to the expert 'We think these craft are coming from somewhere in the region of Uranus.' (And all on the testimony of a hole in the ground!)

England is of course a country of eccentrics and it has produced an enormous amount in the UFO field which reflects this national characteristic more than anything ufological. To name them might be unfair but any reading of the UFO material from the 1960s would paint a strange sociological picture.

Less than eccentric, but far more dangerous, are some of the characters that have sought to attach themselves to the bandwagon. British ufology has suffered in the past from researchers who claim to have undertaken regression hypnosis sessions on a great number of abduction witnesses and then believe that they 'own' the witnesses and will even threaten injunctions against anybody who even mentions 'their' cases. Indeed they seem to feel that a second line of income from UFOs can be obtained through compensation from dubious court cases against a UFO community not easily able to defend itself in a legal system which, in Britain, is more designed to protect the rich crook than the poor honest man. Their first line of income comes, of course, from publication – but primarily only in sleazy tabloid newspapers.

For the future, the signs are that this kind of profiteering is going to proliferate both in the United States and in Europe, probably changing the UFO phenomenon dramatically, and for the worse.

In any case, the UFO phenomenon will undoubtedly mutate as it has always done and what the future for Europe will hold is uncertain. I think it likely that Europe will take centre stage over and above the United States eventually, as the United States is more and more seen to be not adhering to the ETH so much as clinging to it by breaking fingernails. Although recently, many of the US scientific groups are beginning to develop a more European approach so that what might emerge is a transatlantic unification. Openness and analysis will slowly attract the respect of the scientific community from which ufology will then be able to grow and from which those scientific disciplines will also be able to expand. Apart from the core of true mystery which lies at the heart of ufology, sociologists could learn a lot from a study of the development of the phenomenon. Folklorists could also do so and the psychologists will find an enormous amount of material in among 'true' ufological material.

But speculation is idle as it has always been in this subject. The next major event could well turn out to be on some other continent, which would then allow it to take centre stage. As Europe more than any other continent so adequately indicates, UFOs are a truly global phenomenon. The national boundaries are important only in as much as they bring into focus the national characteristics of their people, which simply affect the *perception* of a phenomenon. But the phenomenon itself seems generally quite uniform and the key which unlocks the great ufological mysteries could lie in any part of the world at any time.

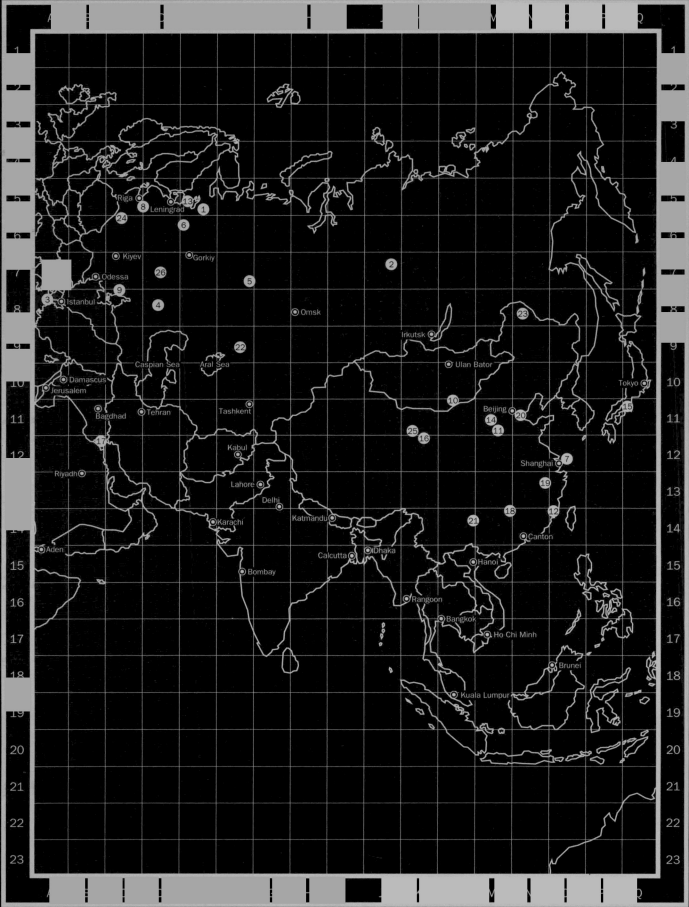

THE EAST

AS EARLY AS 1946 – THAT IS, EVEN BEFORE THE

'OFFICIAL' COMMENCEMENT OF THE 'AGE OF

THE FLYING SAUCER' – PROFESSOR KAZANTSEV

WAS SPECULATING PUBLICLY ABOUT THE

POSSIBILITY OF EXTRA-TERRESTRIAL

INTERVENTION IN THE HISTORY OF MANKIND.

KEY TO MAP OF THE EAST

① The Robozero Lake Sighting, Robozero Lake, USSR
② The Tungus Event, Tungus, Siberia, USSR
③ Hill 60, Suvla Bay, Gallipoli, Turkey
④ Pushkino, USSR
⑤ Sverdlovsk, USSR
⑥ Rybinsk, USSR
⑦ Shanghai, China
⑧ The Green Triangle, Ogre Observatory, Lativia, USSR
⑨ Ukraine, USSR
⑩ Gobi Desert, China
⑪ Dingxian City, Hebei Province, China
⑫ Zhang Po County, Fu Jian, China
⑬ Petrozavodsk, USSR

⑭ Shanxi Airport, China
⑮ Amano Abduction, Sayama City, Japan
⑯ Lintiao Airbase, Gansu, China
⑰ Kuwait Close Encounter, Umm Alaish, Kuwait
⑱ Hunan Province, China
⑲ Lan Xi, China
⑳ Tientsin Airport, China
㉑ Spiral UFO, Guizhou, China
㉒ Baikonur Attack, Baikonur Space Centre, USSR
㉓ Heilong Jiang Province, China
㉔ Aeroflot Flight 8352, Lake Chud, Near Minsk, USSR
㉕ Gansu Province, Lanz Hau, Gansu China
㉖ The Russian Park Giants, Voronezh, USSR

UFOs AND FREEDOM OF INFORMATION

If UFOs are extra-terrestrial spacecraft, we would expect them to make their appearance more or less impartially throughout the globe. If they are natural phenomena, though they might be affected by local variations of terrain and climate, it is even less likely that they would be selective with regard to the locations in which they appear. Consequently, researchers for many years have been puzzled about what to make of the relative rarity of UFO reports from the Soviet Union, China, and the Eastern bloc generally.

So far as underdeveloped countries were concerned, the absence of UFO reports could be accounted for quite simply, on grounds of low level of education and the absence of appropriate channels of reporting. How would people know *what* to report, and *where* would they report it to?

Ironically, among the earliest suggestions made when flying saucers were first reported in the United States was that they might be secret military devices of Soviet origin. In the Cold War era, the suggestion was not so preposterous. However, it soon became evident that this idea was not viable, with the result that most came to favour an extra-terrestrial origin.

Whether, left to themselves, the Soviet people would have come to the same conclusion, can only be a matter of speculation. The authorities imposed their own explanation and, with it, a blanket on all alternative explanations. So, in 1953, listeners to Moscow Radio were officially informed that 'Flying saucers are a fantasy invented by Western militarists to frighten their taxpayers into accepting higher defence budgets'.

True, there were occasional tantalizing indications that despite official explanations, UFOs that did not seem to be mere fantasy were appearing in Soviet skies. In 1972 a book by the Romanian/Dutch team Ion Hobana and Julien Weverbergh, *UFOs from behind the Iron Curtain*, chronicled sufficient cases to make it clear that UFO activity was not entirely a cultural contrivance of capitalist propaganda. But the authors were able to list only fifty-one sightings in the entire Soviet Union. Did this mean the Russian people weren't seeing UFOs, or that they were not reporting them, or that their reports were being ignored or quashed? The strict restraints on publication meant that it was impossible for outsiders to gauge the real situation underlying the apparent lack of activity.

It was not long, however, before it became evident that the lack of activity was more apparent than real: a deliberately created illusion. What gave the game away was the way in which fluctuations in the public reporting of UFO activity synchronized with fluctuations in official policy. Whenever, as happened from time to time, the authorities temporarily softened their hard line, private groups were formed, articles would be published, only to vanish when the authorities changed their mind again.

From China, too, occasional reports would emerge which suggested that UFO activity was not unknown there, either. For example, in 1980 the Chinese newspaper *Beijing Wanbao* published a photograph showing a shapeless blob of light. This, it appeared, had been taken by Xin Seng and Bi Jiang. While camping near the Great Wall on 23 August, they woke at 4 a.m. to see a luminous object in the sky over Beijing: it hovered silently for more than half an hour. This enabled the campers to take the photograph published in the newspaper, which was hailed as China's first UFO photograph.

Moreover, though the sighting is unremarkable in itself, it is significant that it is only one of many – several of them multiple – to have been reported in China in the course of that month. If we suppose that only a small fraction of those seen were reported, we may infer that a fairly massive UFO wave occurred at that time in that place. Had it occurred in the United States, say, it would have been easy to put it into the perspective of UFO sightings as a whole. But because so little was known about the situation in China, it was not clear whether the August 1980 'flap' was a one-of-a-kind event or a glimpse of on-going UFO activity in China comparable to that experienced in other parts of the world.

The true state of affairs was revealed a year later when journalist Shi Bo and a colleague launched the journal *Exploration UFO*, and received more than 3,000 reports in the course of a year. Though these included a small percentage of tricks and sensationalist claims, the great majority seemed to be honest reports by sincere witnesses. Clearly, the silence which had apparently prevailed hitherto was not an accurate reflection of what the Chinese man and woman in the street were actually experiencing.

This was confirmed in 1982 when Shi Bo's book *China and the Extra-terrestrials* was published in France, documenting reports going back to the early nineteenth century as well as more recent activity which compared pretty well with experience elsewhere in the world. The English-language compilation *UFOs over modern China*, independently published in the United States by Paul Dong and Wendelle Stevens, confirmed both the quantity and the diversity of sightings. Many of the cases in one book did not appear in the other, hinting that there was probably a vast reservoir of undisclosed material.

A regrettable consequence of the political isolation between the Eastern and Western blocs has been that information flow has been very limited. In the cases of the UFO phenomenon, it is characteristic that such East-West exchange of data as has taken place has been for the most part of the poorest and most sensational material. Unless he/she is lucky enough not only to read English but also to have access to serious UFO publications, an Eastern ufologist would have no choice but to get his/her knowledge of Western UFO research from those books which happen to have been translated. These, with rare exceptions, are the silliest and most sensational items, books which any serious Western researcher would dismiss out of hand. By contrast, the work of serious investigators is almost wholly unknown.

Of course the same thing is liable to happen in reverse. Typically, the one UFO event in the Soviet Union which made its impact on the entire world was the mid-1989 report that extra-terrestrial entities had actually landed at Voronezh in the Soviet Union. Was this truly an expression of the new freedom in Soviet cultural life, or was Soviet propaganda striking again – this time with a deliberate attempt to defuse interest in the subject by ridiculing it?

Taken at face value, the reports could be seen as a sign that the same freedom which was manifesting itself throughout the Eastern bloc now included flying saucer reports. If this is so, they also showed that, given that freedom, the Soviet people and the Soviet media would, between them, generate the same kinds of sensational absurdity as the rest of the world.

In his 1967 dossier 'UFO Sightings in the USSR' (never published) Felix Zigel rejects landings and encounters with UFO occupants as fiction or hallucination – as most serious ufologists in the West are inclined to do. But just as in the West there is a substantial body of opinion which believes that these events take place on a matter-of-fact level, so it is certain that there will spring up schools of thought, each favouring different viewpoints, in the Soviet Union, China and elsewhere in the Eastern world.

Nor is that the only problem ufologists in the East will have to learn to deal with. It has been clearly established that the Soviet government, on several occasions in the 1970s, used the 'flying saucer myth' as a convenient camouflage for secret rocket launches. The Soviet authorities deliberately allowed their citizens to develop a panic situation, causing fears of American nuclear attack and all kinds of anxiety and hysteria as occurred at Petrozavodsk on 20 September 1977, rather than reveal their space activities to the rest of the world. Such disinformation is something ufologists have to accept as just one of their problems, whether in the East or in the West.

Paradoxically, the new freedom in the Soviet Union may make it more rather than less difficult for effective UFO research to be conducted. From now on, serious UFO researchers in these countries, like their colleagues in Western Europe, Australia and the Americas, are going to find that their first and most difficult task is to separate the signal from the noise.

HILARY EVANS is the overseas liaison consultant and a specialist publications editor for the British UFO Research Association. He is a researcher of many years standing, an author of many books and articles on UFOs and paranormal experiences, and a regular contributor at UFO symposia throughout the world. Hilary has been co-editor with John Spencer on two compilations in the UFO studies field.

DATABASE

PRE 1900

NAME THE ROBOZERO LAKE SIGHTING

DATE 15 AUGUST 1663

PLACE ROBOZERO LAKE, USSR
MAP REF: E5

EVENT CLOSE ENCOUNTER OF THE FIRST
KIND

Part four of the historical files compiled and issued by the Archaeological Commission contains a report submitted by the St Cyril monastery of a strange sighting over Robozero Lake in the USSR in the year 1663.

On 15 August many of the inhabitants of the district of Belozero had gone to church in the village of Robozero. While they were in the church there was a sudden crash from outside and many people left to see what had happened. One of the witnesses, Levka Pedorof, saw what happened and even had an explanation for it: it was a sign from God.

At approximately midday a huge ball of fire had descended over Robozero from a cloudless sky; the fire was approximately 148 ft (45 m) wide and projecting in front of it were two beams. It disappeared (there is no description of how) but approximately an hour later it re-appeared over the lake, travelling towards the west where it vanished. Later it returned and hovered over the lake for an hour and a half.

Fishermen on the lake were severely burned by the closeness of the object and the lake water was lit up to the depth of some 29 ft (9 m). According to the report, even the fish fled to the banks . . .

1900s

NAME THE TUNGUS EVENT

DATE 30 JUNE 1908

PLACE TUNGUS, SIBERIA, USSR
MAP REF: J7

EVENT PRE-ATOMIC AGE ATOMIC
EXPLOSION?

At approximately 7 o'clock on the morning of 30 June 1908 a massive explosion was heard from the forests of the Tungus region of Siberia. It had been preceded by reports from many hundreds of farmers, hunters and fishermen of the remote region who had witnessed an object travelling at great speed through the sky emitting a light 'more dazzling than that of the sun'. Most of the inhabitants of the village of Vanovara saw the light travelling along the horizon and following the explosion they reported a sinister-looking, mushroom-shaped cloud.

Even 500 miles (800 km) from Vanovara, in the village of Kansk, the explosion was heard as a deafening noise and one train driver in that town even stopped his train thinking that one of his own freight cars had exploded.

Above the Taiga (forests) an enormous hurricane began to tear away from the Tungus region destroying roofs of houses and shattering windows. Huge waves flooded the banks of the Angara river. In London, shock waves were recorded on barographs.

The Tungus explosion has become legendary and the precise

Forest devastation following an airborne explosion in the Tungus region of Siberia in 1908.

details of what is fact and what is fiction are obscure but what is very clear is that a massive explosion took place in, or more probably over, the Tungus forests on that day. It was not until the 1920s, following the Russian Revolution, that an expedition could be put together to visit the region – on the basis that they were going to recover a giant meteorite that was believed to have caused the explosion.

What they discovered was not a meteorite crater, which was disappointing to them because the Americans had just recently announced that they had proven a meteorite origin for their huge crater in the Arizona desert. The suggestion had to be, therefore, that it was not a meteorite which had caused the devastation.

Of the devastation itself, the searchers found a forest of destruction which basically consisted of trees lying flat on the ground and strewn outwards from one central point. In the very centre some material still standing suggested an explosion directly overhead.

Analysis of a tree trunk from the epicentre of the explosion also shows that the tree accelerated in growth after the catastrophe, which would imply a dosage of radiation.

Comparisons between the devastation in the Tungus and the devastations at Hiroshima and Nagasaki are very clear and there is every appearance in the Tungus of an airborne nuclear explosion.

What exploded in the air above the forests may never be known but it has been speculated that rather than merely a meteorite it could have been the malfunctioning power source of a crashing space craft, which in 1908 would point very much towards an extra-terrestrial origin.

1910s

NAME HILL 60

DATE AUGUST 1915

PLACE SUVLA BAY, GALLIPOLI, TURKEY
MAP REF: A8

EVENT THE LOST REGIMENT

Many respected UFO researchers refer to the phenomenon of 'cloud UFOs' and this is certainly the most extraordinary example of the phenomenon on record.

At the break of day, under a clear Mediterranean sky, the 1st 4th Norfolk regiment was poised to march on 'Hill 60' near Suvla Bay, during the Gallipoli campaign. The regiment noticed six to eight identically shaped clouds hovering near the hill which in spite of a breeze were not altering position or shape at all. Beneath them and on the hill itself was a larger cloud some 800 ft (244 m) long and 200 ft (61 m) wide looking almost solid.

The 1st 4th Norfolk regiment, consisting of over 1,000 men, marched up the hill to reinforce troops further forward. Their march was witnessed by twenty-two men of a New Zealand field company. They reached the cloud and they marched into it, taking almost an hour before all the men had disappeared from the observers' sight. The cloud unobtrusively lifted off the ground joining the smaller clouds above and then they all moved away towards the north. In three quarters of an hour they had all disappeared from view.

Since the 1st 4th Norfolk regiment did not return it was reasonably assumed that the Turkish armies had captured them. With the Turkish surrender of 1918 Britain demanded the return of its regiment. Turkey had not captured the regiment, had not made any contact with it, and was quite unaware of it. Of the 1,000 men who marched into the cloud none have ever been seen since.

Lacking the sinister characteristics of the Hill 60 phenomenon, these classic examples of lenticular clouds are both common and harmless.

1940s

NAME PUSHKINO

DATE SEPTEMBER 1943

PLACE PUSHKINO, USSR
MAP REF: D8

EVENT CLOSE ENCOUNTER OF THE FIRST
KIND

Spanish volunteers fighting alongside the Germans in Russia, in the Azul Division, were in a bunker during a battle between German and Russian Air Forces.

The witnesses were astonished to see a disc shaped UFO stationed above the planes in combat 'as if watching the battle' as one of the witnesses described it.

After a time the UFO disappeared at speed without revealing its source.

1960s

NAME SVERDLOVSK

DATE 1961

PLACE SVERDLOVSK, USSR
MAP REF: F7

EVENT PERMANENT ABDUCTION

A report said to arise from the Moscow Aviation Institute tells of a mail delivery plane, an Antonov AN-2P, with seven people aboard, which was flying between Sverdlovsk and Kurgan. Approximately 100 miles (161 km) out, the pilot radioed ground control and then the aircraft disappeared from radar screens. As ground control could not raise them again a search party was dispatched.

Helicopter-borne troops went straight to the scene of the last communication and recovered the plane immediately. The aircraft was in a small clearing in a densely wooded forest. It was undamaged and intact but its position made it impossible for it to have landed since there were no runway facilities or clear patches. The authorities' comment was that it could only have been lowered gently into the clearing. The mail cargo was present and on testing the engine it started without difficulty. But none of the seven on board were found either then or since.

The report also states that a UFO was tracked on radar at the time of the disappearance and a 100 ft (30 m) wide circle of scorched grass was found some 300 ft (92m) from the aircraft suggesting the landing or near landing of a circular object.

DISAPPEARING PHENOMENA

Aircraft disappearances occur all over the world. Perhaps the most famous is that of 'Flight 19' and its associated rescue flying boat (RIGHT). A flight of five TB Avenger aircraft (LEFT) took off from Florida on a routine training flight never to return.

The incident occurred in the infamous Bermuda Triangle and the loss is generally attributed to that phenomenon, although exactly what occurs in this extraordinary corner of the world has yet to be discovered.

NAME RYBINSK, USSR

DATE SUMMER 1961

PLACE RYBINSK, USSR
MAP REF: E6

EVENT CLOSE ENCOUNTER OF THE FIRST KIND

The appearance of a fleet of flying saucers hell-bent on breaching Moscow's air defences caused an unfortunate reaction from a battery commander and forced an interesting response from the UFOs.

In the summer of 1961 missile emplacements were being set up near Rybinsk as part of the Moscow defences. Suddenly an enormous flying saucer appeared, flying at 60,000 ft (18,208 m) and surrounded by smaller attendant UFOs. Despite the height the battery commander authorized firing a salvo at the objects and all exploded before reaching the target. Before any harm could be done the small attendant UFOs apparently stalled all the electrical apparatus of the base and then flew back to rejoin the larger craft; only then did the electrical apparatus start up again.

NAME SHANGHAI

DATE 1 JANUARY 1964

PLACE SHANGHAI, CHINA
MAP REF: O12

EVENT DISTANT ENCOUNTER

A large cigar shaped UFO was seen by many of the population of Shanghai in January 1964. Apparently MIG fighters were scrambled to pursue it but were not able to engage the object.

Officially it was stated that the object was an American missile, proving yet again that UFOs in whatever country they appear tend to end up being blamed on foreign superpowers!

Cigar-shaped UFOs such as the one in this illustration are one of the most commonly reported configurations in the world.

NAME THE GREEN TRIANGLE

DATE 25 JULY 1965

PLACE OGRE OBSERVATORY, LATVIA, USSR
MAP REF: D5

EVENT DISTANT LIGHT

Astronomers Robert and Esmeralda Vitolniek and Yan Melderis at Ogre Observatory in Latvia, USSR, witnessed what they at first thought was a solid triangular object. Once they examined it through the telescope they saw that it consisted of a large object surrounded by three smaller green balls and they estimated the large central sphere to be some 300 ft (92 m) wide.

Their best estimate of altitude was that it was at approximately 60 miles (96 km) high but they could offer no identification of the sighting.

NAME UKRAINE

DATE 29 SEPTEMBER 1967

PLACE UKRAINE, USSR
MAP REF: C8

EVENT VEHICLE INTERFERENCE

An IL-14 aircraft on the Zaporoje to Volgograd air route, flying over the Ukraine, encountered a UFO at an altitude above its own flight level. Alarmingly, the plane's engines cut out and it glided down towards what would have been a major disaster. However, 2,625 ft (800 m) from the ground the UFO disappeared and the aircraft's engines restarted, leaving a shaken crew to complete the remainder of the journey uneventfully.

Of all the vehicle interference reports received from around the world full power failures on aircraft are rare and, curiously, seem to be most reported in Asia although many 'interferences' are reported in all forms of transportation.

NAME GOBI DESERT

DATE APRIL 1968

PLACE GOBI DESERT, CHINA
MAP REF: L11

EVENT CLOSE ENCOUNTER OF THE SECOND KIND

While working on an irrigation project in the Gobi desert, Gu Ying and a companion witnessed the apparent landing of a UFO. They saw an illuminated disc-shaped object, red-orange in colour and about 10 ft (3m) wide approximately half a mile from where they were. When it landed, the commander of the military unit which was undertaking the engineering project requested the regiment to send investigators. Motorcycle troops were dispatched on a fact-finding mission.

It is believed that the approach of the motorcycles was detected by the object as it took off immediately they closed in. It was heading towards the northern border of the USSR.

As they were not well informed about UFOs, the general feeling was that this was a new form of reconnaissance craft from the Soviet Union. Examination of the landing site showed burn marks on the ground, confirming the physical reality of the report.

1970s

NAME DINGXIAN CITY

DATE SEPTEMBER 1971

PLACE DINGXIAN CITY, HEBEI PROVINCE, CHINA
MAP REF: M11

EVENT DISTANT ENCOUNTER

Chen Chu was serving with the People's Liberation Army during an assignment north of the city of Dingxian in September 1971 when he witnessed a UFO event. It was approximately 7.30 in the evening and Chen Chu, and others, witnessed a globular object rising slowly and emitting a misty gas. After apparently hovering, it fired a strong jet and rose higher, then remained stationary for a time before descending again. Eventually it descended out of sight.

The incident was reported immediately and the army unit sent a car to investigate. On returning, the unit claimed to have chased the object around the mountain roads before losing it.

The witness's credibility is strengthened by his own attempts at down-to-earth explanation: he confessed that having tried to explain it as a plane, a balloon or some other 'normal' object he had always felt unable to do so.

NAME ZHANG PO COUNTY

DATE 7 JULY 1977

PLACE ZHANG PO COUNTY, FU JIAN, CHINA
MAP REF: O14

EVENT MASS SIGHTING

Although the vast majority of UFO activity is reported in the Americas and in Europe, it seems that every continent and indeed every country has its own spectacular and unique involvement in the UFO phenomenon. Such is the case in this event though regrettably the uniqueness amounted to mass panic and death.

Early in the evening of 7 July 1977, at Zhang Po County, Fu Jian, China an open air film was attended by some 3,000 people. Suddenly two glowing orange UFOs descended towards the crowd so low and so close together that panic ensued. The witnesses could feel the heat of the objects and hear a low humming sound and they claimed that the objects passed so low that they virtually landed.

The sighting was of short duration and the objects ascended and disappeared very quickly; unfortunately in the ensuing panic 200 hundred people had been injured and two were killed. Examination of the film being broadcast showed that it was not the result of any optical illusion or light effect caused by the transmission.

NAME PETROZAVODSK

DATE 20 SEPTEMBER 1977

PLACE PETROZAVODSK, USSR
MAP REF: E5

EVENT DISTANT ENCOUNTER

Although a relatively undramatic case in terms of sighting, it had interesting repercussions because of the government's attitude.

AURORA BOREALIS

The Aurora Borealis, or Northern Lights, like its counterpart in the southern hemisphere, the Aurora Australis, or Southern Lights, is a natural atmospheric effect which can be observed at near-polar latitudes. Although usually seen as bands of light shimmering over a long period, there are sightings of smaller, quicker 'flashes' which can account for some of the distant sightings that are reported.

Auroras are caused by charged subatomic particles from the sun interacting with atoms and molecules in the Earth's upper atmosphere. They occur at high latitudes on account of the fact that the particles from the sun are concentrated over the poles by Earth's magnetic field.

Of the case itself there were many reports by residents of Petrozavodsk that a giant, glowing jellyfish shaped UFO was hovering over the city. It was never seen except from a distance and was seen for only a ten to twenty minute period, during which time it amounted only to a light phenomenon. It appears to have manoeuvred over the city, apparently shining down fine rays that appeared to be like rain. The object then became a bright semi-circle, red in the centre with white around it until it finally disappeared.

The case produced a sudden outburst of mass hysteria. There were many excited responses from the population, and legendary tales, unsupported, of holes being bored into the pavements, of bizarre electromagnetic effects driving vehicles off the roads and even one claim that it was the forerunner of a nuclear attack on the city.

The Russian government made no statement and this was taken to be an official acceptance of the UFO phenomenon. It may be that the Russians decided to use the UFO phenomenon to cover up a particular event of their own and, if so, must have felt somewhat embarrassed to be paid back in pounds for their pennies of outlay.

Western observers believe that the Russian government did not want to admit to the launch of a military satellite or any other form of secret satellite from nearby Plesetsk; a subject which the Russian government typically never commented on.

NAME SHANXI AIRPORT

DATE 26 JULY 1978

PLACE SHANXI AIRPORT, CHINA
MAP REF: M11

EVENT DISTANT ENCOUNTER

Flying instructor Sha Yongkao was giving flying instruction at 10,000 ft (3,048 m) when both he and his pupil saw two glowing UFOs circling the airport and then flying away. Yongkao attempted pursuit of the objects and was told by radio that there were no other aircraft in the area and that they were not returning on radar.

The same witness had a second encounter less than a year later when he witnessed a fast moving UFO at a height of approximately 3,000 ft (914 m).

NAME AMANO ABDUCTION

DATE 3 OCTOBER 1978

PLACE SAYAMA CITY, JAPAN
MAP REF: Q11

EVENT ABDUCTION

Late in the evening on 3 October 1978 Hideicho Amano drove to the top of a mountain near his home to take advantage of the good reception on his CB radio. He was planning to use this to talk to his brother. His two-year-old daughter, Juri, was also in the car.

At the top of a mountain, with the radio on, the car was suddenly illuminated. Amano looked around but could see no obvious source. But the source had located Juri!

Suddenly Amano became aware that his daughter was lying across the rear seat of the car with an orange beam shining onto her stomach. Before he could react he felt a metal object press against his forehead and he looked up to see a strange, hideous entity: short and with no obvious nose.

Although paralyzed there appears to have been some kind of communication attempted; he felt the presence of visual images being played into his mind and heard high pitched screaming noises. After an indeterminate period of time the entity disappeared and the electrical circuits of the car and radio which had died, suddenly came back to life.

Amano was in a state of panic and drove down the mountain as rapidly as possible, not even looking back at his daughter. At the bottom, he turned to her, she appeared unharmed by the experience and requested only a drink of water.

Amano retired to bed with a severe headache and then remembered that the entities had planted something into his brain to alert him to their presence, and they have promised to return.

NAME LINTIAO AIRBASE

DATE 23 OCTOBER 1978

PLACE LINTIAO AIRBASE, GANSU, CHINA
MAP REF: K12

EVENT MULTIPLE WITNESS SIGHTING

Early in the evening on 23 October 1978 a large crowd of people including many military personnel were gathered in an open air theatre. Together they witnessed the approach of a UFO.

It was a cloudless night and the stars were clear when from the east a huge object approached. It was apparently oblong, had two powerful searchlight beams in front and trailed a luminous wake from its rear. There seemed to be a fog surrounding the object. Fighter pilots had the object in sight for more than two minutes and were certain they were looking at a large object near the ground flying relatively slowly.

Apparently nobody had a camera and was able to photograph it, which was a cause for some regret. They could be comforted by the fact that in the West a great many witnesses have made the same lament, while those who did have cameras lamented over the fact that their photographs proved very little!

NAME KUWAIT CLOSE ENCOUNTER

DATE 9 NOVEMBER 1978

PLACE UMM ALAISH, KUWAIT
MAP REF: B12

EVENT CLOSE ENCOUNTER OF THE FIRST KIND

On the night of 9 November 1978 there were reports of flying saucers over the Kuwait oil centre near Umm Alaish to the north of Kuwait city. The reports claimed that once observed the flying saucer had dimmed its lights and disappeared.

On the following night employees of the centre witnessed a more extraordinary encounter: a huge cylindrical object larger than a jumbo jet approached the site. The seven witnesses described the dome and flashing red lights and watched the object for seven minutes before it disappeared. During the duration of the object's stay the pumping system automatically shut down which suggested there had been some kind of electrical failure. It restarted when the UFO left, which should be physically impossible since after any shut-down the system has to be manually reset.

According to one report cameras were handed out to field workers near the site should the object return and on 21 November it did – several photographs were allegedly taken but never published.

NAME HUNAN PROVINCE

DATE 12 SEPTEMBER 1979

PLACE HUNAN PROVINCE, CHINA
MAP REF: M14

EVENT THE GREAT CHINESE BLACKOUT

City blackouts associated with UFOs have frequently been reported in the West, and particular reference is made to the Great North-Eastern Blackout of the United States (see page 50).

China too has been able to offer its own version from September 1979 when in the early hours of the evening there was a power failure in Xuginglong and Huaihua, cities of Hunan Province. A brilliant UFO was seen over the towns emitting white rays before vanishing without a sound.

It is believed that there have been other power failures associated with UFOs but that the government has felt the need to suppress information about these.

NAME LAN XI

DATE 13 OCTOBER 1979

PLACE LAN XI, CHINA
MAP REF: 013

EVENT CLOSE ENCOUNTER OF THE THIRD
KIND

Witnesses to UFO events act quite
differently to one another and one
such example comes from Lan Xi in
China's Shekiang province in
October 1979. A truck driver, Wang
Jian Min, driving at 4 o'clock in the
morning, encountered a parked car.
Inside the car, the driver described
a strange craft that he had seen
landing ahead of him and told Wang
Jian Min that he was too scared to
approach it.

Wang Jian Min was apparently
not so afraid and led the way up the
hill, with the other car following, to
confront the object. The dome
shaped UFO was sitting across the
road emitting a blue glow and beside
it were two short entities dressed in
silver. The witness noticed they also
had what appeared to be lamps
beaming from their helmets. Still not
discouraged, Wang Jian Min picked
up a crowbar from his truck and
sallied forth.

The UFO and its occupants had
obviously heard of the expression
'Discretion is the better part of
valour'; both the entities and the
UFO disappeared.

1980s

NAME TIENTSIN AIRPORT

DATE 16 OCTOBER 1980

PLACE TIENTSIN AIRPORT, CHINA
MAP REF: N11

EVENT RADAR DETECTED ANOMALY

Radar control at Tientsin Civil
Aviation Bureau were plotting Flight
402 when the radar screen returned
an anomalous echo. During the
approach to the airport the plane's
return on the screen lost contact for
several seconds. On contacting
Flight 402 they discovered that what
they were watching on the screen
did not correlate with the aircraft,
indeed it should not have been
showing up on that particular radar
at the time. Later during the
approach the anomalous radar
return came back again, and this
time it was visible alongside the
return of the aircraft itself; the
image lasted a few seconds and
disappeared again.

Most extraordinarily there was a
second flight in the air at the time,
Flight 404, which could not have
been the source of the UFO since it
was moving in a different direction.

Radar-detected UFOs are among the most
common types of 'sightings', all the more
authoritative when visually confirmed.

However, the captain of the flight
indicated that in trying to lock on the
automatic direction finder the plane
had locked on to an unknown
transmission source; later, the plane
successfully locked on to the proper
transmission.

The last anomaly in the case was
during the touchdown of Flight 404
when one of the control tower
personnel heard interference on the
radio and believed someone was
tuning in to the control tower. In
addition to the tower, the aircraft
crew and radar personnel listened to
the interference but no-one could
identify the source.

PATERNOSTRO ©87

NAME SPIRAL UFO

DATE 24 JULY 1981

PLACE GUIZHOU, CHINA
MAP REF: L14

EVENT SPIRAL UFO

Of one thing we can be certain about the spiral UFO seen in China in 1981, it is that it was a real physical object. It was reportedly seen by many hundreds of people giving independent reports from all over the province.

Farmer Tian Jin Fu, in the late evening, first saw the object when it was about the size of the moon and later saw a tail appearing from it forming a concentric spiral around the original object.

Across parts of the province people were frightened by the apparition, while others were excited; an understandable cross-section of reaction to something so strange.

Wang Aining in Henan described what he saw as a wash-basin some 60 ft (18.3 m) wide, spinning and dispersing flashes of blue light. He also noticed it was surrounded by white fog. Li Zhengai of the People's Liberation Army believed he was looking at the moon until he recognized it was in the wrong part of the sky. The local weather stations confirmed the sighting but were unable to confirm its identity.

University professor Shi Zunsheng reported seeing a UFO with a row of portholes and drew a sketch of a classical saucer although up until that date he had been severely critical of UFO claims.

If all of this were not remarkable enough, ever more remarkable was the fact that the sighting had been predicted a month earlier! Astronomer Zhang Zhousheng of Yun'nan Observatory had announced that between 10 and 30 July UFO activity would intensify and there

An artist's impression of an incoming meteor. The fiery glow is caused by friction which occurs as the meteor enters the Earth's atmosphere.

would be many sighting reports, which indeed occurred. Zhang Zhousheng also described the UFO that would be seen; he said it would be larger than the moon, would appear to be a disc shape and possibly spiral, would rotate clockwise and be bright in the centre with a fog surrounding it. Zhang Zhousheng also commented that the sighting should last some ten minutes.

Actually Zhang Zhousheng was using very simple scientific principles rather than any psychic powers. He had been tracking the path of a meteor shower due to pass through the atmosphere at the time of his prediction and in this way he had foretold the effects that they would have.

NAME BAIKONUR ATTACK

DATE 1 JUNE 1982

PLACE BAIKONUR SPACE CENTRE, USSR
MAP REF: F9

EVENT CLOSE ENCOUNTER OF THE FIRST
KIND

On 1 June 1982 two UFOs were seen hovering over the Baikonur Space Centre, one paying particular attention to the launch pads.

Examination of the pads the following day revealed that there had been considerable structural damage, with loose rivets and

The Baikonur Cosmodrome.

broken welds. At the nearby housing complex where the other UFO had been there were thousands of panes of glass damaged or broken out. The centre was out of action for two weeks for repairs.

NAME HEILONG JIANG PROVINCE

DATE 18 JUNE 1982

PLACE HEILONG JIANG PROVINCE, CHINA
MAP REF: N8

EVENT CLOSE ENCOUNTER OF THE FIRST
KIND

During a localized wave of UFO activity over Heilong Jiang Province in China in June 1982 a flight of five

Chinese Air Force pilots patrolling the North China border reported an extraordinary, and potentially dangerous, encounter.

The danger came with the first alert of the sighting when the jet fighters' electrical systems malfunctioned and their communication and navigation system cut out. Ahead of the planes was an unidentified object approximately the size of a full moon, glowing yellow-green. As it closed in on the planes it grew to resemble a mountain of green mist within which certain black objects could be seen. Because of the electrical system failures the planes were forced to return to their base.

NAME AEROFLOT FLIGHT 8352

DATE 1985

PLACE LAKE CHUD NEAR MINSK, USSR
MAP REF: C6

EVENT DISTANT NIGHT LIGHTS

This report, which comes from both the *People's Paper* and also the official news agency Tass, was publicized in 1985 though no date was given for the event.

According to the report Flight 8352 was flying from Tbilisi to Tallin when at approximately 4 o'clock in the morning the plane, a Tupolev TU-134 encountered 'cloud UFOs'. The first trace of the sighting was apparently when the second officer noticed a bright star-like object above and to the right which seemed to fire a laser-like beam down toward the ground. Other crew members confirmed the sighting.

The laser-like beam of light thinned out into a more diffuse cone of light; all the crew of the Tupolev estimated that they were looking at something coming from approximately 30 miles (48 km) high. The cone of light had been

In October 1989 the Soviet News Agency Tass reported that two giant entities were spotted near their flying saucer in a suburban park 300 miles south of Moscow.

scanning the ground and illuminating the landscape very clearly, suddenly it turned on the aircraft itself obscuring the crew's vision.

Suddenly the star-like source of the beam seemed to increase in size becoming almost a yellowish-green cloud and it looked as if it was rapidly approaching the craft. For this reason the captain ordered radio details to be confirmed of the sighting to air traffic control in Minsk, which was unable to verify the sighting visually or by radar.

The cloud UFO exhibited some non-ballistic movement finally swinging round to behind the Tupolev and pacing its flight. The crew noticed smaller lights zigzagging inside the cloud. Finally, air traffic control admitted they could see flashes of light on their horizon which was in approximately the correct position for the transmission from the Tupolev.

Remarkably, the cloud at one point seemed to be trying to camouflage its shape, replicating the outline of the Tupolev itself! The passengers were now somewhat alarmed by the cloud and the captain instructed them to be told that they were seeing the Aurora Borealis.

A second aircraft flying in the opposite direction also confirmed the sighting when the two aircraft were some 10 miles (16 km) apart. As they were examining the cloud UFO with Lakes Chud and Pskov in the background they were able to make a reasonably accurate estimate of the size of the cloud, some 25 miles (40 km) wide. When the Tupolev landed at Tallin the radar control there confirmed that radar had detected not just the aircraft but two additional returns.

In March 1985 the USSR Academy of Sciences announced 'The Aeroflot crew of Flight 8352 had encountered "something we call UFOs".'

NAME	GANSU PROVINCE
DATE	11 JUNE 1985
PLACE	LANZ HAU, GANSU, CHINA MAP REF: K11
EVENT	CLOSE ENCOUNTER OF THE FIRST KIND

China was one of several countries to report an extraordinary UFO during 1985. On 11 June, Civil Aviation Administration Boeing 747, flying from Beijing to Paris, witnessed the object in the late evening, over Lanz Hau in Gansu Province.

The UFO flew across the path of the airliner at extremely high speed causing the captain – Wang Shuting – to consider an emergency landing. Of particular importance was the size of the UFO, also reported in other countries in the same year: an apparent diameter of 6 miles.

NAME	THE RUSSIAN PARK GIANTS
DATE	OCTOBER 1989
PLACE	VORONEZH, USSR MAP REF: D7
EVENT	CLOSE ENCOUNTER OF THE THIRD KIND

The Soviet news agency Tass almost gave way to sensationalism in late 1989 when it reported a flying saucer landing in a suburban Russian park. However, the report certainly had credibility as the involvement of scientists investigating the area showed, and perhaps reflected the liberalization taking place in the country's media.

According to the report, a UFO landed in a suburban park at Voronezh, some 300 miles (483 km) south of Moscow, and witnesses saw two giant entities walking nearby. They were described as tall and thin but with tiny heads and they apparently had a small robot-like

One of two orange globes which appeared in July 1989 in a suburb near the Russian city of Perm.

creature with them. Interestingly, the proportions are the exact opposite of most Western alien descriptions – dwarf bodies, huge heads – though reflect perhaps the folklore of Russia, in which giants feature strongly. The sighting seemed to confirm a previous report from Perm in central Russia when a milkmaid had claimed to meet a taller than average creature with a small head.

Scientists apparently went to the park in Voronezh and found a 60 ft (18.3 m) wide depression in the grass, four deep dents, which are regarded as landing trace evidence. After the giants left there were reports that several of the witnesses had been gripped by a fear for several days.

Investigation of a 'flap' is slow but it appears at the date of writing this that there was indeed a wave of sightings in the area at that time. A full investigation of this will probably take about five years, assuming a reasonable level of access to the material.

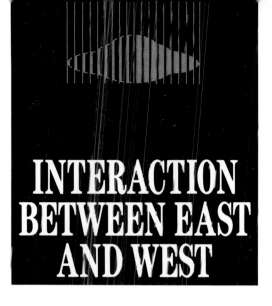

INTERACTION BETWEEN EAST AND WEST

T he introduction by Hilary Evans and the database itself give a very good impression of the state of ufology in Asia, principally the USSR and China *as seen through Western eyes*. However, ufology is a part of a larger spectrum, a spectrum that includes folklore, the paranormal, mythology, sociology, and psychology. The influence of these factors on UFO sightings is crucial to a full understanding of the phenomena. Perhaps reports are coloured by folklore? Perhaps the phenomenon has an in-built ability to react to people's expectations? No true understanding of the phenomenon can be achieved while these sort of questions remain unanswered.

For Western ufologists the problem is that we do not have full access to all that is necessary to really understand the picture of ufology in 'closed' societies. China remains relatively closed, and the Soviet bloc is only just opening up (and it is still early days for any in-depth analysis). We have good reports, of course, from these countries but we can never be certain we have all of the important components.

We need a full interaction between East and West on this subject, with access to government opinions and involvement, and perhaps a fuller understanding of those other 'human' factors which surround those cases. As the world opens its doors a fuller picture will emerge; it is beginning to already.

Several Soviet delegates have been allowed – even encouraged – to attend 'Western' conferences and their input has been most valuable. Hopefully, they obtain much from interaction with us. Researchers such as Paul Norman and Timothy Good have travelled in China, and have been given access to valuable material. Good, effective, civilian UFO research groups have developed in most 'Eastern bloc' countries.

Originally built as an early-warning system, the Great Wall of China remains the largest construction ever built by man and a lasting reminder of China's territorial isolationism.

The picture is the same as in all other parts of the world; the phenomenon is truly global. It is the 'local' interpretations which offer the variety. For all ufologists the problem is to separate source from signal.

The future understanding of this global phenomenon will be richer, but it lies, nevertheless, in the future. A full picture of UFOs in this part of the world will broaden our minds and give us the perspectives we all need – it cannot be quick enough in coming!

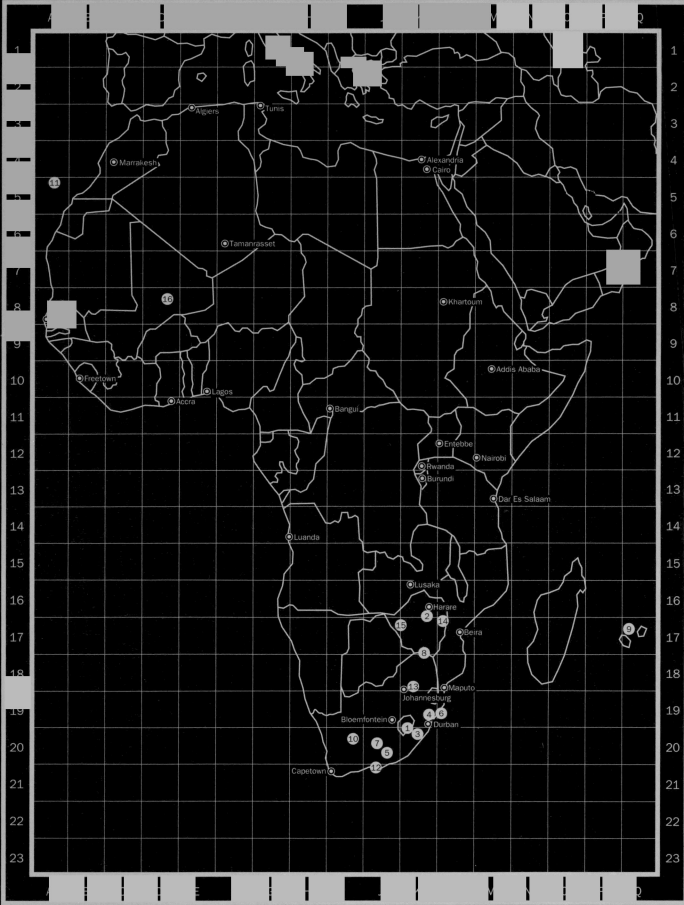

AFRICA

WHILE THERE IS LITTLE SHYING AWAY FROM
REPORTS OF 'GHOSTS', THERE DOES SEEM TO BE A
FEAR OF RIDICULE WHEN SOMETHING
OCCURS WHICH IS THOROUGHLY ALIEN TO A
PEOPLE'S CULTURE.

KEY TO MAP OF AFRICA

① Drakensteen Mountain, Cape Province, South Africa
② Lake McIlwaine, Harare, Zimbabwe
③ Elizabeth Klarer, Drakensberg, South Africa
④ Edwin and George, Patterson's Groyne, Durban, South Africa
⑤ Fort Beaufort, South Africa
⑥ Durban, South Africa
⑦ The Tennis Court, Rosmead, South Africa
⑧ The Beit Bridge Encounter, Zimbabwe/South Africa border

⑨ Antoine Severin, Reunion Island, Indian Ocean
⑩ The Landing at Loxton, Loxton, South Africa
⑪ The Canary Islands Soap Bubble, Canary Islands
⑫ Groendal Reserve, Uitenhage, South Africa
⑬ The Mindalore Encounter, Johannesburg, South Africa
⑭ La Rochelle, Mutare, Zimbabwe
⑮ Matabeleland Encounters, Matebeleland South, Zimbabwe
⑯ The Dogon Tribes, Mali, North-west Africa

UFOs WITHIN AFRICAN CULTURE

In Africa one is faced with a great variety of cultures and beliefs and it is essential that such diverse attitudes be taken into account when dealing with any report. Whereas in Western culture, UFOs are treated with great scepticism by the scientific community, the African cultures readily allow for paranormal happenings. Predictions of death or enemy attack, by Sangomas (witch-doctors), are often accurate although in the former case this is sometimes caused by severe emotional trauma.

However, spacecraft, the Extra-terrestrial Hypothesis, and UFOs, are totally alien to black African literature and folklore. This lack of knowledge is often compounded by lack of foreign currency in the developing countries to purchase books on UFOs from overseas. Thus, when I approach witnesses in cases of supposed sightings or contacts, I can be 99 per cent certain that their interpretation will be representative only of *their* culture.

The one overriding factor which appears in all cultures is that of fear! The unknown can be seen as a physical threat and, despite varying interpretations of the origins of the threat, creates an overwhelming traumatic abyss.

While there is little shying away from reports of 'ghosts', there does seem to be a fear of ridicule when something occurs which is alien to a people's culture. On a recent phone-in broadcast in Zimbabwe, I was contacted by a young African boy of twelve. 'I was in my grandmother's village when I saw this "thing" passing over, and spewing out hot, burning material,' he said. (The village was some distance into the bush and isolated). Later, when I contacted him, he said he could not talk to me. 'My mother and father told me that what I saw was the lights of another village nearby' the boy reported. 'They want me to forget all about it.' Whatever village this was, it had no electricity, only the smoking fires of locally hewn wood. Could that possibly reflect in the sky above him looking like falling, burning embers? But whatever the answer, I got no further.

In the Loxton Case in the Karroo, South Africa (see page 151), there were three other witnesses to Danie Van Graan's sighting of a caravan-like UFO. A young coloured boy (eight or nine years of age) had noticed the object on the ground. He ran to call his mother, Meitjie Devenish, who was sitting with a young man nearby. They all saw the object on the ground, but were so terrified by its implications and the possibility of police questioning, that they left the area, moving towards the S.E. Cape, to East London.

Dave van Rhyn tells a story about a UFO encounter during the War of Independence in Zimbabwe (then Rhodesia) when he was accompanied by his black sergeant, Gilbert. It was about 8.30 pm when Dave was driving the army Landrover from Chiredzi to Mutare in Zimbabwe. They had noted some very bright car headlights behind them when Gilbert pointed out that the vehicle seemed to be travelling above the ground. Realizing there was no landing strip in the area, Dave drew over to the side of the road and stopped. They both got out to look but the light had disappeared; suddenly it rose up from a hollow on their right hand side. Both men had a tremendous fright but Dave stood his ground. The light was huge, like a football field, and it passed over them and then shot up into the sky. When Dave looked for Gilbert, he found him under the vehicle, still trembling with shock. The possibility of a UFO had entered Dave's mind, but the poor sergeant had no idea what was going on.

In the case of Clifford Muchena (see page 153) it must be remembered that I never suggested to Clifford

Vast, unpopulated areas of scrubland and bush make up much of Africa. It is little surprise that UFO sightings on this continent are few and far between.

that he had seen UFO entities; aliens and UFOs were never mentioned at the original interview. Clifford alleged that the men were the 'ghosts of my ancestors' and I never attempted to make him think otherwise. I did, at the end of the interview, ask if he had heard that there were 'men in space' and he immediately reacted. 'Do you mean astronauts?' he asked, although he admitted that he had never seen a picture of one. On subsequent occasions we discussed the probability that the fireball that he and nineteen other witnesses had seen, could have been some sort of omen or vehicle, *not from this Earth*.

The largest number of reports I receive are in the form of balls of light (BOLs). One learns to categorize these and with knowledge gained over the years from books and papers I have read (such as the work of Paul Devereux and Hilary Evans) I can give an identity to most of them. What does still puzzle me is their intelligent movement.

For example, in the Fort Beaufort case in South Africa, (see page 148) the fiery object reacted to the voices of the labourers as they moved about to try to corner the object. When a labourer, Boer de Klerk,

shouted, the fireball moved sideways for about 820 ft (250 m) and disappeared behind a bush. Warrant Officer van Rensburg, the policeman in charge, who had been called in by Bennie Smit, the owner of the farm, said, 'I did notice that when anyone approached it, it shied away behind the bushes.'

Whatever UFOs are: extra-terrestrials or time travellers, psychological imagery or even apparitions, let us not speculate wildly about Africa. I have interviewed many dozens of African people in the course of my research. I only apply the UFO hypothesis when certain factors keep re-appearing, i.e. balls of light or the strange behaviour of lights, entities which *appear* to be totally alien, machine-like craft, ozone (and other) smells, electromagnetic effects on both humans and machines, paralyzing of witnesses, etc. As a field investigator of about fifteen years standing, I believe this is the appropriate way to sift the ufological data from the varied reports.

CYNTHIA HIND is the MUFON representative for Africa, and one of the most experienced researchers on that continent. Her efforts over the years have done much to enrich knowledge of the way in which the UFO phenomenon has arisen there.

DATABASE

NAME DRAKENSTEEN MOUNTAIN

DATE SPRING 1951

PLACE DRAKENSTEEN MOUNTAIN, CAPE
PROVINCE, SOUTH AFRICA
MAP REF: K20

EVENT CLOSE ENCOUNTER OF THE THIRD
KIND

Juan Benitez published this classic alien encounter report in 1978.

The witness, a British engineer working in Cape Province, South Africa, had been driving up the Drakensteen Mountain in his car late at night when a man flagged him down and claimed he needed water. The man was under 5 ft (152 cm) tall, was bald with a domed head and spoke in a strange accent. The witness offered to drive him to a nearby mountain stream.

On returning the man to the original point, the witness saw a disc-shaped craft. The 'man' invited him inside the object and showed him that he needed water because one of his colleagues had burned himself. When the witness asked the entity where he came from the entity pointed at the sky and said "From there!"

NAME LAKE MCILWAINE

DATE 26 JULY 1954

PLACE LAKE MCILWAINE, ZIMBABWE
MAP REF: K16

EVENT DISTANT ENCOUNTER

On 26 July 1954 Squadron Leader A. Roberts and a student pilot, R. Howarth, were flying a Tiger Moth near Lake McIlwaine, in Zimbabwe (then Rhodesia) when the two witnesses saw a saucer-shaped silver object some 1¼ miles (2 km) above them, and about 6 miles (9 km) away. Taking a closer look they saw that 'it turned on its side and flew away at great speed'.

However, as they reached the edge of Lake McIlwaine they saw the object coming towards them, then maintain station some 2½ miles (4 km) away. There were no portholes or external means of propulsion visible; they estimated the object to be approximately 40 ft (12 m) wide. The object disappeared at incredible speed.

NAME ELIZABETH KLARER

DATE 27 DECEMBER 1954

PLACE DRAKENSBERG, SOUTH AFRICA
MAP REF: K20

EVENT CONTACTEE

'Not afraid this time?' Potentially a chilling question, not least when asked by an extra-terrestrial standing beside his hovering flying saucer when you and he are the only people at the top of a deserted hill in a desolate landscape. Fortunately for Elizabeth Klarer not only was she not afraid but felt enormous warmth and trust for the alien; indeed she was to fall in love with him and have his child.

In her young years, in October 1917, Elizabeth saw her first UFO. She was with her sister watching the sunset from a hill near her family farm at Drakensberg in South Africa when an orange-red globe came rushing towards them. This was apparently a meteorite on a collision course with the Earth and Elizabeth watched as the metallic UFO apparently deflected it to avoid a collision. In 1937 while flying from Durban to Baragwanath with her husband they saw a blue-white UFO approach the plane, pace it for a while and then disappear.

Her most extraordinary experience began on 27 December 1954 when she was again at the family farm and was alerted to some activity by the great excitement of young Zulu children outside. She rushed to the hill where she had first seen a UFO and watched as a huge disc-like craft some 60 ft (18.3 m) wide descended and hovered near her. It was flat with a dome, and portholes facing her. Through one of the portholes she could see a humanoid figure surveying her and the landscape. Shortly afterwards the craft flew off at speed.

In April 1956 Elizabeth Klarer felt compelled to return to the family farm apparently aware of something 'waiting for her' there. Early in the morning she climbed the hill, which she had come to call 'Flying Saucer Hill', and discovered on top a similar huge metallic craft resting on the ground. The entity was this time standing outside the ship. He was tall, some 6ft 4in (2 m) high, had clear grey, slanted eyes and high cheekbones. He was wearing a one piece suit. It was at this stage that the alien asked 'Not afraid this time?'

Elizabeth boarded the craft; inside she met a second alien similar to the first and the door was closed. She began to panic in case she was never to return to Earth, and when she went to the windows they too

were closed, but she quickly became aware that she was among friends which she was sure emanated from telepathic communication.

The craft flew up to its mothership, which was full of the same aliens all of whom appeared to be very friendly. On board she was shown 'videos' of the aliens' home planet, known as Meton.

She discovered in her dealings with the aliens that her principal contact was named Akon, that they were a race of vegetarians, they could move freely within the galaxy but could not cross the gulf between galaxies. They lived in a perfect world unaffected by pollution and on their planet they have no politics or money, no wars or hostility and have long ago rid themselves of disease.

In order to communicate effectively with Akon, Elizabeth learnt telepathy. Akon explained to Elizabeth that he needed her for 'stock breeding' but she accepted this happily as she was now in love with her extra-terrestrial. She became pregnant and spent four months of her pregnancy – up to the birth – living on Meton, with Akon. The child was born and now lives there in the care of his father.

Akon told her that he came from a planet four light years away which would seem to put it in the vicinity of Alpha Centauri, the nearest star to the Earth's sun. They are surveying us to ensure that our pollution and nuclear progress is not too damaging. Apparently the gradual and somewhat haphazard exposure of the human race to UFOs was an acclimatization device.

The nature of the experience, and the description of many of its components, have many echoes in the claims of George Adamski (see page 28), Antonio Villas Boas (see page 181) and other claims that have been received across America and Europe in more recent years.

1960s

NAME EDWIN AND GEORGE

DATE EARLY 1960

PLACE PATTERSON'S GROYNE, DURBAN, SOUTH AFRICA
MAP REF: K19

EVENT CONTACTEE

In 1960 Edwin was 13 years old and working as a radio mechanic in a factory south of Durban in South Africa. While he was there, a man named George took the post of supervisor in Edwin's section. The two of them got on very well together and often went fishing at Patterson's Groyne where their friendship grew. George was quiet and gave few clues about his personal life.

One day, responding to a light-hearted question, George said 'I am going to give you absolute proof that lights in the sky are not all Sputniks. Then you will know that spaceships exist.' On one of their fishing trips George took a black bag with him which contained some sort of communication device and when George switched it on they both heard a strange language.

Just fifteen minutes later an anomalous light appeared in the sky which George pointed out to Edwin. It was about the size of a tennis ball at arm's length; George explained that this was a spacecraft zeroing in on the radio. Suddenly, to Edwin's amazement, an English voice spoke identifying itself as belonging to Wy-Ora who was in charge of the spaceship; he and his crew apparently came from the planet Koldas and one of their number was named Valdar. Valdar was in fact none other than George who scoured Earth to find suitable people to spread the word about their mission.

George impressed Edwin in many ways; during this contact he apparently gave instructions to the radio to make the spacecraft undertake certain manoeuvres, which it did. On one occasion when they were at work Edwin watched George – who apparently thought he was alone – physically manhandle a machine into place which had just taken a crane and five people to set

Edwin surveying Patterson's Groyne, where he used to fish with George (Valdar) and where he first saw the UFO with which George was communicating.

it down. According to George there were hundreds of similar aliens living on the Earth, interacting with humans.

One day George handed in his notice and told Edwin that he had to leave. Edwin took George, at his request, to a beach at Richard's Bay where they fished for some time and then George apparently changed from his ordinary clothes into a one piece zip-up coverall and gave Edwin the communication radio. As instructed, Edwin sheltered behind a sand dune and saw the arrival of a 150 ft (40 m) wide disc-shaped flying saucer; he noticed a figure inside a dome on top as the craft landed. George boarded and within seconds the object was merely a distant dot in the sky.

Ever since, Edwin has received messages from George and based on them has collected a cult group around him. Much material has been transmitted, describing the lifestyle of the aliens and the technical features of their craft. In particular some of the messages indicated that there were rival factions of aliens manipulating the Earth.

Investigator Cynthia Hind listened to one of the broadcasts as it was received. It described aspects of the aliens' purpose on Earth. Undoubtedly, the broadcast could have been faked, but it would have been expensive to do so and Cynthia was given freedom to examine the radio receiving equipment at her leisure (though she admitted she was not expert enough to comment on its workings.) She has commented that the affair 'had a disturbing effect on me'. She maintains a healthy questioning attitude towards the UFO phenomenon and she is not in my opinion a gullible person. I echo her own question, raised in her book *UFOs – African Encounters*: 'Can we really afford to laugh it all off?'

1970s

NAME FORT BEAUFORT

DATE 26 JUNE 1972

PLACE FORT BEAUFORT, SOUTH AFRICA
MAP REF: J20

EVENT CLOSE ENCOUNTER OF THE SECOND KIND

In June 1972 an event was to occur near the town of Fort Beaufort in South Africa which, extraordinarily, exhibited an apparent sensitivity towards the sound of the human voice.

Early in the morning the owner of Braeside Farm, Mr Smit, sent one of his labourers, Boer de Klerk, to inspect the farm's reservoir. At 9 o'clock de Klerk returned in a clearly agitated condition.

An hour earlier de Klerk had apparently been at the reservoir when he had noticed a ball of fire near a ridge. Smit went back to the site with de Klerk and also saw the object. It was a fiery red ball some 2 ft (61 cm) wide hovering at treetop height and spitting out flames. Incredibly, when de Klerk shouted, the object appeared to back off by some 820 ft (250 m) behind a bush and reappeared later.

Smit left de Klerk to watch the object while he returned to his homestead to collect his rifle and contact the police. Two officers arrived at 10.30 and Smit took them back to the site where all four – together with three other labourers – watched the object. They shot at it, and apparently hit it once though that seemed to have little effect; eventually it crashed through the undergrowth and disappeared.

The following day an investigation of the area uncovered nine supposed landing traces.

On the 8 July Smit heard two loud explosions from his farm and discovered that the reservoir, which is nearly 30 ft (9.14 m) across and made of heavy brick and cement, had been shattered. Indeed large pieces of its structure were lying some 60 ft (18.3 m) from the site. Smit stated that shortly before the explosions occurred he had seen the UFO again.

NAME DURBAN

DATE 1 JULY 1972

PLACE DURBAN, SOUTH AFRICA
MAP REF: L19

EVENT DISTANT NIGHT LIGHT

During a Boeing 727 flight from Johannesburg to Durban the pilot Captain Chester Chandler, the senior flight officer Graham Smith and the flight engineer G. Koekemoer all witnessed the close approach of a light to their aircraft as they prepared to descend for landing.

It was nearly 9 o'clock in the evening and the sky was clear and dark. Suddenly the crew noticed a light apparently pacing the aircraft. They contacted Durban approach control and reported the sighting, approach control confirmed no other aircraft in the area and no military aircraft operating. The sighting ended when the light accelerated and turned away.

A check of the aircraft indicated no malfunction of instruments on board (as is often reported by UFO approaches). Chandler commented that he accepted there was 'something out there' which pilots could not explain, speaking presumably not only of his own sighting but of UFO reporting generally.

OPPOSITE Following UFO sightings in the area, the tarmac of this tennis court at Rosmead Junior School was found torn up and scattered.

NAME THE TENNIS COURT

DATE 12 NOVEMBER 1972

PLACE ROSMEAD, SOUTH AFRICA
MAP REF: J20

EVENT CLOSE ENCOUNTER OF THE SECOND KIND

Harold Truter, the principal of the junior school at Rosmead, had locked up the house and the attendant tennis court on Friday 10 November when he left for the weekend. On returning in the evening of Sunday 12 November he noticed a strange light in the sky but considered it just an unusual but natural phenomenon. Whether or not this was connected to what he then discovered is unknown. As he was unloading his car he saw that the surface of the tennis court had been broken up; there were holes in it and tar and coal ash had been lifted

up and scattered. The gates were, however, still securely locked. The police were called in.

It is worth noting at this stage that there were many other UFO reports received from the same area at the same time including reports of sightings by police officers.

Investigation of the tennis court indicated a symmetrical pattern of identical holes; some of the tar from the court had been strewn some 600 ft (183 m) away, on to a ridge nearby. Bluegum trees alongside the tennis court had been badly burnt and they died about two months later.

Analysis of samples taken from the site indicated no obvious anomalies though indicated no solution either. Whether or not the tennis court was the landing site of a UFO remains speculated by some, but unproven.

NAME THE BEIT BRIDGE ENCOUNTER

DATE 30/31 MAY 1974

PLACE BEIT BRIDGE, ZIMBABWE BORDER
MAP REF: K17

EVENT A MOST EXTRAORDINARY VEHICLE INTERFERENCE

Peter and his wife Frances (pseudonyms) were travelling from Harare (then Salisbury) in Zimbabwe (then Rhodesia) to Durban in South Africa via Fort Victoria and the Beit Bridge border, crossing over the Limpopo River on the night of 30/31 May 1974.

Approximately 6¼ miles (10 km) to the south of Umvuma, a small farming town amidst the dry desolate scrublands, Peter, who was driving, slowed down considerably as he knew he was well in excess of the speed limit. He thought he saw a policeman on the

The Beit Bridge crossing of the Limpopo River which forms the border between Zimbabwe and South Africa and the scene of Peter and Frances's encounter.

road ahead and the road was noted for its speed traps. As they passed the 'policeman' they noticed that he seemed to be wearing a plastic or metallic-looking suit and when they looked back after passing him they could see nothing at all!

Fifteen minutes later, at 2.30 in the morning, Frances saw a light off to the left hand side of the vehicle apparently keeping pace with them. The car lights began to fade. Other electrical equipment in the car, such as the radio was unaffected; all around them there was a light bright enough to cast shadows. Both Peter and Frances felt remarkably cold and wrapped up in coats and blankets while they were driving.

Peter was again driving fast, between 87-93 miles (140-150 km) per hour and he eased his foot off the accelerator. Nothing happened! The car continued to move at full

speed, without headlights and completely out of Peter's control. He could not stop, brake, steer or in any way control the car. Although Peter was terrified by this he said nothing to his wife who was already concerned enough by the UFO sighting. This continued for some 11 miles (18 km) until reaching a petrol station at Fort Victoria by which time the UFO had disappeared.

It was 4.30 in the morning when they drove into the garage in Fort Victoria and the garage attendant, dressed in vest and shorts, expressed surprise at their remark about how cold it was. An hour later, they set off again.

Six and a quarter miles (10 km) out of Fort Victoria the UFO took up its left hand position yet again and there was also a second UFO directly above. Although this was a potentially busy route, because of the daytime heat many people would have driven at night, and the previous day had been a public holiday, the couple were surprised that the roads were totally deserted.

During this next leg of the drive the couple thought they might be off course because of the strange landscape around them; low bushes, high grass, marshes and swamps. It appeared that they were shrouded in a 'cone of silence'; there was no noise from the engine and no noise of insect life. Yet again, Peter completely lost control of the car now at a speed of something like 125 miles (200 km) per hour. 'I wasn't driving' said Peter. The road from Fort Victoria to Beit Bridge is very curved and twisted but that night it was absolutely straight!

Frances fell asleep at around 6.15 a.m. and at 7.30 they arrived at Beit Bridge. It was now light but the two UFOs were still visible high above them. The clock in the Zimbabwe customs post showed 8.30 a.m. though both Peter's and Frances' watches showed 7.30 as did the clock inside their car. A radio time check indicated it was indeed 8.30.

Analysis of the car was to provide some of the most extraordinary details yet! When he had left Fort

Victoria Peter had set the trip meter to give himself a mileage count and when he looked at it at Beit Bridge it showed that the car had travelled some 10½ miles (17 km). Fort Victoria to Beit Bridge is a distance of 179 miles (288 km). In addition he should now have had to fill the petrol tanks of his Peugeot 404 which should have been virtually drained by the journey; in fact they were still full and took only 22 cents worth of petrol. The tyres provided an even more extraordinary puzzle; in order to save money Peter had fitted cheap retreads for the drive, proposing to replace them with decent tyres more cheaply available in South Africa. At best they should have given him about 746 miles (1,200 km) worth of driving. Peter showed the tyres to investigators; they had done nearly 4,970 miles (8,000 km) and were still as if brand new. Regression hypnosis was to reveal a stunning story!

According to Peter's recall, his wife's falling asleep on the road to Beit Bridge had not been coincidence; it was quite deliberate. After she had gone to sleep a 'space being' had been projected into the backseat of the car and had remained there for the rest of the journey. The space-being apparently told Peter that he would be able to see him as anything he wanted to see; if Peter wanted the entity to look like a duck then it would look like a duck, if he wanted it to look like a monster it would look like a monster. In some strange way Peter also examined the inside of the spacecraft though there appears to be some suggestion that he made an out-of-body trip from the car and into the spacecraft, leaving his physical form to run the vehicle. According to the regression hypnosis the craft was built on three levels divided between engineering, communications, living quarters,

flight deck, etc. It was approximately 90 ft (27.4m) wide and 60 ft (18.3 m) high.

Interestingly, there was a special abduction 'unit' on board the craft; an empty room into which abducted humans could be taken where they could be induced to believe they were still in a (simulated) Earth surrounding. Other parts of the recall indicated that the beings were physical, they had no reproductive organs, they came from the outer galaxies, were like gods and travelled in time rather than space.

It seems that their purpose is to influence the course of the Earth without making direct interference. As part of their contact they apparently live amongst us as businessmen, university students, lecturers, and so on.

NAME ANTOINE SÉVÉRIN

DATE 14 FEBRUARY 1975

PLACE REUNÍON ISLAND, INDIAN OCEAN
MAP REF: Q17

EVENT CLOSE ENCOUNTER OF THE THIRD KIND

It was just after noon on 14 February 1975 when Antoine Sévérin saw a domed UFO in a field at Petite Ile. Small entities some 3-4 ft (91-122 cm) tall got out of it and fired a white beam at Séverin, rendering him unconscious. For several days Séverin suffered from impaired vision and lack of speech which a local psychiatrist interpreted as being reaction to shock.

When the police published their report on the incident their Lieutenant Colonel Lobet said 'It turned out that (the witness) is normally a well balanced, well behaved individual of excellent character, and not given to the perpetration of hoaxes.' He added 'None of the persons who have

testified to us believe Antoine Séverin to have been hallucinating, and they all take his statement seriously.'

NAME THE LANDING AT LOXTON

DATE 31 JULY 1975

PLACE LOXTON, SOUTH AFRICA
MAP REF: I20

EVENT CLOSE ENCOUNTER OF THE THIRD KIND

On the chilly, misty morning of 31 July 1975 Danie Van Graan was walking over a 10 ft (3 m) high earth bank, which protects his village from flood water. In the field below him he saw what looked like the aluminium roof of a caravan.

The 'caravan' was an oval shape and Van Graan could see four people moving about inside as if in slow motion. They were small, thin, pale and wore cream-coloured overalls. They had fair hair, slanting eyes, long faces and high cheekbones – a description reminiscent of the female abductor of Antonio Villas Boas (see page 181).

Van Graan could hear a humming sound and when he approached approximately 15 ft (45 m) from the machine, the entities inside suddenly looked up at him. At that moment there was a slight click and a flap opened at the side of the object; a bright beam of light hit him in the face. The light disorientated him and indeed from that time he has suffered blurred and double vision, though prior to that he had had no trouble with his eyes. At the time, Van Graan also noticed that he had suffered a nose bleed, which was later confirmed by an acquaintance. Suddenly the humming noise became louder and the machine took off very fast and very smoothly. Within about twenty seconds it had disappeared from view.

Subsequent investigation at the site revealed landing leg traces. Of the alfalfa field where the UFO had rested, the landing site itself was barren, the soil hard baked. Van Graan, echoing Maurice Masse in France a decade earlier, stated 'Ever since that machine landed here nothing will grow in this spot' (see page 89).

There is some suggestion that the entities may have done a survey outside the craft before Van Graan encountered them. Investigator Cynthia Hind located a second witness, Jan Van Der Westhuizen, who had seen nothing but had heard a humming noise at approximately 7.30 in the morning. Since he thought it was a helicopter he did not investigate. If that noise was the machine landing then it was there for twenty minutes before Van Graan came across it. At the far corner of Van Graan's field there was a virtually dried up duck pond and Van Graan found footprints in the ground unlike those of any of his workers. Although he had not seen them outside the craft it is possible that they had made an excursion.

Van Graan was asked what he felt when they left and he said, 'What I did think, although it wasn't at that very moment, was what a pity it was that I couldn't go up to the machine and talk to those people'.

NAME THE CANARY ISLANDS SOAP BUBBLE

DATE 22 JUNE 1976

PLACE CANARY ISLANDS
MAP REF: A5

EVENT CLOSE ENCOUNTER OF THE THIRD
KIND

There were many reports of this UFO as it flew on what is presumed to be a course from Fuerteventura island to Tenerife, via Gran Canaria. According to the sightings the object was moving at some 1,865 miles (3,000 km) per hour.

On Gran Canaria, a doctor and three others in a taxi saw the UFO as an enormous electric-blue ball hanging stationary some 6 ft (183 cm) from the ground, 150 ft (46 m) away with two tall entities inside it. In the twenty minutes that the four of them watched the object it changed size dramatically. It was like an enormous soap bubble approximately the size of a two-storey house at first but when the taxi turned its spotlight onto the object it rose, getting larger all the time, until it was the size of a twenty-storey building although the entities and equipment inside remained the same size.

This was enough for the witnesses who fled to a nearby house but remained watching the object through the windows. Suddenly the object changed shape, surrounded itself with a white halo and disappeared rapidly towards Tenerife giving off the sound of a screaming whistle. Investigation revealed that the object was also detected on radar.

NAME GROENDAL RESERVE

DATE 2 OCTOBER 1978

PLACE GROENDAL RESERVE, UITENHAGE,
SOUTH AFRICA
MAP REF: J21

EVENT CLOSE ENCOUNTER OF THE THIRD
KIND

On Sunday 1 October 1978 four boys aged between twelve and sixteen were hiking in the Groendal Reserve and had arranged to be collected by the mother of the eldest on the following day, Monday. At approximately 11.15 in the morning the four saw a silver object between the trees about a half mile away and also two silver-suited entities, wearing suits similar to those worn by fire fighters, some 900 yards (823 m) away. Witnesses noticed that they did not seem to walk but rather to glide, a feature common to many UFO reports.

One of the entities had a silver case or box with him but how it was being held is unclear as none of the witnesses could identify any arms. Indeed even the legs were indistinct appearing from the knees downwards almost 'like a fin'. According to the investigator, Cynthia Hind, none of the boys had been exposed to UFO literature or films and did not consider the possibility that the entities were alien in any way until after the event.

The witnesses watched the entities move over a fence and up a hill though noticed that they did not appear to move as humans would, bending forward, but rather gliding erectly up the hill. Before reaching the top they suddenly disappeared and the UFO was also gone.

Although the sighting had only lasted for some 60 seconds it was felt that their speed of movement was exceptional for normal people. Indeed at one point a third entity had joined the other two though no-one could remember exactly how.

Trackers in the reserve were unable to offer an explanation.

NAME THE MINDALORE ENCOUNTER

DATE 3 JANUARY 1979

PLACE MINDALORE, JOHANNESBURG, SOUTH
AFRICA
MAP REF: K18

EVENT ABDUCTION

Meagan Quezet and her son André left their house and walked up the road to bring the family dog in for the night. It was around midnight. As they were walking along they noticed that there was a pink glow

on the road and Meagan said 'Look, they've got lights on that road up there'. André replied that there were no street lights up there, as he knew the road well.

As they got closer they saw that the pink light was emanating from an egg-shaped craft standing on landing legs, not dissimilar to the American lunar landing module. The overall height of the object was some 12 ft (3.65m), the width possibly the same and each leg was about 4 ft (122 cm) high. Apparently neither witness was afraid because they thought at the time it must be some sort of experimental aircraft.

Suddenly five or six people stepped out of the opening and onto the ground. They approached and two of them came close to the witnesses and began speaking to them in something that sounded like a high pitched Chinese language. They were dressed in coveralls and one of the men had thick hair and a beard; they were of normal height.

Suddenly Meagan got the feeling that something was not quite normal and said to André 'Go and get Daddy, and run, please run'. André ran and Meagan continued her conversation but the next thing she remembered was the entities jumping back into the craft with no apparent difficulty even though it had no steps. There was a buzzing sound and the craft rose up although still apparently on its legs, the legs extending. Shortly after this it took off into the sky and disappeared. André did not get very far before returning to his mother when he saw the craft take off and together they went back to the house. Meagan chose not to wake her husband, who would have been tired following a very long shift at work. It was not until the next day when he was already at work, that André telephoned him and told him the story, telling him that his mother

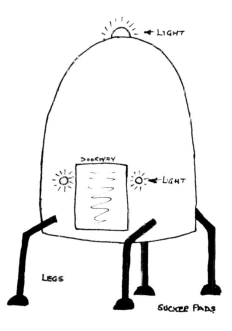

Andre Quezet's drawing of the object onto which he and his mother were abducted.

had also seen the object. Paul suggested phoning the newspapers.

Meagan agreed to take a lie detector test but was reluctant to undergo hypnosis and summed up her reluctance as 'Things happen under hypnosis. The hypnotist might say "What happened when you went into the craft?" and he could be suggesting things to me which I know I didn't do'.

In fact, however, Meagan eventually did agree to regression hypnosis and during this session it came out that the aliens strongly attempted to lure her into the craft and that at one point both she and André climbed in. Inside, she described chairs and 'funny lights' and they apparently imparted a message to her that shocked and surprised her but in fact which she has never been able to remember. Apparently before any kind of physical examination (which might have been expected given 'normal' abduction stories) the witnesses were able to jump out of the craft and it was at this point that Meagan shouted to André to run quickly and get his father.

It must be noted that the doctor was not supportive of the testimony under hypnosis and commented 'The impression I have is that this is a hysterical fantasy . . . and the material that she then produced, was very fanciful.' André has always resisted hypnosis and has also turned away from further investigation into the event.

1980s

NAME LA ROCHELLE

DATE 15 AUGUST 1981

PLACE MUTARE, ZIMBABWE
MAP REF: L17

EVENT CLOSE ENCOUNTER OF THE THIRD
KIND

La Rochelle is a large estate just outside Mutare in Zimbabwe. It forms part of the Nyabara Forest Training School and is a tourist attraction.

At around half past six in the evening Clifford Muchena, the principal witness, saw a ball of light near the tearoom on the estate. Many others also saw it. It was big and rolling towards the tearoom. It reached the observation tower, seemed to roll up it and appeared to set light to the inside of the tower although it later rolled back down the tower leaving no marks of burning behind. The fireball gathered itself and moved across the lawns to a building known as 'The Fantasy' which was an outhouse designed for the protection of orchids grown on the estate.

It was then that Clifford saw three men standing on the lawns. He thought it must have been a warden, Andrew Connolley and others but then realized the figures were too tall. When Clifford called out Mr Connolley's name the men turned towards him, turning their whole

Clifford Muchena fell to his knees after first witnessing a ball of fire streak through the Zimbabwean estate in which he worked, and then being confronted by silver-suited aliens.

Clifford Muchena (RIGHT) with Naison, the head gardener, two of the main witnesses to events at La Rochelle.

bodies and not just their heads. They were wearing shiny silver suits but Clifford could not see their faces as the light shining from them was so bright. Clifford fell to his knees and it is not clear whether this was from fear or because of some force emanating from the men or fireball. The men were now only 10 ft (3 m) away.

Another witness, Eunice Kachiti, also recalled seeing the fireball on the lawns near a cassia tree in the centre of the lawn. She saw two strange men holding what seemed to be torches in their hands. Her description is of them wearing something like blue jeans and may therefore not be the same sighting as Clifford's. Nonetheless she was excited enough to make her report. Neither of the witnesses actually specified a connection between the ball of light and the men though clearly two concurrent events may well have been associated.

Suggestions have been made that the men were merely visitors who

had perhaps arrived without paying and that Clifford has misinterpreted what he had seen, though this seems unlikely. Of the ball of fire it has been suggested that this could have been ignited methane or swamp gas or even ball lightning but none of these explanations quite bear out the details of the sighting, particularly the fact that where the fire was there were no burn marks or even marks of heat.

It is interesting to note that the witnesses did not attribute UFOs to their sightings. Clifford believed that what he was seeing may have been spirits of his ancestors. Clifford is described as pleasant, not highly educated but able to read and speak reasonable English. The fact that he does not have the technological or sophisticated background of those of us in the West who study UFOs could well account for his own particular interpretation of these events. It might also be that our technological background distances us from the truth. Perhaps we should be considering the spirits of our ancestors theory alongside more technologically orientated ones such as the extra-terrestrial theory.

NAME	MATABELELAND ENCOUNTERS
DATE	22 JULY 1985
PLACE	MATABELELAND SOUTH, ZIMBABWE MAP REF: K17
EVENT	DISTANT ENCOUNTER

During the 22 July 1985 a rash of UFO sightings occurred in the urban areas of Matabeleland South. At a quarter to six in the evening two Hawk fighters from the Zimbabwe Air Force were scrambled to intercept them.

The fighters intercepted the UFO at 7,000 ft (2,130 m) but it launched itself upwards reaching 70,000 ft (21,336 m) in under a minute. Unable to chase, the Hawks returned to Formhill Airbase where the UFO was seen disappearing at high speed on a horizontal path.

Air Commodore David Thorne made the comment that follows: 'As far as my air staff is concerned, we believe implicitly that the unexplained UFOs are from some civilization beyond our planet'.

NAME	THE DOGON TRIBES
DATE	c 200 BC TO PRESENT
PLACE	MALI, NORTH-WEST AFRICA MAP REF: D8
EVENT	TRIBAL KNOWLEDGE

Examination of the claims of the Dogon tribesmen of Mali indicates that they appear to have extraordinary knowledge of the star Sirius. According to Robert Temple in his book *The Sirius Mystery*, the Dogon tribe had knowledge for over 2,000 years of the star Sirius B, which was only discovered by astronomers in the West in 1862.

Temple believes that we must consider that the information the tribesmen have, was passed to them by intelligent beings from planets around Sirius.

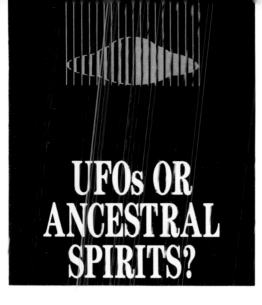

UFOs OR ANCESTRAL SPIRITS?

African ufology, like its South American counterpart, is hindered by the immense size of the continent and the few good researchers available to collect the raw data. It is a fact of life in areas where it has been tested that when there are people available to report to, then the reports come in. Unfortunately, reports are not the only requirement. For an effective, meaningful study the reports must be well investigated, and a few people on a large continent are hard pressed to do the work.

Cynthia Hind is one of the best, if not the best. Certainly her energy in travelling, sometimes days, to investigate one report is one of the most important factors in our having any real understanding of the phenomenon in Africa at all. Furthermore, she has a well balanced approach to the subject and an open mindedness that is always refreshing.

Perhaps most importantly, she has an understanding of the basic tribal overtones that influence the reports being received. Cynthia has taken the trouble to learn about tribal divisions and their beliefs. As a result of this she is able to sift out the raw data from the interpretations and provide the necessary input to a global view of the phenomenon. Those tribal overtones are important, though to be fair to Cynthia, researchers including myself are sometimes at odds to know how to react properly to them. When Clifford Muchena saw silver-suited entities (see page 153) he considered they might be the spirits of his ancestors. Cynthia never suggested otherwise, which was vitally correct. We in the West, and Cynthia too, who comes from a Western background, sift away those interpretations and – in effect – replace them with our own. Silver-suited entities have time and time again been seen in association with flying saucers, therefore we might reasonably ask if in fact Clifford saw flying saucer entities and merely mistook them for his

Dogon tribesman. This people's knowledge of the star Sirius dates back 2000 years and Dogon folklore suggests possible contact with extra-terrestrials.

ancestors. Conversely, perhaps we should also consider that our technological interpretations have no more substantiation than Clifford's theory. Perhaps 'our' classic cases in fact represent the spirits of *our* ancestors. Who can say for sure? This question is one that researchers must come to grips with. Each of us must recognize that we have a world view which may be as erroneous as the next person's.

The question must be raised again, can the phenomenon react to the culture, rather than be dependent on it? Can it send extra-terrestrials to Europe and North America, and spirits to Africa, as a way of being appropriately noticed? The answer to that question contains the answer to the phenomenon, but will we ever be able to find it?

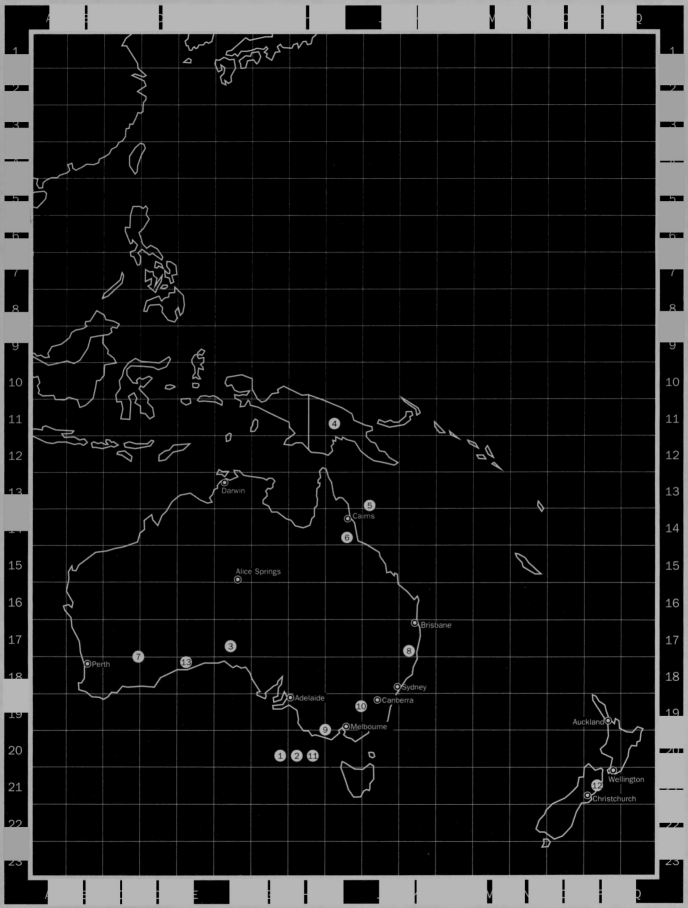

AUSTRALASIA

'THE ROYAL AUSTRALIAN AIR FORCE IS
INTERESTED IN ALL WELL REPORTED SIGHTINGS
[OF UFOs], WHICH ARE INVESTIGATED . . . DETAILS
OF THESE INVESTIGATIONS ARE NOT MADE
PUBLIC . . .' IT WAS A POLICY THAT BEGAN TO
CHANGE SIGNIFICANTLY DURING THE
1970s AND 1980s.

KEY TO MAP OF AUSTRALASIA

① Submarine UFO, Bass Strait, Australia
② The Beaufort Bomber, Bass Strait, Australia
③ Maralinga, South Australia
④ The Father Gill Sighting, Papua New Guinea, Australasia
⑤ Bougainville Reef, Queensland Coast, Australia
⑥ Horseshoe Lagoon, Queensland Coast, Australia

⑦ Gardin/Smith Encounter, Near Kalgourie, Australia
⑧ Kempsey, New South Wales, Australia
⑨ Mooraduc Road, Near Melbourne, Australia
⑩ Jindabyne, Snowy Mountains, Australia
⑪ The Valentich Encounter, Bass Strait, Australia
⑫ The Kaikoura Controversy, Kaikoura, New Zealand
⑬ Nullarbor Plain, Western Australia

THE AUSTRALASIAN PERSPECTIVE

ustralia is not just the only island continent but also a continent of extreme contrast. Despite this it has an amazingly similar record of UFO reports to those of other continents. I learned this when becoming associated with the Victorian UFO Research Society (VUFORS) in the early 1960s. Ever since my first voyage to Australia when serving in the American Navy, I had wanted to return.

My involvement in UFO research prompted me to make inquiries with regard to what was being carried out both privately and officially in this field. Recommendations came from individuals actually engaged in UFO investigations, who were not only doing private research but associated with the military community as well. It was from these pioneers of ufology that I learned of the original Melbourne group and follow-up organization founded by Peter Norris LLB. He headed the Victorian group which is one of the most reliable in the world.

After emigrating to Australia in 1963, I found that I had been the recipient of good advice and have never regretted my association with a group where the policy is to mind its own business and to co-operate with individuals and groups when that co-operation is reciprocal.

Soon after my arrival, I learned the official attitude concerning the subject from The Royal Australian Air Force who stated: 'The RAAF is interested in all well reported sightings, which are being investigated . . . Details of these investigations are not made public . . .' It was a policy that began to change over the next two decades.

The first Australian UFO conference took place in Ballarat, Victoria, organized by the astronomical society of that city. The conference was not only attended by ufologists and astronomers but by officials from the RAAF as well, including the former Air Marshall, Sir George Jones; an indication that some co-operation even at that time existed between individuals from the ranks of officialdom and the Australian UFO research community.

One of the first definite indications that official investigators were not in agreement with the overall official policy concerning UFOs came to light during a meeting in Canberra, with an officer who had investigated one of the most interesting Australian encounters. When we showed him a letter from headquarters concerning the case, he said the letter was altogether different from the actual report he had submitted.

There have been many examples when personnel in all branches of the services have assisted private researchers in trying to ascertain the whither, whence and why of the UFOs. Time and time again the scientific community has been called on for assistance only to be told by some 'professor of possibility' (or armchair ufologist) that UFOs are nonsense.

Restrictions on the free exchange of information on UFO encounters are applied. For instance, a UFO was filmed by the captain of an airliner during a flight from Australia to Port Moresby (see page 163). The captain reported the encounter to Townsville air traffic control. He was instructed not to have the film developed until his return to Australia. Upon his return two officials were on hand to take the film from him. Although VUFORS was aware of the incident, it was a few years before we discovered the captain's identity.

The most outstanding event in Australian ufology is the Frederick Valentich encounter (see page 169). The incident has done more to change the attitude of some officials than any other UFO related event. VUFORS, located near the Moorabbin Airport from where the ill-fated flight commenced, undertook the bulk of the investigations. Information concerning this greatest mystery in Australian aviation history has been published around the world.

The most outstanding encounter with a UFO and humanoids in Australasia occurred on 26 and 27 June 1959 at Boianai, Papua New Guinea (see page 162). Reverend Gill who witnessed the event was interviewed by Dr J. Allen Hynek on his visit to Australia in 1973. Many other witnesses who had close encounters were interviewed as well.

While researching in this part of the world, I have had the pleasure of meeting top researchers from New Zealand. My first visit to the country coincided with the visit of Dr Hynek, where we met again at the home of Harold Fulton. Harold did much 'spade work' for ufology in the late fifties and early sixties. During this visit, I met another well known pioneer of ufology, Henk Henflairr. The highlight of this visit was to receive first-hand information on the outstanding Moreland encounter from Henk who was a close friend of the Morelands.

The Morelands owned a small farm near Blenheim, where the encounter occurred. Mrs Moreland was on her way to the shed early one morning to milk two cows. Something caused her to look up when she saw two green lights 'like eyes' coming down through the clouds. As the object descended she saw it was headed for the spot where she was standing so she ran several yards, frightened that otherwise she would be crushed. By the time she reached her new position the object was hovering at about 15 ft (4.5 m), as estimated from some pine trees. The object was described as having a dome and inside were two human-shaped beings. Mrs Moreland was wondering what would happen next when the object tilted, rose above the pine trees then flew away with a whining noise. At the same time there was an odour like ozone.

The incident created confusion in the household because Mrs Moreland's husband was a security guard at the nearby Woodburn Air Force Base. Mr Moreland decided to contact the authorities so the sighting could be identified. Mrs Moreland was interviewed by the Air Force psychologist who put her through some tests. After the news became known, locals visited the farm in large numbers. Henk knew the witness as a down to earth, credible person. Mrs Moreland's attitude was that of revulsion. She would not like to go through the experience again.

The most outstanding series of UFO encounters in New Zealand took place between October 1978 and January 1979 when mystery objects were observed by pilots who flew along the coasts of North and South Island. A journalist, Quentin Fogarty, was on holiday when his manager, Leonard Lee, requested him to fly the route and interview one of the pilots who had made several sightings. It came as a surprise when the crew and passengers found themselves flying amid a whole fleet of UFOs.

News of this encounter, broadcast on a Melbourne radio station, appeared to be similar to the radar/visual encounters which occurred during the Washington Flap (see page 25). The same sort of pattern was unfolding in the New Zealand case. Objects were detected on radar in Wellington and Christchurch; at the same time they were being filmed by the cameraman and witnessed by those on board the aircraft. At one stage the aircraft was being paced by the UFOs.

Two days later excerpts of the film were broadcast worldwide. Not familiar with the extent of UFO activity, the news programme was mistakenly presenting the case as the 'first ever' film of UFOs. Soon after the broadcasts, 'explanations' were coming in from the scientific community worldwide, all contradictory, none satisfactory. The leading New Zealand astronomer was 99 per cent sure that the planet Jupiter was the answer. Sir Bernard Lovell at Jodrell Bank Observatory in England, was sure the objects were meteorites. The objects refused to burn out. They kept buzzing the aircraft! An ornithologist in New Zealand held the view that the objects were mutton birds flying inland to mate. If true, they were anxious to get on with the job: the birds were out-flying the aircraft. The New Zealand Air Force explained them as reflections from squid boats although no fishing boats were in the position required to cast such reflections. A more plausible explanation would have been a formation flight of flying fish at 10,000 ft (3,048 m)!

Australasia is experiencing its share of extraordinary and fascinating phenomena and the database which follows bears out that fact. Much of the continued high profile of Australasian ufology is due to VUFORS which operates as an authoritative, highly active body adding a valuable Australasian perspective to any international study of the subject.

PAUL NORMAN, of the Victorian UFO Research Society, is one of the most active ufologists in Australia. He is a supporter of, and valued guest at, many international congresses and symposia and has contributed articles on the subject to publications all over the world.

DATABASE

NAME SUBMARINE UFO

DATE SUMMER 1942

PLACE BASS STRAIT, AUSTRALIA
MAP REF: G20

EVENT CLOSE ENCOUNTER OF THE FIRST
KIND

In the summer of 1942 a Royal Australian Air Force pilot was patrolling the Bass Strait in response to reports from local fishermen of night lights over that area. He watched as a UFO came out of the overhead cloud cover.

It was daylight, before 6 o'clock in the evening, and the pilot had good visibility. The UFO was described as shining, bronze in colour, some 150 ft (46 m) long and 50 ft (15 m) wide. On top of the UFO something like a plexiglass canopy could be seen. For a while the UFO paced the aircraft and then pulled away at remarkable speed and dived straight into the ocean.

NAME THE BEAUFORT BOMBER

DATE FEBRUARY 1944

PLACE BASS STRAIT, AUSTRALIA
MAP REF: H20

EVENT AIRCRAFT INTERFERENCE

What appears to be Australia's earliest case of vehicle interference took place in February 1944. A Royal Australian Air Force Beaufort bomber was flying at 4,500 ft (1,372 m) and almost 250 miles (400 km) per hour over the Bass Strait – the scene of so much UFO activity including the remarkable Valentich

case of 1978. The pilot reported that a large dark shadow was keeping pace with the plane just 100 ft (30 m) or so away. Something resembling exhaust appeared to come from it.

During the encounter, which lasted approximately twenty minutes, the bomber's radio and navigational instruments were knocked out. The encounter ended when the object accelerated away at speed.

As Australian researcher Bill Chalker points out, this particular type of plane 'figured heavily in the official Royal Australian Air Force list of planes that went missing without trace during World War II in the Bass Strait area – an area that was not linked to any significant enemy activity'.

NAME MARALINGA

DATE OCTOBER 1957

PLACE MARALINGA, SOUTH AUSTRALIA
MAP REF: F17

EVENT CLOSE ENCOUNTER OF THE FIRST
KIND

Maralinga in South Australia was one of the nuclear testing ranges used by the British government. Following such testing in October 1957 a Royal Air Force corporal and other servicemen stationed at the base witnessed a UFO hovering nearby. It was shiny and silver-blue with portholes along the edge of its clear metallic structure.

Investigation with the local airfields indicated that there should have been no aircraft activity in the

area at the time. Unfortunately because of the high security at the base there were no cameras available to take photographs of the object which stayed for some fifteen minutes or so before leaving.

NAME THE FATHER GILL SIGHTING

DATE 27 JUNE 1959

PLACE PAPUA NEW GUINEA
MAP REF: I11

EVENT CLOSE ENCOUNTER OF THE THIRD
KIND

June of 1959 brought a UFO 'flap' to Papua New Guinea. There were, in all, seventy-nine detailed sighting reports from Boianai, Banaira, Giwa, Menapi and Ruaba plain. The most important of these would seem to be the Boianai mission encounter of 27 June although the story most probably starts the night before.

At 6.45 p.m. on 26 June Reverend William Gill went out of the main mission to look for Venus which should have been conspicuous in the sky at the time. He saw Venus but also noticed a very bright sparkling object above it that seemed to be descending towards the mission. He called two of the mission's staff, Stephen Moi and Eric Langford and later other men from the mission joined them to witness the object.

The object was circular with a wide base. It appeared to have an upper deck with something resembling legs beneath it. A blue light was beamed up into the sky periodically and on top of the object, which appears to have been some sort of 'cabriolet' flying saucer, four

humanoid entities could be seen. Some of the witnesses reported seeing portholes around the side of the object. There were also small UFOs in the sky at the time, flying in an irregular pattern. The large object disappeared at 9.30 at tremendous speed towards Giwa.

The following night the same or a similar object was seen. Again there seemed to be four entities on the top of the saucer and Reverend Gill noticed that one of them seemed to be operating equipment somewhere in the centre of the disc but out of their line of vision. Reverend Gill stretched out his arm and waved and the figures waved back! More of the mission staff started waving and then all of the four entities waved back, astonishing the staff.

Reverend Gill used a torch to flash a series of lights at the UFO and the UFO seemed to be responding by making a pendulum-like motion waving backwards and forwards. The UFO closed in on the witnesses but after a while the entities disappeared below deck.

At 6.25 in the evening two of the entities came back on deck and seemed to be working by the light of the blue spotlight. Five minutes later, rather bored with this limited interaction, Reverend Gill decided to go in for dinner and did not come out again for half an hour by which time the UFO, though still visible, was now away in the distance.

In total, Gill and thirty-seven other witnesses at the Boianai mission saw the objects in the sky.

In 1977, Gill was specifically questioned about breaking off the sighting for dinner and stated: 'We were a bit fed up that they wouldn't come down after all the waving . . . this is the difficult thing to get across to people . . . here was a flying saucer; therefore it must have been a traumatic experience. It was nothing of the kind.'

The Australian Department of Air suggested 'Most probably they were reflections on a cloud of a major light source of unknown origin'. Such an explanation hardly seems to do justice to the sheer weight and quality of witness reports.

1960s

NAME BOUGAINVILLE REEF

DATE 28 MAY 1965

PLACE BOUGAINVILLE REEF, QUEENSLAND COAST, AUSTRALIA
MAP REF: J13

EVENT CONFISCATED FILM

In the early hours of the morning of 28 May 1965 Captain John Barker was flying an Ansett DC-6B airliner from Brisbane to New Guinea when he found he was being paced by a UFO. He described the object as oblate, with an exhaust. It was also seen by the co-pilot and stewardess.

The sighting was reported by radio to Townsville control in Queensland; Barker radioed that he was taking photographs of the UFO.

When he landed at Port Moresby, in New Guinea, Barker was instructed not to have the film developed but to return with it to Australia. On his return he was flown to Canberra where both the film and his own plane's flight recorder were confiscated.

Captain Barker's official statement includes the comment 'I had always scoffed at these reports, but I saw it. We all saw it. It was under intelligent control, and it was certainly no known aircraft'.

NAME HORSESHOE LAGOON

DATE 19 JANUARY 1966

PLACE HORSESHOE LAGOON, QUEENSLAND COAST, AUSTRALIA
MAP REF: I14

EVENT 'CORNFIELD' CIRCLES

Circles of flattened grasses are perhaps most famous for their frequent appearances in the southern counties of England. Contrary to popular mythology, in this area they are rarely linked with actual UFO sightings.

A 'landing nest' of flattened grass allegedly created by a UFO witnessed by George Pedley at Horseshoe Lagoon.

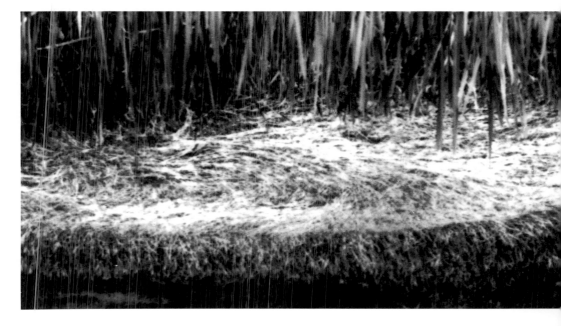

The Boianai Mission in June 1959 responded warmly with waving hands to a visitation by four humanoid entities in their 'cabriolet' flying saucer.

However, one such circle that very clearly *was* associated with a UFO sighting occurred in the swamps at Horseshoe Lagoon in Australia and was witnessed by a banana grower by the name of George Pedley.

While he was driving his tractor at 9 o'clock in the morning he suddenly heard a loud hissing noise like rushing compressed air and saw just 25 yds (23 m) ahead a blue-grey spinning UFO rising from the ground. It was approximately 25 ft (7.62 m) wide and 9 ft (2.74 m) high and when it reached a height of about 60 ft (18.3 m) it shot off at terrific speed.

On investigation Pedley discovered that under its landing, or at least hovering, site there was a circular area of flattened grasses. Other investigators to the site discovered a total of five such circles and also obtained many other reports from other witnesses who had seen the same UFO.

The precise mechanism which forms the so-called cornfield circles is not fully understood. Investigation of the mechanism in the United Kingdom by such people as Dr Terence Meaden of Tornado and Storm Research has indicated that they are caused by wind vortices; however, there are other energy forms associated which may well of course be perfectly natural. One such energy appears to be an ionization of the air which creates a glow above the area where the vortices are touching the ground; this could be the explanation for the UFO that Pedley saw, though usually it is described as red rather than blue-grey.

Australia, however, came up with a few unique suggestions of its own; birds featured heavily with species like the blue heron or the bald headed coot being blamed for the impressions on the ground. Another

theory was that the circles are the love nests of mating crocodiles. If the UFO phenomenon produces nothing else, it produces variety!

NAME GARDIN/SMITH ENCOUNTER

DATE 22 AUGUST 1968

PLACE NEAR KALGOURLIE, AUSTRALIA
MAP REF: C17

EVENT VEHICLE INTERFERENCE

I am grateful to Paul Norman for clarifying certain details of this case.

Captains W. Gardin and G. Smith flying from Adelaide to Perth on 22 August 1968 suffered electromagnetic interference when encountering a fleet of UFOs. The plane was an eight-seater Piper Navajo, flying at 8,000 ft (2,438 m) at approximately 200 knots; only the two captains were aboard. Smith was woken by Gardin and asked to come to the cockpit to confirm what he had seen.

Ahead of the plane and at approximately the same altitude was a formation of UFOs. In the centre was a large craft and around it were four or five smaller objects which seemed to have flown out of the parent craft. During the sighting the main craft broke into several sections and the whole formation appeared to be making strange interactive manoeuvres.

Kalgourlie communication centre was radioed for information but the captains were informed that there was no air traffic in the area. The captains reported the sighting and at that time the radio suffered some form of breakdown.

After approximately ten minutes the UFO formation gathered itself together 'as if at a single command' and disappeared from sight at remarkable speed; immediately following their departure radio communications came back to life.

1970s

NAME KEMPSEY, NEW SOUTH WALES

DATE 2 APRIL 1971

PLACE KEMPSEY, NEW SOUTH WALES, AUSTRALIA
MAP REF: K17

EVENT ABDUCTION?

At approximately 10 o'clock in the evening on 2 April 1971, after a spate of UFO sightings in the area, a middle-aged aborigine at Kempsey in New South Wales seems to have suffered a most incredible form of abduction. The man was in his kitchen obtaining water for a drink when he suddenly saw a small entity outside the window. He felt a sucking force which picked him up into the air and rendered him unconscious.

When he came to it appears that he had been sucked clean through the window and he was discovered cut and bruised some 7 ft (2m) away from the smashed glass. More incredibly, the window was secured by an iron bar across the middle, which had not been broken, leaving the only possible exit for the aborigine a 32 by 10 in (81 by 25.4 cm) space!

NAME MOORADUC ROAD

DATE 1972–1973

PLACE MOORADUC ROAD, NEAR MELBOURNE, AUSTRALIA
MAP REF: H19

EVENT CONTACTEE/ABDUCTION

For witness Maureen Puddy the encounter began on 5 July 1972 when she was driving between Frankston and Dromana along the Mooraduc Road, south-east of Melbourne. From above and behind her car she saw a blue light approaching, which she first took to

be a helicopter ambulance (quite commonly used in this region of wide open spaces). She stopped the car and stepped out to look, noticing no sound from the light. What she saw was incredible. A huge object approximately 100 ft (30 m) wide was hovering and completely overlapping the road at about twice the height of the telegraph poles. It was shaped like two saucers; there were no signs of welds or rivets, windows, portholes or other details and it was glowing intensely and blue. At this time Mrs Puddy noticed there was a faint humming noise though she could see no sign of movement from the object at all.

Terrified, she leapt back into the car and sped off but she noticed that no matter how fast she drove the object always maintained station exactly behind her. After 8 miles (13 km) it seemed the chase was over and Mrs Puddy noticed the object streaking away in the opposite direction.

Mrs Puddy reported the event to police, friends and family though generally speaking it was received with banter and humour and probably for this reason she decided to say nothing more about it. The 25 July 1972 was to change her mind!

On this day at more or less the same time and in the same place on the Mooraduc Road she was driving again, home to Rye after visiting her son in hospital at Heidelberg. Suddenly there was a blue light all around her car and her first reaction was 'Oh hell! Not again!'

Immediately thinking of the encounter of twenty days earlier she accelerated to get away and to her horror discovered that far from succeeding the engine of the car cut out, she lost control of her steering and the car rolled off to the verge of the road.

All around, the trees and bushes were bathed in the blue light and

VUFORS investigators Judith Magee and Paul Norman.

Mrs Puddy gripped the steering wheel in real fear. Looking upwards through the top of the windscreen of her car she could see part of the rim of the object directly above her. She began to receive messages!

A voice – in her head rather than her ears – said 'Tell the media . . . do not panic . . . we mean no harm.' It went on to say 'All your tests will be negative.' And then, 'Tell me dear comrade, do not panic, we mean no harm.' Incredibly there was a final message 'You now have control' at which time the car engine started up. Near to panic, Mrs Puddy drove quickly to the police station and in an agitated and upset condition reported her encounter. The police reported the event to the Royal Australian Air Force.

Mrs Puddy made several illuminating observations about her own sighting to the UFO researchers; she pointed out that the word 'media' was not one that she would be likely to use. She also commented that she did not know what could be meant by 'tests' since she did not have any test results.

The Royal Australian Air Force commented that they could not explain the sighting but could confirm there were no aircraft in the area at the time and, interestingly, the *Flying Saucer Review* (FSR) report states 'She was advised to remain quiet about the incident rather than chance causing panic'.

There were corroborative sightings which suggest Mrs Puddy's encounter was a very real one. A Mr Maris Ezergailis was in the south-east suburb of Melbourne, Mount Waverley, at approximately three quarters of an hour after Mrs Puddy's encounter and he states that he saw a flash of blue light travelling horizontally. Mrs Puddy herself commented on Mr Ezergailis' report 'That's the way it looked when it took off the first time I saw it'. At around the same time as Mrs Puddy's encounter another couple, a Mr and Mrs Beel, also reported seeing an unusual light 'Something unlike anything we had seen before'.

The report in *Flying Saucer Review* ends by saying that 'Mrs Puddy says she won't drive along that road again at night unless she has company'.

On 22 February 1973, following the publication of *FSR*'s report, she did again drive along that road and with most illustrious company indeed. The results were extraordinary.

Throughout that day Mrs Puddy had heard voices saying 'Maureen, come to the meeting place'. She realized that this was a further telepathic message from those who had contacted her those months ago. Mrs Puddy telephoned Judith Magee who, along with Paul Norman, agreed to meet her at 8.30 in the evening on the Mooraduc Road. They went to exactly the same place the previous events had occurred and Ms Magee, getting into Mrs Puddy's car, commented 'I was experiencing a tingling sensation like a mild electric shock. It shortly passed off'.

An extraordinary part of the encounter had already taken place. Mrs Puddy commented that she had nearly driven off the road on the way to the meeting because, as she had been driving, a gold-foil-suited entity had appeared inside her car between the two front seats and then disappeared again!

The convoy of Mrs Puddy's car (containing Mrs Puddy and Ms Magee), followed by Paul Norman in his car, arrived at the site. Paul Norman left his car and got into the back seat of Mrs Puddy's. There they discussed the materialization of the entity. Suddenly he reappeared again and Mrs Puddy in a frantic state grabbed Ms Magee and said 'There he is! Can't you see him? He is in the same clothes.' The figure was walking towards the car and had stopped by the left headlight.

There was a catch! Neither Judith Magee nor Paul Norman could see the entity though it must be stated at this stage that Ms Magee was quite certain that the agitation felt was real and that 'Maureen Puddy was not consciously fabricating . . . she was really upset'.

The entity was apparently beckoning to Mrs Puddy to follow it and even though Ms Magee offered to go with her the witness was resolute in her determination not to move and continued to tightly clasp the steering wheel. Even more extraordinary events were ahead!

Suddenly Maureen Puddy was screaming that she had been kidnapped and she was describing the inside of the UFO and shouting that she could not get out because there were no doors or windows. Throughout all of this she never left the driving seat of the car nor the sight of the two investigators but her agitation was very real. Now apparently inside the UFO, she described a mushroom-like object in the room with a jelly moving about inside it; she relaxed into an almost entranced state and then suddenly the experience was over.

This case, probably more than any other, raises questions about the true nature of abduction experiences. If Mrs Puddy had been alone then almost certainly she would have reported the event with all the clarity of a physical experience and it is only the presence of the investigators that confirms that this was not the case. On the other hand it would be too simplistic to dismiss the abduction here as purely psychological; for one thing it follows corroborated sightings and for another the witness's reaction was not one of trance throughout most of the experience. Of particular importance is the fact that this abduction is very similar to many others and we have to consider how many of those others reporting a physical presence would have been contradicted had there been corroborative witnesses to say otherwise.

In the event that we conclude that the abduction experience here, and elsewhere, was not a psychological event but an external one imposed on the witness, then a possible conclusion is that the abduction experience is more in the nature of a message being received than of a visitation.

NAME JINDABYNE

DATE 27 SEPTEMBER 1974

PLACE JINDABYNE, SNOWY MOUNTAINS, AUSTRALIA
MAP REF: 119

EVENT ABDUCTION

Two young men, one aged nineteen and the other only eleven, were hunting in the Snowy Mountains near Jindabyne when they saw a bright white light on the horizon and heard a deep humming noise.

Approximately nine years later the eleven-year-old witness, now himself a young adult, had dreams which suggested an abduction memory of that earlier time. In the dreams he recalled being drawn towards the object, floated inside and laid on a bed or table (in a manner similar to Hickson and Parker's abduction in Pascagoula, USA – see page 59).

Tall, thin, grey entities conducted some form of examination of him including measuring the electro-magnetic fields around his body. The younger witness also recalls the elder witness being drugged to prevent resistance. The witness told investigator Mark Moravec 'We were not afraid but we were not really conscious either'. They were apparently annoyed at the feeling of having been used like specimens.

On the night following their bright light sighting, saw the same light again. Part of Moravec's

investigation was to establish whether this was the same object which was seen in the first instance. If this had been established there would have been good reason for believing the UFO to be a star or planet. If this were the case then the dreams the younger witness experienced were either shielding some deeper memory or the dreams were a psychological event triggered by a mundane sighting.

NAME THE VALENTICH ENCOUNTER

DATE 21 OCTOBER 1978

PLACE BASS STRAIT, AUSTRALIA
MAP REF: H20

EVENT FATAL ENCOUNTER

In 1978 there occurred one of the largest UFO flaps in Australian history with a great number of sightings concentrated around the south-eastern quarter of the continent, and the highest concentration around the Bass Strait. On 21 October 1978 one case is made all the more interesting because of the corroboration by other witnesses and the circumstances of the witness's own report. It is unfortunately also tragic as it has almost certainly resulted in the witness's death.

At 6.19 p.m. on 21 October a young Australian pilot, Frederick Valentich, took off from Moorabbin Airport, Melbourne; he was flying to King Island, just off the coast of Victoria. His flight took him over the Bass Strait, one of the most ufologically active areas in Australia.

At 6 minutes and 14 seconds past 7 o'clock that evening Valentich (aircraft designation DSJ) radioed Flight Service (FS) with an enquiry, the consequences of which he obviously was unable to foresee at the time. What follows is the transcript of the communication

between Valentich and Flight Service from that point to just over 6 minutes later – the last time Valentich was ever heard from.

I am grateful to Paul Norman of VUFORS for supplying me, through BUFORA with the following transcript.

1906:14
DSJ *Melbourne, this is Delta Sierra Juliet. Is there any known traffic below five thousand feet (1,520 m)?*
FS *Delta Sierra Juliet, no known traffic.*
DSJ *Delta Sierra Juliet, I am, seems to be a large aircraft below five thousand.*
1906:44
FS *Delta Sierra Juliet, What type of aircraft is it?*
DSJ *Delta Sierra Juliet, I cannot affirm, it is four bright . . . it seems to me like landing lights.*
1907:00
FS *Delta Sierra Juliet.*
1907:31
DSJ *Melbourne, this is Delta Sierra Juliet, the aircraft has just passed over me at least a thousand feet above.*
FS *Delta Sierra Juliet, roger, and it is a large aircraft, confirmed?*
DSJ *Er – unknown, due to the speed it's travelling, is there any air force activity in the vicinity?*
FS *Delta Sierra Juliet, no known aircraft in the vicinity.*
1908:18
DSJ *Melbourne, it's approaching now from due east towards me.*
FS *Delta Sierra Juliet.*
1908:41
[open microphone for two seconds].
1908:48
DSJ *Delta Sierra Juliet, it seems to me that he's playing some sort of game, he's flying over me, two, three times at speeds I could not identify.*
1909:00
FS *Delta Sierra Juliet, roger, what is your actual level?*
DSJ *My level is four and a half thousand, four five zero zero.*

FS *Delta Sierra Juliet, and you confirm you cannot identify the aircraft?*
DSJ *Affirmative.*
FS *Delta Sierra Juliet, roger, stand by.*
1909:27
DSJ *Melbourne, Delta Sierra Juliet, it's not an aircraft it is* [open microphone for two seconds].
1909:42
FS *Delta Sierra Juliet, can you describe the – er – aircraft?*
DSJ *Delta Sierra Juliet, as it's flying past it's a long shape* [open microphone for three seconds] *cannot identify more than it has such speed* [open microphone for three seconds]. *It's before me right now Melbourne.*
1910:00
FS *Delta Sierra Juliet, roger and how large would the – er – object be?*
1910:19
DSJ *Delta Sierra Juliet, Melbourne, it seems like it's stationary. What I'm doing right now is orbiting and the thing is just orbiting on top of me also. It's got a green light and sort of metallic like. It's all shiny on the outside.*
FS *Delta Sierra Juliet.*
1910:46
DSJ *Delta Sierra Juliet* [open microphone for five seconds]. *It's just vanished.*
FS *Delta Sierra Juliet.*
1911:00
DSJ *Melbourne, would you know what kind of aircraft I've got? Is it a military aircraft?*
FS *Delta Sierra Juliet, confirm the – er – aircraft just vanished.*
DSJ *Say again.*
FS *Delta Sierra Juliet, is the aircraft still with you?*
DSJ *Delta Sierra Juliet, it's* [open microphone for two seconds] *now approaching from the south-west.*
FS *Delta Sierra Juliet.*
1911:50
DSJ *Delta Sierra Juliet, the engine is rough-idling, I've got it set at twenty-three twenty-four and the thing is coughing.*

A shining, green, starfish-shaped object was observed in the skies over the Bass Strait on the day that Frederick Valentich and his blue and white Cessna 182 went missing.

FS *Delta Sierra Juliet, roger, what are your intentions?*
DSJ *My intentions are – ah – to go to King Island – ah – Melbourne. That strange aircraft is hovering on top of me again,* [open microphone for two seconds]. *It is hovering and it's not an aircraft.*
FS *Delta Sierra Juliet.*
DSJ *Delta Sierra Juliet, Melbourne* [open microphone for seventeen seconds].
[No official conclusion has been given for the strange sound which was heard that interrupted the pilot's last statement].

Neither Valentich nor his blue and white Cessna 182 have ever been heard from again.

This was a case which brought UFOs 'into the open' as far as the Royal Australian Air Force were concerned. They made the request of a UFO witness that he be interviewed by the press in the hopes of encouraging other witnesses to come forward, so concerned were they to investigate the pilot's last minutes. There was other official activity; the Forestry Commission requested fire lookouts to report UFOs, police officers interviewed UFO witnesses and aircraft pilots were asked to notify their traffic controllers of any unusual object in the sky.

VUFORS is based at Moorabbin and was ideally placed to follow up this most important investigation; immediately it did so. They uncovered no less than twenty people at different points around the Bass Strait who were reporting a green light in the same location and in the same time-frame that Valentich was describing his contact with the green light or object.

One most interesting report came from a bank manager and his wife who were driving near Melbourne and observed, over the

Frederick Valentich.

Bass Strait, a green lit starfish-shaped object, which could well have been the object Valentich was reporting. Indeed for several days VUFORS was flooded with reports from around the Bass Strait area confirming if nothing else that something was in the sky on the evening of Valentich's disappearance – a something not just mysterious enough to cause puzzlement in witnesses but also to cause sufficient puzzlement and curiosity to make them need to report what they had seen.

The other reports suggest that a truly external event had played a major part in the case. Some abductions and indeed even more mundane UFO reports are uncorroborated or there are very good reasons for believing they are mostly an internal, self-generated reaction to mundane stimuli. Many cases certainly have no corroboration where there ought to be some. But cases such as Valentich's prove beyond doubt that there is a hard core of objective reality in the subject of UFOs, which must be resolved, if not just for curiosity's sake but also to put the

spirit of Valentich to rest, wherever he now is.

There have been rumours, some dubious, surrounding Valentich's present whereabouts; one suggested that he crashed into the Bass Strait and that the Cessna was on the seabed. The claim came from divers who stated they had taken sixteen photographs and were offering them for 10,000 Australian dollars. There were few takers for this offer although a potential salvage operation was suggested. It has come to nothing and is generally regarded as a hoax.

A second story even had Valentich alive and working at a gas station in Tasmania. This seems to be a not uncommon reaction among those who try to involve themselves in any major event and is in the same league as suggesting that Elvis Presley is still alive or that half a dozen gunmen were responsible for shooting President Kennedy. In truth, it is highly likely that Valentich's whereabouts are not known with any certainty by anyone.

The official reaction to the case reveals elements of a cover-up. Bill Chalker who has been given access to the Royal Australian Air Force UFO files found that this particular case was not among their number. It was eventually explained to him that the Valentich case was listed as an 'air accident investigation' rather than a UFO case, therefore not coming within the framework of what they were prepared to allow him to see.

Of the air accident investigation report two rather obvious statements conclude the matter as far as the official line goes:
1. Degree of injury – 'presumed fatal'.
2. Opinion as to cause – 'The reason for the disappearance of the aircraft has not been determined'.

NAME THE KAIKOURA CONTROVERSY

DATE DECEMBER 1978

PLACE KAIKOURA, NEW ZEALAND
MAP REF: P21

EVENT DISTANT SIGHTING

On 31 December 1978 a film crew hired by Channel O of Melbourne filmed a UFO during its flight over the Kaikoura area of New Zealand.

On 21 December 1978 Captain Vern Powell and Captain John Randle in an Argosy cargo aircraft were flying from Blenheim to Christchurch and then on to Duneden when they made a number of radar and visual sightings.

On 31 December 1978 Channel O in Melbourne chartered an Argosy plane in order to retrace the first Argosy's flight path. This was not, it must be stressed, to search for UFOs but to obtain background material for their report on the earlier sighting. Channel O's reporter, Quentin Fogarty, (who was on holiday in New Zealand at the time) was asked to undertake the investigation; the plane was crewed by pilot Bill Startup and co-pilot Robert Guard. The film crew consisted of Fogarty along with David Crockett and his wife Ngaire. The first Argosy took off at 11.46 p.m. from Wellington airport on 30 December 1978.

Less than 25 minutes later at 12.10 a.m. (now 31 December 1978) the film crew were in the loading bay filming background material, the plane was flying at 117 knots at 10,000 ft (3,048 m) and suddenly Startup and Guard spotted lights in the direction of Kaikoura. They radioed Wellington control and requested information and were told 'There are targets in your 10 o'clock position at 13 miles (21 km) appearing and disappearing; not showing at present, but they were a minute ago.' For a while after that

Wellington radar reported a series of targets up to 4 miles (6.4 km) from the plane.

At 12.22 a.m. Wellington radar reported another target and the Argosy confirmed a visual sighting saying 'It's got a flashing light'. Crockett took twelve seconds of film showing bright oval blue-white images and then a further five seconds of film showing horizontal lights flashing on and off. Four minutes later, before switching frequencies to join Christchurch air traffic control, Wellington confirmed that the targets were now behind the Argosy. Throughout the remainder of the flight various targets were visually spotted and confirmed on radar. The plane landed shortly after 1 o'clock in the morning

At just gone a quarter past two in the morning the Argosy took off again flying back to Blenheim to obtain more film footage.

Thirty-two miles (51 km) out of Christchurch a huge target was reported in the 3 o'clock position some 12 miles (19 km) from the plane but unfortunately Wellington radar was too distant to pick up the return. Film footage showed oval shaped objects with rings of light. 'A sort of bell shape with bright bottoms and less bright tops.'

At 2.51 a.m., 7 ft (213 cm) of film was taken showing further bright lights. At 3.10 a.m. the plane landed at Blenheim.

There have been endless suggestions as to what was being filmed: Venus, Jupiter, weather phenomena, wave reflections, Japanese squid boats, birds reflecting light, bubbles of pollution and so on. No final conclusion has ever been drawn.

Alleged UFO photographed from an aircraft over Kaikoura, New Zealand, in 1978.

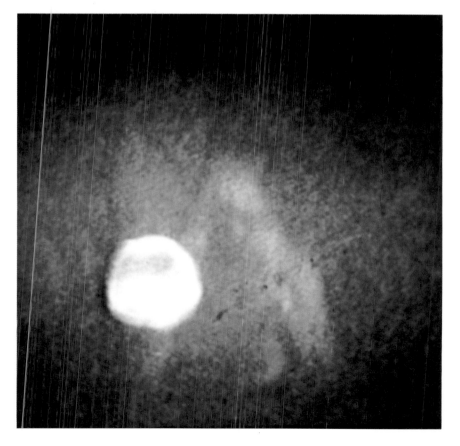

1980s

NAME NULLARBOR PLAIN

DATE 21 JANUARY 1988

PLACE NULLARBOR PLAIN, WESTERN
AUSTRALIA
MAP REF: E18

EVENT VEHICLE INTERFERENCE

I am indebted to Paul Norman of VUFORS for sending me details of his report into this incident.

The mother and three sons of the Knowles family from Perth were driving towards Mundrabilla when they saw lights ahead of them. As they were in the outback they realised these could be no ordinary street lights. Just a quarter of an hour before the lights were seen the car radio had begun malfunctioning.

As the car got closer to the 'lights' it became obvious that it was in fact one strangely glowing light hovering above the ground just off the side of the highway. In fact they seemed to be seeing a light that was hovering over another vehicle and they had to swerve to avoid a

collision. Sean, the son that had been driving, made a U-turn and chased the light which in due course changed its course and headed back towards the Knowles' own car. Sean turned again but this time the object sped up to the car and landed on its roof with an audible thump.

The car seemed to be being dragged upwards and the family was unsure what course of action to take. The two dogs in the car became very agitated and one of the sons, Patrick, said he felt as though his brains were pulled from his head. In fact the family did not really realize that the car was in the air until it dropped back to the ground bursting one of its tyres. Incredibly, while the object had been attached to the roof, the mother, Faye, had rolled down the window and reached up and touched the object which felt warm and spongy, possibly a suction pad. If the description is accurate,

The Knowles's family car, complete with burst tyre, being examined by investigators from VUFORS following a close encounter on the Nullarbor Plain.

then this is the most crude form of abduction we have yet seen.

Dust surrounded the car and came in through an open window and there was a smell like decomposing bodies. One of the sons, Sean, stated that he had missed some of the details as he had 'gone out cold' at one stage. Once back on the ground Sean stopped the car and the family jumped out and hid in the bushes along the side of the highway until the UFO was gone.

From outside, they described the object as a white light approximately the same size as the car with a yellow centre and making a sound like electrical humming. The family changed the tyre and drove on to Mundrabilla where they discussed the experience with truck drivers.

Paul Norman and a colleague investigated the radio and found that it was now operating perfectly even though it had been malfunctioning during the encounter. On the roof of the car they found an indentation matching the description given by the family. Of the tyre, it was in good condition and should not have blown but in fact was ripped all the way round its edge.

Laboratory analysis of the dust revealed oxygen, carbon, calcium, silicon, potassium and other traces and a possible trace of astatine which is a radioactive chemical that can only be produced synthetically. However, the half life of astatine is only a few hours and any normal isotope of this element would have deteriorated before the investigation was under way.

Investigation by VUFORS revealed that there were other UFO reports around the Nullarbor plain on the night of the encounter. Paul Norman's comment on this case remains level-headed. 'Before we know what is happening, there are more reports to check out and much more research remains to be done'.

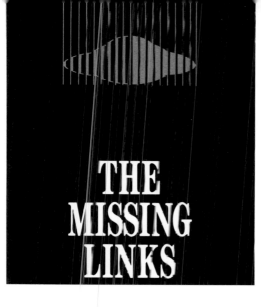

THE MISSING LINKS

ustralasia, the Asian islands, New Zealand and principally Australia, is a ufologically rich part of the world. The introduction by one of its most active researchers – Paul Norman of VUFORS – and the database itself gives a good idea of the variety of the reports coming from that area of the world, and of the importance of such cases as Father Gill, the Valentich case and the Mooraduc Road case; all of which have been most thoroughly investigated.

I would like to concentrate my summary of this continent on what is *not* there. What is missing from Australia in particular is of great importance to researchers who seek an overall understanding of the phenomenon on a global basis. Why, for example, does Australia have no crash retrieval cases? It is certainly reasonable to expect them given the availability of wide open spaces, good lines of communication and good researchers. The country even has military and space programme installations. All of these components exist in Australia as they do in North America. Yet 'aliens' (to take the classic line)

clumsily drop saucers all over North America – at the last count there could be as many as forty saucers and over a hundred alien cadavers stored for examination there – yet they never get clumsy over Australia. (The absence of crash retrieval cases in South America and Africa is more understandable given the size of the continents, the meagre scattering of researchers, and poor communications.) So why is this type of phenomenon absent from Australia? Is it a factor of the people, the researchers, or the phenomenon itself? If it is a factor of the phenomenon itself then one could reach a bizarre conclusion: they drop saucers in the United States because they want them to be found there!

Until we can understand the answer to that question then no real understanding of UFOs is possible; we may still be a long way from a real perspective that will allow us to appreciate the truth. A study of the development of Australian ufology in comparison with other areas of the world will provide some of the pieces necessary to complete the jig-saw.

Ayers Rock, a mysterious but much admired feature in this land of vast open spaces.

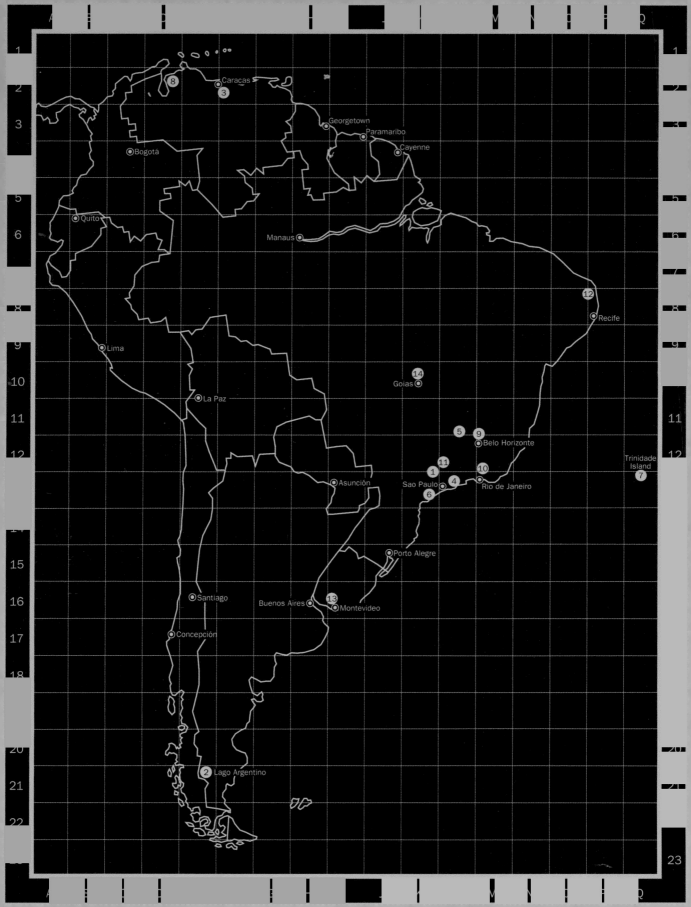

SOUTH AMERICA

WITH THE DEVELOPMENT OF RESEARCH,

ESPECIALLY IN BRAZIL, ARGENTINA AND CHILE,

PEOPLE HAVE BECOME AWARE THAT THEY

SHOULD CALL A UFOLOGIST WHEN THEY NOTICE

SOMETHING UNUSUAL IN THE SKY.

KEY TO MAP OF SOUTH AMERICA

① Baurú, Brazil
② Lego Argentino, Argentina
③ Caracas, Venezuela
④ Ubatuba, Brazil
⑤ Antonio Villas Boas, Minas Geraes, Brazil
⑥ The Fort Itaipu Attack, Fort Itaipu, Brazil
⑦ Trindade Island photographs, Trindade Island, Atlantic Ocean

⑧ Lake Maracaibo, Santa Rita, Venezuela
⑨ Familia Sagrada, Belo Horizonte, Brazil
⑩ The Niteroi Deaths, Rio de Janeiro, Brazil
⑪ Bebedouro, North of Belo Horizonte, Brazil
⑫ The Bananeiras Bus, Bananeiras, Brazil
⑬ Isla de Lobos, Uruguay
⑭ Elias Seixas Abduction, Conceiçao de Araguaia, Goias, Brazil

THE SOUTH AMERICAN VIEWPOINT

South America is such a large continent (Brazil is, itself, the size of a continent) that it is hazardous to offer generalizations on any one subject. Nonetheless, UFOs are a common phenomenon around the world, and close encounters of all kinds are basically the same here as they are throughout the rest of the world.

However, here the 'grays', which are the more alien-looking aliens known in North America and to some extent in Europe, are less frequently met. In the cases I have investigated, entities, even when they involve smaller beings, have not behaved in a hostile manner. Many are very human looking, and some are taller than humans. To take for example the Elias Seixas Abduction (see page 188), a human being's semen was forcibly extracted, yet the abductee has no ill feelings about this. He sees the positive side of his UFO experience. Generally, we feel that it is the human being's personal attitude towards his captors that is important.

With the development of research, especially in Brazil, Argentina and Chile, people have become aware that they should call a ufologist when they notice something unusual in the sky. In the past they only called the national astronomical observatories, or the control towers at airports, always obtaining the same reply, 'You must have seen a meteorological balloon'. (Official astronomers seem to have no imagination – why do they never say anything else when they wish to debunk a sighting, are they complying with orders they have received?)

On one occasion, however, they were not involved. On 19 May 1986, radar screens were saturated with lights (which were also observed visually) and echoes, first in Sao José dos Campos, then Brasilia and the Santa Cruz Air Base in Rio de Janeiro. This caused confusion in the air traffic

South America is rich in cultural history and images of ancient gods like these on Easter Island. Some see in these figures the reflection of ancient astronauts . . .

controls, so FE Mirage jets were scrambled by the Air Force to intercept the UFOs. Finally the Air Minister himself, Brigadier Octavio Moreira Lima came forward on TV and stated that UFOs had been observed and promised to give a full report within two months. He did not keep his word, obviously pressure was brought to bear, but by whom?

On TV two or three days later the Brigadier presented all the pilots and air traffic controllers, ten altogether – who had participated in this unearthly 'hunt'. All had watched the lights, none were able to intercept them, their speed having been beyond 930 miles (1,500 km) per hour. Another interested witness was Ozires Silva, then taking up his post as President of PETROBRAS, who was travelling in his private plane, when he witnessed the UFO. He has now just been appointed Minister of Infrastructure in the new Collor government, so ufologists have hopes for a more open attitude on the subject.

We have good ufologists in Brazil. One of them, Engineer Claudeir Covo, interviewed all the pilots, studied every facet of the case, and published his findings. Captain Basilio Baranoff, of Sao José dos Campos, who works at Technological Aeronautics Institute (I.T.A.), also compiled a very extensive, detailed report. I myself gathered a collection of over thirty reports of lights seen in the sky on, or around the 19–20 May, some of which were very interesting and implied close encounters. This was published by the review *UFO*. Then Fabio Zerpa, President of ONIFE, Buenos Aires, brought out a complete monograph on the subject, after he too visited Brazil and met some of the witnesses. This, for him, was a follow up to a similar UFO flyover the preceding year in Argentina. Chile also contributed its share – Eugenio Bahamonde of Ponta Arenas told me how UFOs had flown over his country at that time.

As to the true extent of UFOs, well documented cases such as the one above do much to enlighten the population, especially people with enquiring minds.

Multiple-witness sightings are important as at times they involve thousands of spectators, however, *abductions* are far more interesting and more frequent than imagined by even a keen ufologist.

Several really outstanding cases have come my way, others were first examined by colleagues in Brazil. Argentina and Chile have their share of them too, though I know less about Uruguay, Bolivia, Paraguay and other smaller countries in South America for lack of sufficient data. However, in Colombia there is the famous Engineer Rincon case, 1973, which has a wealth of interesting data. This engineer,

with his own UFO group, received a message in which he was told to meet extra-terrestrials at a certain place and date. He complied, and found a metallic sphere on his way that led him to the meeting place. There he met several extra-terrestrials who had landed in a UFO. He had met one of them before, here on Earth. There is a similarity here with the South African case of Edwin, who met 'George' (see page 147), as described in Cynthia Hind's *African Encounters* and in *Koldas* by C. Van Vlierden and W. Stevens.

In Brazil we also accept the contactee as part of the picture and give their cases as much care as the nuts-and-bolts accounts. As to what *interpretation* is given them, that is the researcher's responsibility.

Ufologists – in South America as in the rest of the world – have different attitudes according to their outlook and belief systems. On the one hand we have 'advanced ufology', which is mystical, yet well-rooted in culture and folklore. We also have the die-hard scientific ufologists, who discard all but scientific data. Finally there are those, like myself, who are deeply interested in the esoteric and spiritual aspects of ufology, yet work on a data-gathering basis, with a view towards future communication with our extra-terrestrial visitors. Brazilians are interested in alternative culture, which includes healing and homeopathy, chromotherapy, astrology, para-psychology and so on, and includes ufology. I know that Europeans do not accept such a seemingly hybrid combination – but if they lived here, perhaps they would. The situation in Argentina is much the same as here. In Argentina, Fabio Zerpa published *Cuarta Dimension*, which has been in existence for the past thirty-one years. In Brazil, I was editor of the first scientifically oriented UFO review which closed down in 1980. Now for the past few years we have had *UFO*, edited by Gevaerd in Mato Crosso do Sul, and *Planeta*, published in Sao Paulo, that intermittently features information about UFOs.

I believe the difficulties for ufology are the same everywhere in the world, but I am also sure that persistence will break down all barriers.

IRENE GRANCHI is one of the most respected ufologists on the South American continent, and has been an active researcher for many years. She is president of CISNE, the Centro de Investigacoes Sobre a Natureza dos Extra-Terrestres. She has been involved in most of the major cases on that continent, she is a regular contributor to UFO literature and a valued speaker at many symposia.

DATABASE

1940s

NAME BAURÚ, BRAZIL

DATE 23 JULY 1947

PLACE BAURÚ, BRAZIL
MAP REF: K13

EVENT CLOSE ENCOUNTER OF THE THIRD
KIND

On 23 July 1947 José Higgins was one of a group of workers who witnessed the landing of a 150 ft (46 m) wide grey-white flying saucer at Baurú in the state of Sao Paulo, Brazil. Higgins was left alone when the other workmen fled the area and he was confronted by three entities about 7 ft (213 cm) tall wearing inflated transparent suits and carrying boxes on their backs. Their clothing, visible through the suits, appeared to be made of brightly coloured paper. All the entities had large rounded bald heads, huge eyes, no eyebrows and long legs. Oddly, Higgins found them beautiful.

They seemed to be trying to lure him into the saucer but he eluded them. He hid in some bushes and then, amazingly, watched them appear to play. They spent half an hour leaping and jumping and tossing huge stones. Eventually they re-entered the craft and it vanished towards the north. At one point they had drawn what Higgins took to be a map of the solar system which seemed to indicate that they had come from Uranus.

Of particular interest was the distinct rim around the edge of the flying saucer which gave it a 'Saturn-shape' (see Trindade Island photographs incident page 185).

1950s

NAME LEGO ARGENTINO

DATE 18 MARCH 1950

PLACE LEGO ARGENTINO, ARGENTINA
MAP REF: E21

EVENT CLOSE ENCOUNTER OF THE THIRD
KIND

In the early evening of 18 March 1950 rancher Wilfredo Arévalo witnessed the landing of a flying saucer while a second companion saucer hovered overhead, as if guarding the first. Arévalo walked to within 400 ft (120 m) of the craft noticing an intense smell 'like burning benzine'. The craft was giving off a blue vapour through which Arévalo could see that the surface of it seemed to be made of something like aluminium.

Even when it landed, part of the disc remained revolving 'like a gramophone record'. In the glass cabin Arévalo could see four tall, well shaped men dressed in something like cellophane.

The men shone a search light at Arévalo then the craft took off, leaving an area of burnt grass later confirmed by other ranchers.

NAME CARACAS

DATE 28 NOVEMBER 1954

PLACE CARACAS, VENEZUELA
MAP REF: F2

EVENT CLOSE ENCOUNTER OF THE THIRD
KIND

In the early hours of 28 November 1954 Gustavo Gonzalez and José Ponce were driving a van in the suburbs of the Venezuelan capital. They stopped when they saw a glowing globe some 10 ft (3 m) wide hovering over the road.

What was to follow is a most unusual contact claim. Gonzalez ended up brawling with a hairy, dwarf like entity which was wearing a loin-cloth, had glowing eyes and displayed deceptive strength. Although it was very light, it was able to knock Gonzalez some 15 ft (4.5 m) without any obvious effort. The brawling ended when another creature from inside the globe blinded Gonzalez with a ray from a tube he was carrying. Ponce, in the meantime, watched creatures carry soil and rocks into the globe after marching out from nearby bushes.

Gonzalez had a long scar on his side from the fight and the two men were placed under medical observation for a few days. It was first assumed that the men must have been drunk but later one of the doctors treating them admitted that he accepted their story because on driving back from a night time call he had actually seen the fight with the entities! The doctor was apparently sufficiently curious to take up discussion of the case with American authorities in Washington.

NAME UBATUBA

DATE SEPTEMBER 1957

PLACE UBATUBA, BRAZIL
MAP REF: L13

EVENT CRASH RETRIEVAL

Reports from Ubatuba, Brazil in September 1957 indicated that a flying saucer had approached

fishermen who had then seen it explode, scattering material everywhere. There was some doubt about the authenticity of the claim as the exposure was through a newspaper columnist, and the fishermen were never available for questioning.

It was thought that they might have been asked to remain silent by the government.

Some of the alleged material was recovered and analyzed; the analysis indicated that it was a pure magnesium, of a purity beyond the capabilities of our own metallurgical processes, therefore indicating an extra-terrestrial origin. Clearly this may be overstating the case though it is interesting that in Ashland, Nebraska when patrolman Schirmer was abducted (see page 54) he was told that the flying saucers were made from 100 per cent pure magnesium. Various inconclusive tests were carried out, and at the present time it is believed that all the recovered material has now been either used up or lost.

The Ubatuba retrieval has become a great debating point for ufologists seeking either support for, or denial of, the Extra-terrestrial Hypothesis. Unfortunately it is one of those cases about which far more is written than is known.

NAME ANTONIO VILLAS BOAS

DATE 15 OCTOBER 1957

PLACE MINAS GERAES, BRAZIL
MAP REF: L11

EVENT ABDUCTION

The most extraordinary and now famous case of Antonio Villas Boas actually started in the first week of October 1957. Villas Boas and his brother Joao saw a brilliant beam of light coming from the sky as they looked through their bedroom window. It seemed to scan their home but they could not see its source.

On 14 October around 10 o'clock in the evening, Villas Boas and his brother were ploughing the family's fields. In the high temperatures of Brazil it is customary for the land-owning class to work through the night and employ labourers to work during the hot daytime hours. They saw a ball of red light, which was too brilliant to look at directly, hovering approximately 300 ft (92 m) above their field. Villas Boas asked his brother to accompany him to investigate the light but his brother refused so he went alone.

As he approached the light, it evaded him at high speed and for some time Villas Boas chased it back and forth across the field. He gave up after approximately twenty attempts to catch up with the UFO and returned to his brother. They watched as it remained around for a short while, sending intermittent rays in random directions.

On the following night Villas Boas was ploughing alone and shortly after midnight he saw the red ball again. Although still hovering at some 300 ft (92 m) he got close enough to see that it contained a bright oval shaped object. Perhaps because of its closeness, Villas Boas lost his enthusiasm of the previous night to catch up with the object and considered making a getaway in his tractor. He was not successful!

The object landed some 40 ft (12 m) in front of him on three metallic legs; it was an egg-shaped craft with a rotating dome.

Villas Boas left the tractor and ran but was chased by five entities and overcome. They carried him aboard. The entities wore grey tight-fitting suits and helmets which revealed only their small blue eyes. From the helmets, tubes ran into their clothes at the back and sides.

Villas Boas found himself in a small room with polished metal walls, brightly lit and with no visible signs of the door he had entered through. Eventually his captors led him through several rooms to one in which they forcibly undressed him. Curiously at the time, but perhaps understandable with hindsight, one of the entities spread a thick, transparent liquid over his skin and then he was taken into a small room where a blood sample was taken from him. This operation left a scar which investigators verified in the subsequent investigation.

For over half an hour Villas Boas was left alone in a virtually featureless room sitting on a kind of couch bed. He noticed pipes in the walls from which small puffs of smoke were spreading, the smell of which made him feel sick; indeed he vomited in one corner of the room.

After half an hour had passed Villas Boas was treated to an extraordinary twist which took his experience beyond the realms of the usual abduction phenomenon. His solitude was broken by the arrival of another alien. 'Her body was much more beautiful than any I have ever seen before. It was slim, and her breasts stood up high and well separated. Her waistline was thin, her belly flat, her hips well developed, and her thighs were large.' This new distracting arrival was a human-like naked woman with blonde hair, pale skin, large blue slanted eyes, reduced lips, nose, ears and high flat cheekbones that gave the impression of a sharply pointed chin. She was short and came towards Villas Boas in silence.

As Villas Boas later put it, she was 'looking at me all the while as if she wanted something from me'. She certainly did! She hugged Villas Boas and rubbed her face and body against his. In the circumstances,

Villas Boas's solitude was broken by the arrival of a naked, humanoid alien whose body he described as 'more beautiful than any I have ever seen before'. She approached in silence.

any lack of interest from Villas Boas would have been quite understandable but in fact he became excited by the contact, responding to her touch with enthusiasm. He later considered that the liquid spread over him may have been a sexual stimulant.

The embrace ended on the couch where the couple had a normal act of sexual intercourse which Villas Boas found exciting and pleasing. She reacted as any healthy woman would with one slight exception: she never kissed him (though she did bite him softly on the chin). She also had a somewhat disconcerting habit of growling and barking occasionally.

Later, Villas Boas was to understand that they wanted him only for breeding stock which made him somewhat angry and if that was the case then presumably the object of the exercise had already been achieved. However, unfulfilled in some capacity or the other the woman did not stop at this point but continued petting, arousing Villas Boas to a further successful act of sexual intercourse. It was after the second act that she apparently became frigid and withdrawn and it was then that he realized he had been used, which caused him, too, to become frigid.

In an interview twenty-one years later Villas Boas added one detail to the encounter which had not hitherto been revealed. After this second act of sexual intercourse the woman also extracted a sperm sample from him which he assumes was preserved for later use.

Before she left him the woman pointed at her belly and then at the sky. Villas Boas said 'I interpreted the sign as meaning to say that she intended to return and take me with her to wherever it was that she lived. That is why I still feel afraid; if they came back to fetch me, I'd be lost.' Researchers have also interpreted this gesture as a sign that she would be taking his seed back and a child would be born.

Villas Boas was allowed to dress and was given a tour of the craft during which time he attempted to steal one of the instruments as a proof of his experience; one of the aliens caught him and took the object from him. Rather brusquely he was turfed off the craft and left in a field to watch the object take off at astonishing speed. Villas Boas had spent over four hours on board.

Later, medical examination revealed a scar where the blood sample had been taken and what may have been radioactive burning on parts of his skin. Top Brazilian researcher Mrs Irene Granchi spoke to Villas Boas's wife, Marlena, at the time and asked her how she felt about the possibility of her husband having an extra-terrestrial offspring. She said she did not mind and indeed was rather proud of the idea.

The case has attracted considerable speculation, the most obvious of which was the suggestion that Villas Boas was subject to an erotic fantasy.

Whatever the reality, Villas Boas never retracted his claims despite being annoyed at the way his experience had been exploited by the media (the encounter has even been the subject of a French comic strip) and throughout his life his recall was never contradictory.

NAME THE FORT ITAIPU ATTACK

DATE 4 NOVEMBER 1957

PLACE FORT ITAIPU, BRAZIL
      MAP REF: K13

EVENT POSSIBLE UFO ATTACK

Evidence of possible hostility on the part of UFO occupants comes from a remarkable case that occurred in Brazil in 1957.

At approximately 2 o'clock in the morning two guards at Fort Itaipu saw a bright light above them; they thought they had seen a nova, or exploding star. Quickly they realized that they were looking at an object descending directly towards them at rapid speed. About 1,000 ft (304 m) above them the UFO reduced speed and descended slowly to a height of approximately 150 ft (46 m).

The guards were able to see that inside the constant orange glow the object was circular, some 100 ft (30 m) wide and appeared to be under intelligent control. Although both guards were armed with powerful submachine guns, neither made any aggressive gesture towards the UFO. The UFO, however, appears to have made one towards them.

The guards heard a humming, generator type sound and were then hit by a sudden blistering heat. There was no flame or visible ray but an instant overwhelming feeling of burning and it seemed to the guards that their bodies were actually on fire.

The screams of the guards alerted other troops but, before they could organize themselves, a power failure plunged the base into darkness. Shortly afterwards, when the heat disappeared and the power came back on, the soldiers saw the glowing UFO as it streaked away into the sky. The unfortunate guards were in a serious condition and required considerable medical attention for their burns.

Brazilian military officials were so concerned that a request was made to the United States for assistance and officially the case has never been closed. There is a question that has never been answered: were the guards the unfortunate victims of a backlash of power emission from the UFO or where they the target of an attack by it?

NAME TRINDADE ISLAND PHOTOGRAPHS

DATE 16 JANUARY 1958

PLACE TRINDADE ISLAND, ATLANTIC OCEAN
MAP REF: Q13

EVENT CLOSE ENCOUNTER OF THE FIRST
KIND/PHOTOGRAPHIC CASE

'A flying saucer sighting would be unlikely at the very barren island of Trindade, as everyone knows Martians are extremely comfort loving creatures.' The above comment might well have been written for a tabloid newspaper. In fact, it was part of an official report by the U.S. Navy attaché on a photographic case involving forty-eight witnesses.

The ship *Almirante Saldanha* of the Hydrographic and Navigation Service of the Brazilian Navy was anchored in Trindade Island on 16 January 1958 preparing to sail to Rio de Janeiro. Trindade Island is approximately 750 miles (12,070 km) from the Brazilian coast.

Apart from the ship's normal crew complement there was also a team of divers on board who had been taking underwater photographs around the island. They included the principal witness, Almiro Barauna, a professional photographer. At the time the UFOs approached the island there were around forty-eight witnesses on the deck watching the incident. Below deck the captain, Carlos Alberto Bacellar, was unaware of events.

As preparations were made to get underway, Barauna was getting ready to take photographs of the ship-to-shore transfer boat and was at the time feeling unwell not having taken the seasickness pills he customarily took. At just after noon a bright object was suddenly seen approaching the island and in the general mêlée several people shouted to Barauna as if to indicate that he should photograph it.

Barauna took six photographs within a fifteen second time span; the first two as the object approached the island, the third as it emerged from behind Desegado Mountain, two photographs that missed the object and a sixth photograph was taken as the object was moving away.

Despite the brief duration of the sighting the case has become one of the most famous and the photographs have been perhaps the most widely published in UFO history. The object in the photographs appears to be a flattened globe surrounded by a central ring not unlike the planet Saturn. The image is hazy, which may reflect the characteristics of a camera, but witnesses confirmed that the object was 'blurred'.

Captain Bacellar took immediate steps to safeguard the authenticity of the film Barauna had taken. He insisted that it be developed immediately in a washroom which was converted to a darkroom on the spot. As an extra precaution Bacellar insisted that Barauna, before going into the darkroom, should strip to his swimming trunks in order to make it impossible for

UFO photographed over Trindade Island on 16 January 1958.

him to conceal a previously developed film and thereby produce any kind of hoax photograph. This indicates the degree of seriousness which followed the event.

The Brazilian Navy undertook photographic analysis of the film and it was pronounced genuine. Indeed, the photographs were released to the Press by none other than Mr Juscelino Kubitschek, the President of Brazil. Subsequent investigation revealed that there had been at least seven other sightings between the end of 1957 and early 1958, witnesses to these included Captain Bacellar.

The Brazilian government appears to have been very open about the photographs although it did not make all details of its own investigation public. They seem to accept that an unknown object was observed over Trindade Island by the witnesses. The paragraph with which this section opened, by the US Naval attaché in Rio, hardly seems respectful in view of the Brazilian government's own sensible appraisal of the situation.

1960s

NAME LAKE MARACAIBO

DATE 6 OCTOBER 1961

PLACE SANTA RITA, VENEZUELA
MAP REF: D2

EVENT CLOSE ENCOUNTER OF THE FIRST
KIND

Panic caused by the close approach of UFOs can sometimes have tragic consequences. On the night of 6 October 1961 a large UFO flew low over the town of Santa Rita, Venezuela, its radiance apparently lighting up the entire town. It moved slowly over the nearby Lake Maracaibo causing considerable panic. Most of the fishermen leapt overboard and swam ashore but sadly Bartolme Romero, drowned.

NAME FAMILIA SAGRADA

DATE 28 AUGUST 1963

PLACE FAMILIA SAGRADA, BELO HORIZONTE,
BRAZIL
MAP REF: M11

EVENT CLOSE ENCOUNTER OF THE THIRD
KIND

One of the most striking features of South American humanoid reports is their incredible variety. In this case, the description of the entities appears quite unique.

The witnesses to the event were three boys aged about twelve who were playing in the garden when they saw a large, transparent, glowing globe with four entities inside. One of the entities descended on a beam of light.

All of the entities were tall, around 7 ft (213 cm), and were wearing brown 'divers' suits' and high black boots. Their heads were round and bald and they wore transparent helmets. They had no ears or nose, a 'strange mouth', a vivid red complexion and only one large brown eye.

One of the boys tried to throw a brick at one of the entities but was prevented from doing so by a beam fired from the entity's chest which paralyzed the boy's arm. The boys were left unharmed as the sphere floated back into the sky.

NAME THE NITEROI DEATHS

DATE 20 AUGUST 1966

PLACE NITEROI, RIO DE JANEIRO, BRAZIL
MAP REF: M12

EVENT UNEXPLAINED DEATHS/UFO CONTACT

Late in the evening of 20 August 1966 police at Niteroi, a suburb of Rio de Janeiro, received a report from a woman that a UFO had landed on a nearby hillside. Police climbed the hill on a routine, and probably light-hearted, survey.

Near the top of the hill lay the bodies of two men, their faces covered with lead masks. A note was found with the bodies reading 'At 4.30 p.m. we will take the capsule. After the effect is produced, protect half the face with lead masks. Wait for agreed signal.' It has been suggested that the men were preparing to make contact with the the UFO occupants and if so it was a contact that went badly wrong.

Laboratory tests on the bodies indicated no clue as to the cause of death and stated only that there was no medical reason 'Our lab men have ruled out the possibility of poison, violence or asphyxiation'.

No official connection between the deaths and the UFO sighting has been admitted to, but the Brazilian press suggested a modification to the usual official conclusion in such cases (death caused by person or persons unknown) and suggested instead 'death caused by beings or persons from the unknown'.

NAME BEBEDOURO

DATE 4 MAY 1969

PLACE BEBEDOURO, NORTH OF BELO
HORIZONTE, BRAZIL
MAP REF: L12

EVENT ABDUCTION

On a sunny afternoon in May 1969 Brazilian soldier José Antonio da Silva became the target of a most extraordinary UFO abduction.

Da Silva was fishing when at approximately 3 o'clock in the afternoon he was aware of figures moving behind him. Suddenly he saw a beam of light which hit him in the legs and caused a paralysis, bringing him to his knees.

He was seized and dragged away by the two entities that had closed in on him; they were approximately 4 ft (122 cm) tall, wearing dull silver suits, their heads covered by metallic helmets.

The entities dragged him to a craft described as being a tall cylinder with a saucer on top and bottom, standing upright. The device was apparently 6 ft (183 cm) high and 8 ft (244 cm) wide.

Da Silva and the entities were secured to the seats and a sensation of movement combined with a humming sound indicated to da Silva that the craft had taken off. They landed and, blindfolded, da Silva was dragged from the craft into what appeared to be a different room. When the blindfold was removed the beings had removed their spacesuits and stood before him. They were stockily built, had long beards and wavy red hair falling down to below their waist. Their faces appeared almost troll-like with big noses, bushy eyebrows, large ears and toothless mouths. Their eyes were a shade of green.

On a wide bench in the room with them were the dead bodies of four humans and da Silva speculated that

this may have been designed to encourage his compliance.

The entities searched through da Silva's belongings retaining such items as bank notes and his identity card. Somehow da Silva felt they were asking him to be their spy on Earth. Da Silva refused, which caused some consternation.

Suddenly da Silva saw what appeared to be a Christ-like entity, barefoot and wearing a long monk-like dark robe. The figure spoke fluent Portuguese and gave da Silva a message which da Silva stated he was told he should not pass on for several years. Even now da Silva is hesitant to give details.

Da Silva was blindfolded again, led back to the craft and again taken on a journey. The same jolt announced that the craft had landed, his helmet was pulled off and da Silva was unceremoniously turfed off the craft. He drank from a nearby stream, caught a fish which he cooked and ate and found to his amazement that he was near the city of Victoria, some 200 miles (322 km) from where he had set out. Even more incredibly, it was now over four days since the time of his abduction! On returning to Belo Horizonte, da Silva reported his story which some suggested he invented to explain his absence which seems both out of character and unwisely attention-seeking.

1970s

NAME THE BANANEIRAS BUS

DATE 17 NOVEMBER 1971

PLACE BANANEIRAS, BRAZIL
MAP REF: P8

EVENT CAMOUFLAGED UFO?

An extraordinary case occurred in 1971 when two men, leaving a

THE PALENQUE ANCIENT ASTRONAUT

The position of the central figure in this ancient carving from Palenque, Mexico (BELOW) bears an uncanny resemblance to the Mercury astronaut (ABOVE).

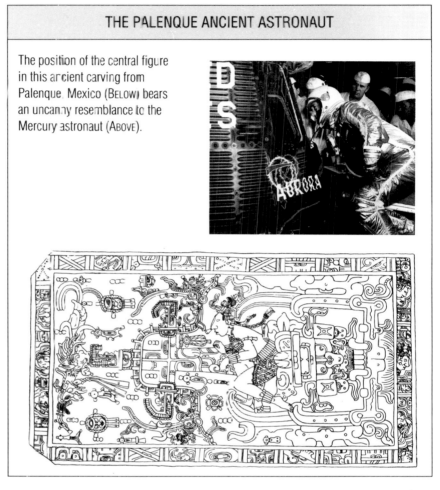

business meeting, were driving in the early evening through the town of Antividad de Carangola. The principal witness was one Paulo Gaetano, travelling with Mr E. B. As they passed the town of Bananeiras, Gaetano felt that the car was not responding properly. The engine then stalled and Gaetano parked on the side of the road.

It seems highly probable that the malfunction of the car was not due to a normal mechanical failure because just next to where it had come to rest Gaetano noticed a red ray of light radiating from a parked object out of which several small creatures emerged and were now approaching!

Gaetano was apparently abducted from the car and taken aboard the craft where he was subjected to a

medical examination which included having a blood sample taken. This left a scar which UFO investigators from the research group SBEVD witnessed and photographed some days after the event.

E. B. apparently did not see an extra-terrestrial craft. He saw a bus! His story of events is that when the car had slowed down and stopped Gaetano had got out, fallen to the ground and E. B. had had to pull him to his feet and take him by bus to Itaperuna, to a first aid clinic.

Did Gaetano see a bus and for some unexplained internal reason related to his own mental make-up suffer a fantasy of alien abduction? Or, did an alien abduction take place which did not involve E. B., who had a false memory planted in his mind to remove the details of the attack?

NAME ISLA DE LOBOS

DATE 28 OCTOBER 1972

PLACE ISLA DE LOBOS, URUGUAY
MAP REF: I16

EVENT CLOSE ENCOUNTER OF THE THIRD
KIND

On the evening of 28 October 1972
five men manning a 200 ft (61 m)
lighthouse were to receive
extraordinary visitors.

Just after ten o'clock in the
evening Corporal Juan Fuentes left
the others to inspect the generators
at the base of the lighthouse. As
soon as he left the quarters he
noticed an object apparently parked
next to the lighthouse on top of a flat
terrace. Fuentes immediately
returned to the garrison house to
collect a gun from his room.

As he walked towards the object
Fuentes noticed shining white,
yellow and purple lights which
illuminated a humanoid figure.
Almost immediately Fuentes noticed
two others, one apparently
descending from the flying saucer to
the terrace where he was.

Fuentes was a decisive man and
on seeing the sight, and at some 80
ft (24 m) from the object, he raised
his arm – pointing the gun forward
ready to shoot. The entities
prevented him from shooting at
them. How they did this, Fuentes is
unclear. The entities re-boarded the
craft which started rising and then
disappeared at fantastic speed.

White as a sheet and gun in hand
Fuentes returned to the other men
and told them he had seen a flying
saucer. They appear to have been
very practical men and his story was
not well received. It was Fuentes'
intention to tell his story to the
media but before doing so he
reported to a higher ranking officer,
who then apparently conferred with
personnel at the American
Embassy.

Because of the single-witness
factor the investigating group, CIOVI,
obtained professional help to put the
witness through over nine hours of
psychological testing which seemed
to support the validity of his claims.

1980s

NAME ELIAS SEIXAS ABDUCTION

DATE 25 SEPTEMBER 1981

PLACE CONCEIÇAO DE ARAGUAIA, GOIAS,
BRAZIL
MAP REF: K10

EVENT ABDUCTION

I am grateful to Irene Granchi of
CISNE for supplying this report.

Elias Seixas, his cousin and a
friend were crossing the State of
Goiás, near Conceiçao de Araguaia
on 25 September 1981. Elias was
driving his truck and was returning
to Rio de Janeiro, where the three
lived. Odd things started happening:
headlights blinked on and off, Elias
felt a cold liquid pressing against the
back of his head. He turned off the
engine, but the lights continued
blinking. He stopped the car and the
three got out, the two others also
having noticed a blue flash cross the
sky. They now saw something that
looked like a bonfire in the distance
across the plains, but realized it
could not be a bonfire: it was a UFO,
pulsating light. Elias took his newly
acquired Super-8 camera and filmed
it for a few seconds. The film later
revealed flashes of light coming from
a 20 ft (6 m) wide fiery-red object.
Back in the truck, Guaraci's straw
hat, wedged between his neck and
the seat, flew off. There was no
wind. The three felt drowsy, and the
journey was long. When they
reached a petrol station in Guaraí,
Elias discovered that *five* hours
were missing in their lives: it was
4.30 a.m. Later, he found that he

had used up only 0.22 gallons (1
litre) of diesel, having covered a
distance of 89 miles (143 km). Once
in Rio de Janeiro, Guaraci placed his
own station-wagon in front of the
truck, and the station-wagon started
blinking its lights on and off,
although neither vehicle had its
engine on. On reaching home, Elias,
walking in front of his truck, saw the
bonnet (hood), which had always
given him trouble in opening, lift by
itself and bang down again.

A wart on Elias's hand
disappeared mysteriously. Later
recollections revealed that semen
had forcibly been drawn from his
penis. This caused him temporary
impotence, visits to a psychiatrist
and a near divorce.

Irene Granchi met the three men
after a talk she gave at a
symposium, and they asked her to
fix an appointment with Dr Silvio
Lago for regression hypnosis. Two
sessions with him were most
revealing: Elias described his
abduction, the aliens he met, the
place he visited, his return journey.
Whereas the ship he was first taken
into had only one tall, long-limbed
man with penetrating lilac-blue eyes,
the beings he saw after landing were
the small, large-headed ones, and he
also saw two human beings he was
not allowed to speak to. He bears no
ill feelings towards his captors, in
spite of everything. Shortly after
undergoing hypnosis he started
developing paranormal powers and
discovered that he could heal. He
has now been working for free for
years with a famous Brazilian doctor
and parapsychologist, Dr Sobral,
where he helps to make diagnoses
with a group of channellers of
ethereal or psychic energies.

The memory of Guaraci, was
entirely blocked, but the third in the
group gave a description which,
although less detailed than that of
Elias, had certain points in common.

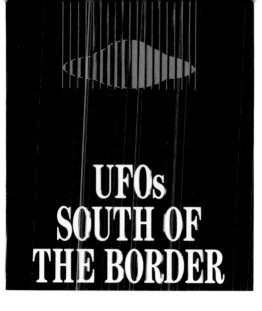

UFOs
SOUTH OF
THE BORDER

The database of South America bears out the belief that the UFO phenomenon is a uniform experience throughout the world, as far as we can understand it. This point goes hand in hand with the suspicion that 'local' cultural overtones can colour the picture. South America provides by far the clearest examples of this, which makes this aspect of its ufology rich for researchers.

There is a much higher rate of reporting sexual encounters from South America. Taking the case of Antonio Villas Boas (see page 181), which while strange and perhaps frightening seems to have many pleasant, even sexually satisfying, components. Why should this be?

A further characteristic of ufology in this area is that the 'entity' descriptions coming from South America are much more varied. Across Europe and North America (ufologically worlds apart in many other ways) there is some standardization in the form of dwarf-like entities with large heads and prominent, alien eyes. In South America there is really no standardization: one report even has red-skinned creatures with one eye!

What is apparent in South America is that reports are frequent where there are people to report to. There seem to be great chunks of the continent devoid of large numbers of reports, almost certainly because there are no easy channels of communication. Experience in other countries suggests that when the investigators are available, the reports come in.

South America does have some of the finest researchers in the world: Mrs Irene Granchi, who wrote the introduction to this section, is very well respected and has been involved in many of the important cases. Our understanding of the phenomenon is made all the clearer because of the work of such people as herself. What we have learned

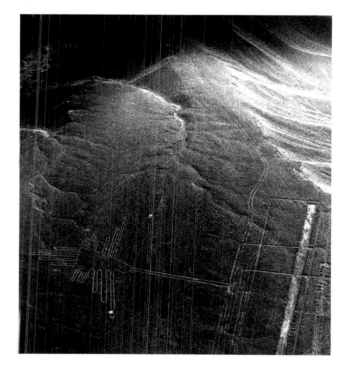

These extraordinary images were created centuries before any form of successful airborne impulsion on a scale that can only be appreciated from air. For whom were they drawn?

to-date has been strongly influenced by their work.

Another factor that almost certainly helped to bring the South American cases to the general UFO world is the involvement of Gordon Creighton. He was fluent in many languages and did much to publish the material coming from that continent.

As contributions to our understanding of UFOs as a global phenomenon continue to emerge from South America, so we edge that bit closer to the final solution. But I suspect it will be a long road, with few easy answers.

INDEX

AFTERWORD

As the current chairman of the International Committee for UFO Research (ICUR) – and a former chairman of the British UFO Research Association (BUFORA) – I am very pleased to be invited to provide an afterword.

The subject of UFOs, as we have seen in this *Casebook* is a truly international one. The database cases reveal how certain types of phenomena transcend cultural boundaries. But if the events being reported are similar, the interpretations could not be more different. A sighting of silver-suited aliens in Africa is interpreted as being a visitation by ancestors while the same sighting in Europe or the USA is classified as an 'alien encounter'. It is clear from this that an understanding of different cultures is paramount in the world study of UFOs and *UFOs: The Definitive Casebook* is much enhanced by the local knowledge of specialist contributors.

UFOs is a fine example of the cooperation which is beginning to develop between UFO groups from all over the world. The better this is, the more investigators there are, and the more authoritative the information that is exchanged, the nearer we will be to providing explanations of phenomena. The International Committee for UFO Research (ICUR) is committed to this approach.

As a final note, I appeal for even greater cooperation between groups and individuals and a greater tolerance of viewpoints. Let's all pull together!

ROBERT DIGBY, CHAIRMAN,
INTERNATIONAL COMMITTEE
FOR UFO RESEARCH.

ORGANIZATIONS

The British UFO Research Association Limited (BUFORA), 16 Southway, Burgess Hill, Sussex, RH15 9ST, United Kingdom. BUFORA operate a 24-hr UFOCALL LINE: (0898) 121886. It contains UFO national news and information (special charges apply).

The Mutual UFO Network (MUFON), 103 Oldtowne Road, Seguin, TX 78155, USA.

International Committee for UFO Research (ICUR), P.O. Box 314, Penn, High Wycombe, Bucks, HP10 8PB, United Kingdom. ICUR will be pleased to provide the name and address of specific organizations in specific countries on request. Organizations seeking to join the International Committee are invited to apply.

BIBLIOGRAPHY

Basterfield, *K Close Encounters of an Australian Kind* Reed (1981)

Berlitz, Charles; Moore, William *The Roswell Incident* Granada Publishing (1980)

Blum, R and J *Beyond Earth* Corgi (1974)

Bowen, Charles (Ed.) *The Humanoids* Futura (1974); *Encounter Cases from Flying Saucer Review* Signet (1977)

Chapman, Robert *UFO* Granada (1968)

Emenegger, Robert *UFOs Past, Present and Future* Ballantine (1974)

Evans, Hilary *The Evidence for UFOs* The Aquarian Press (1983); *Visions, Apparitions, Alien Visitors* Aquarian Press (1984)

Evans, Hilary; Spencer, John (Eds.) *UFOs 1947-1987* Fortean Tomes (1987)

Evans-Wentz, W *Fairy Faith in the Celtic Countries* Oxford University Press (1911)

Festinger/Reichen/Schacker *When Prophecy Fails* Harper & Row (1964)

Flammonde, Paris *UFO Exist!* Ballantine (1976)

Fowler, R *The Andreasson Affair* Prentice-Hall (1979)

Fuller, John G *The Interrupted Journey* Souvenir Press (1966)

Furneaux, Rupert *The Tungus Event* Panther (1977)

Good, Timothy *Above Top Secret* Sidgwick and Jackson (1987)

Hind, Cynthia *UFOs – African Encounters* Gemini (1982)

Hobana, Ion; Weverbergh, Julien *UFOs From Behind The Iron Curtain* Bantam (1975)

Hopkins, Budd *Missing Time* Richard Merrick (1981); *Intruders* Random House (1987)

Hynek, Dr J Allen *The Hynek UFO Report* Sphere (1978)

Jung, C G *Flying Saucers: A Modern Myth of Things Seen in the Skies* Arc (1987, first published 1959)

Keel, John *Operation Trojan Horse* Putman (1970); *Strange Creatures from Time and Space* Sphere (1976); *Visitors from Space* Panther (1976 first published as *The Mothman Prophecies*); *The Cosmic Question* Panther (1978)

Keyhoe, Major Donald E *Flying Saucers from Outer Space* Tandem (1969); *Aliens from Space* Panther (1975)

Leslie, Desmond; Adamski, George *Flying Saucers Have Landed* Futura (1977, first published 1953)

Lorenzen, Coral E *Flying Saucers* (originally: *The Great Flying Saucer Hoax*) Signet Books (1966)

Lorenzen, Jim and Coral *UFOs Over the Americas* Signet Books (1968)

Michel, Aimé *The Truth About Flying Saucers* Corgi (1958)

Randle, Capt. Kevin, USAF (ret) *The UFO Casebook* Warner Books (1989)

Randles, Jenny *UFO Study* Robert Hale (1981); *Abduction* Robert Hale (1988)

Rimmer, John *The Evidence for Alien Abductions* Aquarian Press (1984)

Rogo, D Scott *Alien Abductions* Signet (1980)

Saunders, David; Harkins, Roger *UFOs? Yes!* Signet Books (1968)

Smith, Warren *UFO Trek* Sphere (1977)

Spencer, John; Evans, Hilary (Eds.) *Phenomenon* MacDonald (1988)

Spencer, John *Perspectives* MacDonald (1990)

Stanford, Ray *Socorro Saucer* Fontana (1978)

Steiger, Brad (Ed.) *Project Blue Book* Ballantine (1976); *The UFO Abductors* Berkley (1988)

Stringfield, Leonard *Situation Red* Fawcett-Crest (1977)

Time-Life Editors *Psychic Powers* Time-Life (1988)

Vallée, Jacques and Janine *Challenge to Science* Neville Spearman (1967)

Vallée, Jacques *Passport to Magonia* Spearman (1970); *The Invisible College* Dutton (1975); *Dimensions* Souvenir Press (1988)

Magazines and Periodicals

BUFORA Journal and Bulletin (1968-1988)

Cuadernos de Ufologia (Editors Julio Arcas and Jose Ruesga)

Italian UFO Reporter (Editors Gian Grassino, Eduardo Russo, Paolo Toselli and Maurizio Verga)

The Journal of Transient Aerial Phenomena (1980-1988)

Mystery of the Circles BUFORA Publications (Compiled by Paul Fuller and Jenny Randles)

MUFON UFO Journal (Editor Dennis Stacy)

OVNI Presence (1988) (Editor Yves Bosson)

A sample survey of the incidents of geometrically shaped crop damage C P Fuller (1988).

SOBEPS News (Editor Michel Bougard)

UFO Brigantia (Editor Andy Roberts)

UFOAFRI News (Editor Cynthia Hind)

UFO Times BUFORA Publications (Editor Michael Wootten)